Kinship and Politics

KINSHIP & POLITICS

THE JUSTICES OF THE UNITED STATES
AND LOUISIANA SUPREME COURTS

DONN M. KURTZ II

LOUISIANA STATE UNIVERSITY PRESS

Baton Rouge and London

Copyright © 1997 by Louisiana State University Press
All rights reserved
Manufactured in the United States of America
First printing
06   05   04   03   02   01   00   99   98   97   5   4   3   2   1

Designer: Rebecca Lloyd Lemna
Typeface: Minion
Typesetter: Impressions Book and Journal Services, Inc.
Printer and binder: Thomson-Shore

Library of Congress Cataloging-in-Publication Data

Kurtz, Donn M.
        Kinship and politics : the justices of the United States and
    Louisiana Supreme Courts / Donn M. Kurtz II.
                p.   cm.
        Includes bibliographical references and index.
        ISBN 0-8071-2064-2 (cloth : alk. paper)
        1. Judges—Louisiana—Biography.   2. Judges—Louisiana—Family
    relationships.   3. Kinship—Louisiana.   4. Judges—United States—
    Biography.   5. Judges—United States—Family relationships.
    6. Kinship—United States.   I. Title.
    KF354.L6K87   1996
    347.73'2634—dc20
    [347.3073534]   96-28330
                                                             CIP

An earlier version of Chapter 2 appeared as "Inheriting a Political Career: The Justices of the
United States and Louisiana Supreme Courts," in *Social Science Journal*, 32 (1995), 441–57.

The paper in this book meets the guidelines for permanence and durability of the Committee
on Production Guidelines for Book Longevity of the Council on Library Resources. ∞

To David, Robert, James, and William

CONTENTS

TABLES

FIGURES

PREFACE

A few comments about the research that preceded this volume will serve to explain my interest in both political families and the judiciary. In the 1970s I presented and published several papers dealing with the social background and career characteristics of various sets of Louisiana leaders. This research resulted in the development of a fairly large database on state and local political figures. In the mid-1970s I also began teaching a course on Middle Eastern politics using Bill and Leiden's book, *The Middle East: Politics and Power* (1974). Their analysis of informal groups and the family was the basis for several lectures and class discussions on kinship. Increasingly I found myself illustrating their points about the salience of the family with examples from Louisiana politics.

One afternoon I decided to look through the data on Louisiana leaders to see what I had collected but overlooked in terms of parent-child combinations of officeholders. I thought that if I could find about a hundred such cases I might be able to write an interesting conference paper. That paper did take form, but without much difficulty it was based on over 250 cases (Kurtz 1986). The next effort (1989) was more systematic but still focused on Louisiana, and I refer to it frequently in the text. In that article I was able to develop a number of concepts that have proved to be of some enduring value.

At that point I felt that enough could be said about political families to justify a more ambitious research effort. The original research design for this volume called for an investigation into the families of all the governors, members of Congress, and supreme court justices in Louisiana from 1812 through 1988. I was well into that research when I realized the extent to which I was discovering connections between Louisiana families and similar groups in other states. Up until then I had not been convinced that the subject of families had much applicability outside the South, despite my wife's frequent encouragement to do something with a national group.

Sometime during this period I reread Schmidhauser's article on the United States Supreme Court (1959). Looking at his work from a different perspective convinced me that he had said only part of what could be said about political families. I took my wife's advice and changed my focus to a comparative analysis of the federal and state courts. I chose those two institutions for several reasons. I already had completed much of the research on the Louisiana court, Schmidhauser provided many interesting clues that could be pursued, the two sets of justices were about the same size and totaled a manageable number of cases, and the state-national nature of the data permitted me to formulate some observations about the location of political families at two levels of the political system.

This volume consists of two major parts. First, six chapters describe and analyze the kinship characteristics of the judges from a variety of perspectives. Second, three appendixes present data on the justices and their kinship networks, and list my sources for information on the families analyzed. Most significantly, Appendix A contains the database listing all justices who have politically active relatives along with those relatives, collateral relatives, and connections to other political families.

Some readers will find the analysis more valuable, while others will see more utility in the data itself. I hope that some scholars will use those data for their own purposes; that is the reason for including such a lengthy appendix.

ACKNOWLEDGMENTS

Authors inevitably incur debts that can only be acknowledged but never repaid. Students in three research seminars between 1986 and 1988 did the preliminary investigation on many families included in this book. They were Thomas H. Beasley, Brent D. Burley, James E. Cowan, Colleen P. Danos, Vernicessa Darbonne, Catherine M. DeBlanc, Nicole Fuselier Gil, Lesley R. Gore, Brent H. Gould, Christopher Kimball, Jami L. Legnon, Danny J. Louviere, Sally L. McKissack, Paula V. Milo, Pamela Pena, Louis J. Perret, Angella Bernos Rayon, Timothy K. Reynolds, Charlotte A. Simpson, Carole L. Steen, Corris J. Vallery, Cynthia Voorhies, and Sharon L. Warren. Four students, Michael Magee, William Duncan, Precious Roberson, and Shannon Hicks, proofread parts of the manuscript.

My departmental colleagues have been particularly helpful. Ronald M. Labbe, former department head, offered encouragement throughout this and other endeavors. Janet Frantz, current department head, continued that support and provided critical comments on many aspects of the analysis. Debra Olivier, departmental secretary, helped me with the intricacies of word processing, and she prepared the tables and most of the figures. Kathy Brister produced Figures 13–18.

The University of Southwestern Louisiana was generous in its support by giving me a sabbatical in the summer of 1987, a grant for materials in 1988, and a faculty research grant in the summer of 1989.

Thanks are also due to Mr. and Mrs. James A. Crocker for their financial aid in creating the Crocker Endowed Professorship in Political Science, a position I held while writing this book.

Many details of the family histories and genealogies were available only through the generosity of hundreds of people with whom I corresponded. I am grateful to them for responding to my numerous inquiries.

Kinship and Politics

❧

1

JUDICIAL FAMILIES

He was born in an apartment adjoining the town jail. His father was variously a small-town grocer, hotel owner, timberman, and farmer, as well as the town jailer and later marshall. The son played on the courthouse lawn, and he befriended inmates to the extent of trying to help one escape. When court was in session he would occasionally be invited to sit next to the judge, and he would sometimes accompany his father who, often on horseback, followed the circuit court on to the next county seat. That association with the law and politics was to continue throughout his life, for in 1946 Fred Vinson became the thirteenth chief justice of the United States Supreme Court (based on Hatcher 1974, 246–56).

In contrast, Brockholst Livingston, an earlier member of the court, was literally "to the manor born." His family had maintained vast estates on the Hudson River for three generations. Those extensive property holdings had been established by his great-grandfather, the "First Lord of the Manor." The Livingstons were connected by blood or marriage to the leading families of the Northeast as well as to the families of two other supreme court justices (from various Livingston sources in Appendix C).

As different as their social and economic circumstances were, Justices Vinson and Livingston had one attribute in common. Both were members of political families. Though the political context differed—parochial for Vinson, national and international for Livingston—the result was the same. They were exposed to politics early in their childhood, and that exposure had a lasting impact.

The argument to be developed here is that these cases are not unique and that a significant number of supreme court justices are drawn from families in which kinsmen also held office. In many of those families several members filled governmental positions, often over a period of generations.

Kinship connections in politics are a national phenomenon; they are to be found in a variety of institutional and geographic settings and are not limited to local politics or to certain regions. Many of these families are linked through marriage forming extensive kinship networks that extend backwards to include numerous ancestors and forward to include descendants. These networks also connect officials and families in many states and regions. Finally, it will be demonstrated that this aspect of the American political elite is a current reality, not just a historical curiosity.

The objective of this book is to add to our store of knowledge of the kinship factor in politics by focusing on the public service careers of the families of the justices of the Louisiana and U.S. Supreme Courts. This research will go beyond existing scholarly work (surveyed in Kurtz 1989, 332–35, and Kurtz 1993, 2–8), which is usually limited to a concern with the occupations of the fathers of political leaders in one institutional setting at one point in history. In this volume all the office-holding relatives of the justices from the beginnings of the two courts through 1988 are investigated. This research is unique not only because of its comprehensive historical perspective but also because the database consists of two sets of judges, permitting a comparative analysis of kinship and politics in two institutional locations.

In the first section of this chapter, the key concepts are defined, the database is further identified, and the research methods are explained. The second section develops a profile of the judges' politically active relatives and presents a generational model of political families.

DEFINITIONS, DATA, AND METHODS

A *political family* exists when two or more relatives hold or have held public office.[1] If two or more families are linked by kinship, they are interlocked, forming a kinship network. Relative, family, public office, and kinship network—all of these concepts must be further defined to establish the scope of the study.

The most important concept is *relative,* and it is the most difficult to operationalize because scholars disagree as to the very nature of the American kinship system and because Americans themselves identify their relatives and family members in different ways. This problem is noted only to make the point that any definition of the terms of concern here is subject to

---

1. The sections on definitions and methods are abbreviated versions of a more elaborate discussion in Kurtz (1989, 335–39).

criticism. Realizing this fact, one must offer definitions that are reasonable and useful and then proceed with the analysis.

Two individuals are relatives if they meet one of the following criteria. (1) They are descendants of a common great-grandparent, in which case the most distant relationship would be that of second cousin. (2) One of them married a sibling or a child of the other, in which case the two would be brothers-in-law or father-in-law/son-in-law. This definition corresponds to the civil law model (see Farber 1973, 94, and Stevenson 1979, 215). It commends itself because it is simple and is used, at least in part, in the statutes of many states, including Louisiana (Farber 1981, 7–8).

A *family* consists of any two relatives as just defined and any other relatives of those initially constituting the family. This use of the term is unique; it does not refer to the nuclear, conjugal, or even extended family. In fact, more accurate terms would be *family network* or *network of relatives,* but both are cumbersome, so *family* (or sometimes *family network*) will be used.

Others who have studied kinship connections defined their terms differently. A more restrictive approach may be found in Hess (1966, 2) and in Clubok, Wilensky, and Berghorn (1969, 1040). More liberal definitions are offered by Aronson (1964, 141), Whitley (1973, 626), Purvis (1980, 598n. 9), Merlie and Silva (1975, *passim*), and Hall (1980, 442).

To the extent possible, leaders in the study are grouped into families according to their surnames. Office-holding descendants through a male line would form one family, whereas descendants through a female line would form another. Both units would be linked in a *kinship network* (to be defined in Chapter 4). This system of grouping is arbitrary but necessary to create some boundaries and to identify the families involved.

Creating a few hypothetical situations using Figure 1 will illustrate the various possible combinations derived from the definitions.

1. If both B and G are officials, there is a political family consisting of the uncle/nephew dyad.
2. If B, G, and J hold office and no one else from Lineage II has gone into politics, then J (father-in-law of G) is considered part of the BG family, now BGJ.
3. If B, G, I, and J are all officials, there are two families, BG and IJ, because of the difference in surnames. The two families now form a kinship network linked by the affinal connection of G and J.
4. If the following members of Lineage I—B, G, F, and H—hold office, they are grouped into two distinct families, BG (descendants

FIGURE 1

Kinship Connections

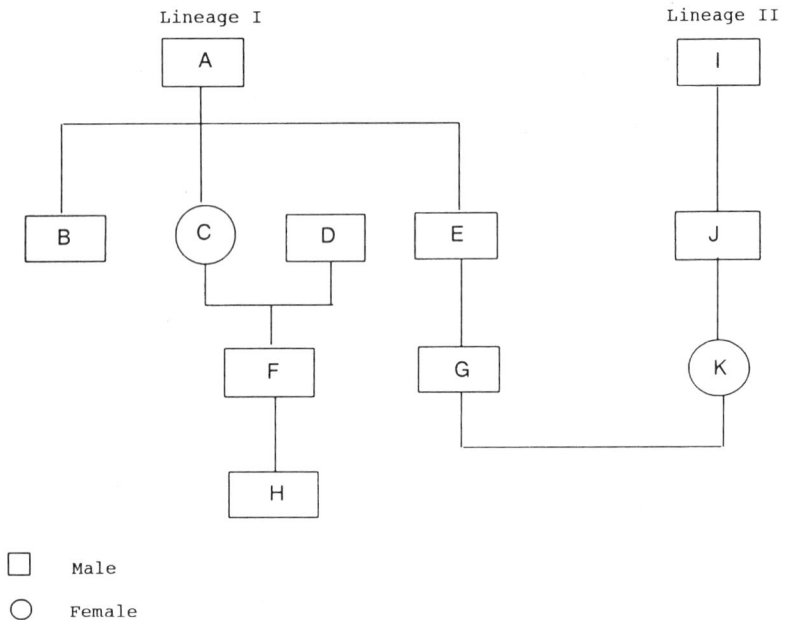

Style adapted from McGoldrick and Gerson 1985

through the male line) and FH (descendants through a female line) because their surnames are different. The two units form a kinship network based on descent from a common ancestor, A.

These definitions are important because they determine the format of Appendix A, the main database of this study, which in turn determines the nature of the analysis and findings.

Chief Justice John Marshall's entries in that appendix may be used to explain the terms more fully. The entry for the chief justice is followed immediately by a number of other entries (Thomas Marshall through William Lewis Marshall). These are relatives of the chief justice in the Marshall family. A second group of individuals, "Relatives from Other Families," includes relatives of John Marshall who are members of other families such as the Dukes, McClungs, and Greens. A third category is "Collateral Relatives," which includes other members of the Marshall family who are not closely related to the chief justice, such as Charles Edward Marshall. He is John

Marshall's first cousin twice removed and thus by definition not a relative. Finally, there is a listing of "Connections to Other Families," which is relevant to the discussion of networks in Chapter 4.

These categories of officials will be combined in different ways depending on the concept being discussed. The term *relative* includes kinsmen in the justice's family and in allied families. A *family* consists of relatives in the justice's family and his collateral relatives as well. Chapters 1 and 2 are concerned primarily with relatives, and Chapters 4 and 5 deal with families in kinship networks.

An individual is considered to have been *politically active* only if he or she has held formal public office. The concept of *public office* is defined as broadly as possible because it is recognized that office holding is but one type of political involvement. All elected officials as well as major political appointees at every level of the system are considered public officers. The above definition has the effect of excluding families in which some members were highly active in politics but did not hold a formal position. In this sense the study begins from the positional or institutional perspective. Limiting the cases in this way is necessary for two reasons. First, it would be difficult to develop a useful operational definition of politically active that included behavior other than office holding; there are too many types of political activity. Second, identifying those who might meet a broader definition would be impossible; no documentary sources are available for unofficial political activity. Other scholars have noted the difficulty of finding family connections without adding the problems associated with less rigid criteria (Hansen and Parrish 1983, 275–76; Bill and Hardgrave 1973, 137–38).

The universe of this study consists of the 98 members of the Louisiana Supreme Court who served between 1812 and 1988 and the 104 justices of the U.S. Supreme Court between 1789 and 1988. One individual, Edward Douglas White, served on both courts and is counted twice. So this study involves 201 individuals and 202 positions. The latter number is the one on which all calculations are based unless the text indicates otherwise.

There were no problems in identifying the members of the federal court, but the state justices require two comments. First, those who served as temporary appointees to the court are not included. Second, John Edward King, a parish judge and son of Justice George Rogers King, served but one day on the court, so he is excluded, too.

As other scholars have noted, the methods employed in identifying the relatives of these 202 judges are best described as eclectic and interdisciplinary (Stone 1971, 47, 67, 73; Griffith 1963, 83; Hareven 1971, 401; Hareven

1977, 1). To discover judicial kinsmen, I took the following steps, although not necessarily in this order.

1. Searched the standard biographical dictionaries.
2. Consulted biographies of individual judges.
3. Investigated genealogies and family histories.
4. Examined local and state histories.
5. Corresponded with a number of justices or their relatives.
6. Consulted a variety of additional sources.

The number and quality of sources varied widely (see Appendix C for a complete list), and that fact must be explained because it has a direct impact on the findings.

1. There was generally more information on federal than on state judges, particularly in terms of comprehensive biographies. The federal justices are of course more prominent, and their careers are of interest to a national rather than to a state community of scholars. Almost nothing is known about ten Louisiana judges, including their dates of birth and death.[2] The fact that eight of the ten served, at least in part, during the Civil War and Reconstruction will affect the analysis of historical periods in subsequent chapters.
2. Information on recent judges and especially incumbents is limited. Extensive biographies tend to be written well after one has left the bench.
3. More data exist on families allied to the Louisiana justices, especially if they were local families, than on those linked to the federal judges.
4. Maternal connections and descendants through female lines were more difficult to trace because of the change in names.
5. More is known about a justice's ancestors than his descendants, particularly if the descendants did not reach high office or eminent standing.
6. Access to information was a problem, as it has been for other scholars (Merlie and Silva 1975, 169n. 4). I was limited to materials in Louisiana collections and to sources available on loan from out-of-state libraries.

2. The justices and their dates of service are Peter V. Bonford, 1863–1864; James G. Campbell, 1853–1854; James L. Cole, 1856–1860, 1863–1865; Albert Duffell, 1860–1865; William B. Eagan, 1877–1878, Rufus K. Howell, 1857–1864; John H. Ilsley, 1865–1868; John Kennard, December, 1872 to February, 1873; George Strawbridge, August to December, 1839; and William Gillespie Wyly, 1868–1876.

7. Finally, I had greater knowledge of Louisiana leaders based on previous research and long-time residence in the state. In addition, a number of students and acquaintances were related to some of the Louisiana families, and they shared information in their possession. Every effort has been made to ensure the accuracy of the relationships and dates of service. Those dates often vary as much as a year or two in many sources. No major effort was made to deal with that issue unless it seemed important. Less time was spent investigating the allied families because the primary focus was on the families of the justices. More extensive research would no doubt reveal that many of the allied families are even larger than reported here. Errors will have been made, but one hopes they are usually errors of omission, in which case the missing entries have the effect of strengthening the argument being presented.

THE FAMILIES

Sixty percent of the Louisiana justices and 72 percent of the United States justices had at least one relative in public office before, during, or after the justice's public service. The discussion in this section will be based on those two sets of judges and their relatives, whether the relatives are members of the justice's immediate family or of other families.

Table 1 indicates that the members of the Louisiana Supreme Court had more relatives in office than did the federal judges. There are two ways to view that difference. Almost half of the federal justices had only one or two relatives in politics, but the comparable figure for the state group is about one-third. Over 40 percent of the Louisiana judges had five or more relatives in contrast to less than 30 percent for the national group. However, the two justices with the largest number of relatives were Brockholst Livingston with thirty-three and John Marshall with thirty-seven, both of the federal bench. These two cases are at the extreme end of the distribution. The next highest in this regard is Robert B. Todd of Louisiana with nineteen.

Most of the office-holding relatives of both sets of judges were spread over two or three generations with the United States justices having a higher proportion of two generations of public service by relatives (41% to 24%) and the Louisiana group having more members (37% to 25%) whose relatives served over three generations. John Jay is the only case of a justice with seven generations of relatives in public office. John Marshall and Brockholst Livingston of the federal bench and George Rogers King and

TABLE 1

Relatives and Generations in Political Office

	% of Louisiana Justices	% of Federal Justices
Number of relatives		
1–2	34%	49%
3–4	24	22
5+	41.5	27
Total	99.5%	98%
Number of generations of office holding by relatives		
1	3%	5%
2	24	41
3	37	25
4	15	16
5	17	9
6	3	3
7	0	1
Total	99%	101%
% of justices with collateral relative in fourth generation	20%	8%
(N)	(59)	(75)

Newton Crain Blanchard of Louisiana all have six generations of kinsmen in office.

Given the definition of *relative*, there can be no more than seven generations in this analysis. In ascending order are the generations of parents, grandparents, and great-grandparents; in descending order are children, grandchildren, and great-grandchildren. The seventh generation is that of the justice himself. However, the research did reveal that 20 percent of the Louisiana and 8 percent of the federal justices have collateral relatives in the fourth generation ascending (great-great-grandparents) or descending (great-great-grandchildren).

A more precise picture of the justices' relatives may be derived from Table 2, which lists each possible relationship grouped according to ascending, contemporary, and descending generations. Within each generational category the various relatives are listed in order of closeness or degree of consanguinity according to the civil law method discussed earlier. The column "all relatives" is a tabulation of the percentage of justices who have a

TABLE 2

Types of Relatives by Generational Group

Generational Group	All Relatives		Closest Relative	
	La.	U.S.	La.	U.S.
Ascending generations				
Parent	47%	51%	47%	51%
Grandparent	32	31	10	11
Great-grandparent	20	17	2	0
Uncle/aunt	17	20	3	8
Granduncle/aunt	17	13	2	3
First cousin once removed	8	12	0	0
Father-in-law	20	28	12	11
None	24	17	24	17
% of jurors who had more than three ancestors	36%	31%		
Contemporary generation				
Sibling	29%	31%	29%	31%
First cousin	12	17	10	13
Second cousin	12	9	5	1
Husband/wife	1.5	0	2	0
Brother-in-law	24	17	8	7
None	46	48	46	48
% of justices who had more than three contemporaries	19%	18%		
Descending generation				
Child	37%	27%	37%	27%
Grandchild	29	9	12	1
Great-grandchild	8	2.5	0	0
Nephew	8	10.5	15	9
Grandnephew	24	6.5	0	1
First cousin once removed	3	12	0	7
Son-in-law	15	17	3	4
None	32	51	32	51
% of justices who had more than three descendants	42%	30%		

particular type of kinsman (*i.e.*, parent, second cousin) in office. There is of course much overlapping because a justice may have several kinds of relatives. The second major column, "closest relative," indicates that relative in each generational category who is most closely related to the judge. The figures for parent, sibling, child, and none will be the same in both columns. If a judge has an office-holding parent (the first variable), then the parent is his closest relative (the second variable).

No major differences exist between the two courts in terms of the various types of ancestors except that the Louisiana justices were somewhat more likely to have no relatives in this group. The most important finding is that about half of the state and federal judges are the sons of public officials. Parents and grandparents are the two closest possible ancestors, and 57 percent of the Louisiana and 62 percent of the federal jurists have a parent or grandparent as their closest kinsman. A particularly interesting finding is that 20 percent of the Louisiana and 28 percent of the United States justices married daughters of political figures. (This observation will be developed further toward the end of this section.) Finally, about a third of both sets of judges have three or more ancestors who held office.

Patterns of public service on the part of contemporaries of the two groups of justices are fairly similar both in the types of relatives and in their closest relatives. That similarity continues when one considers the number of kinsmen who are contemporaries. A large majority of both federal and states judges have fewer than three relatives of their own generation in office. Marriage patterns are again interesting: 24 percent of the state and 17 percent of the federal jurists married sisters of politicians.

The greatest variation between Louisiana and United States justices occurs with respect to descendants. A major finding is that less than one-third of the state judges but a majority of the federal group have no descendants in office. The descendants of federal judges who do hold office tend to be more distant relatives. Louisiana judges are more likely to have transmitted their tradition of public service to subsequent generations, and the state judges have more descendants who went into politics. The justices are similar in the extent to which their daughters married officeholders.

Marriage patterns may now be considered from three perspectives. A justice might marry the daughter or the sister of an official, or the child of a justice might marry a politician. Well over one-third of the members of both courts married daughters or sisters of public officials. By combining these judges with those whose daughters married politicians (and eliminating duplications), we can conclude that about half of the justices are the son-in-law, brother-in-law, or father-in-law of public servants (49% Louisiana and 52% United States). Many of these marriages link two families, creating a kinship network, a subject to be considered further in Chapters 4 and 5.

These findings are not particularly surprising given what is known about the impact of class, occupation, and residence on mate selection. Schmidhauser found that 90 percent of the federal judges came from essentially upper-class backgrounds (1959, 7). Although this study does not address the question of class origins, my impression is that about three-fourths of the state justices were from the upper end of the social ladder, a somewhat higher figure than Heiberg found to be the case in Minnesota, where 55 percent of the fathers of Supreme Court justices had high-status occupations (1969, 911). The fact that one-third of the justices married daughters or sisters of politicians is not too different from the findings of others that between one-fifth (Hatch and Hatch 1947, 403) and one-fourth (Blumberg and Paul 1975, 66) of the marriages listed in the New York *Times* united two individuals who were listed in the *Social Register*. Other studies have noted the tendency of people to choose mates of similar occupational status (Hunt 1940, 504; Centers 1949, 530–35; Mills 1959, 68; Domhoff 1983, 34–37; Pessen 1984, 159–68).

Residential location may also be a factor in the selection of a spouse (Hollingshead 1950, 625). United States justices are residents of the Washington area, and the Louisiana judges are located in New Orleans. Geographical propinquity and probable social interaction with each other as well as with other political leaders increase the possibilities of intermarriage between political families.

Relatives of the justices may be further examined by reference to the types of offices they hold and to the geographical location of their political activity (see Table 3). Membership on either the federal or state supreme court is considered to be a high office. The issue to be addressed here is the extent to which judicial relatives also held positions at or near the peak of the political system. The concept "high office" or "major office" includes the members of either chamber of Congress, governors, federal cabinet officers, ambassadors, and others such as the president, vice president, and significant foreign officials.

Most from Louisiana (58%) have no relatives in major offices, whereas most federal judges (61%) have at least one kinsman who reached a high position, and almost one-third have two or more relatives in major offices. Most jurists (54% state and 59% national) are related to at least one other judge, and more than one-third have two or more judicial relatives.

This is a stronger finding than that of two other studies. Schmidhauser concluded that "thirty-one members of [the] Supreme Court were related to jurists and intimately connected with families possessing a tradition of judicial service" (1959, 14).[3] In his analysis of 744 lower federal judges (constitutional and territorial) who served from 1789 to 1899, Hall found that just under half were related to judges (Hall 1980, 442).

3. Schmidhauser included William Henry Moody as one of those thirty-one judges (1959, 14, n. 20). I was not able to verify that connection. Justice Moody was not included among the seventy-five federal justices in this study.

T A B L E   3

Relatives Holding Political Office

	Louisiana	United States
Number of relatives in major offices		
0	58%	39%
1	20	29
2	15	16
3	5	7
4+	2	9
Total	100%	100%
Number of relatives who were judges		
0	46%	41%
1	15	25
2	22	13
3	8	12
4	2	7
5+	7	1
Total	100%	99%
Number of states in which office held*		
1	75%	51%
2	14	27
3+	12	23
Total	101%	101%

* Includes the states in which the justices were active.

    Most members of both courts have relatives who hold office in the justice's home state. More interesting than the general pattern is the fact that one-fourth of the state and almost half of the national judges have office-holding relatives in other states. The most geographically diverse set of kinsmen were those of Robert Briggs Todd of Louisiana, who had relatives in seven states. Joseph Rucker Lamar, Brockholst Livingston, and Philip P. Barbour all had politically involved relatives in five states. Derbigny, Gray, and Hughes were related to officials in foreign countries.

    A final perspective is gained by classifying the justices according to their generational sequence of public service. *Founders* are justices who represent the first generation to hold office and whose descendants continued the family political activity. A *transmitter* is one who fits between generations of officials; both ancestors and descendants went into politics. If the justice inherited a tradition of public service but did not transmit it to successive generations, he is a *maintainer*. Finally, a *contemporary* is one whose office-holding relatives are all in the justice's own generation.

Table 4 indicates the distribution of both sets of judges in terms of these categories. The first two columns, "% of kin-connected justices," involve calculations based only on the justices who have relatives in politics, the database employed thus far in this chapter.

The principal difference between the two courts is that Louisiana justices tend to be transmitters and United States justices tend to be maintainers (see Table 4). This contrast is related to the earlier finding that federal justices have fewer descendants in politics. This could be a real difference; that is, federal judges may not transfer a political legacy to the same extent that state judges do. However, there is no good explanation in that regard. Another possibility is that national judges do have more politician-descendants than are indicated here, but their service is at a much lower level in the political system. If that is the case, these descendants escaped detection because of the difficulty in identifying low-level positions in other states.

These generational types may be used to create a model of elite kinship connections across generations. Developing an accurate model requires the use of a different data set, one that includes all members of both courts. The second two columns of Table 4, "% of all justices," provides the relevant information. Here, all members of the courts are classified according to their generational category or as having no relatives in politics.

Figures 2 and 3 employ those data in models of the state and federal courts, respectively. The justices are first grouped into two sets. *New mem-*

TABLE 4

| | Generational Type of Supreme Court Justices | | | |
| | % of Kin-Connected Justices | | % of All Justices | |
Type	Louisiana	U.S.	Louisiana	U.S.
Founder	17.5%	8%	10%	6%
Transmitter	49	39	29	28
Maintainer	30	47	18	34
Contemporary	3.5	5.5	2	4
No relatives	NA	NA	41	29
Total	100%	99.5%	100%	101%
(*N*)	(57)	(72)	(96)	(101)

Note: Two state and three federal justices could not be classified.

Generational Model—Louisiana Justices

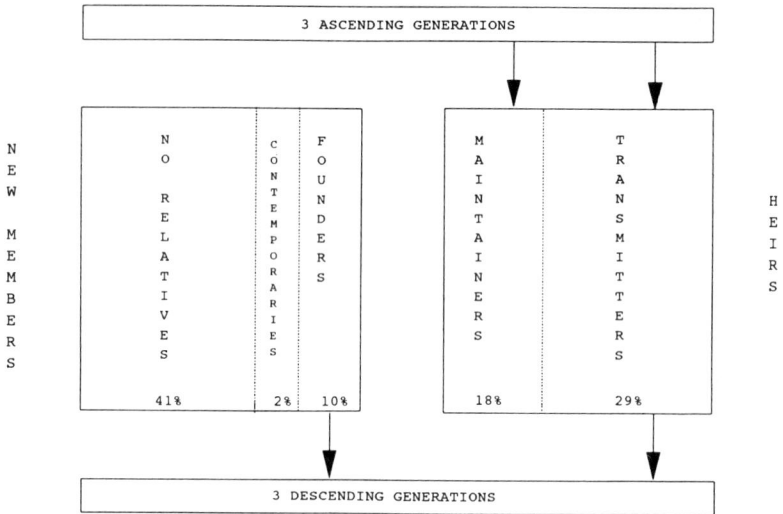

```
┌─────────────────────────────────────────────────────────────────────────┐
│                      3 ASCENDING GENERATIONS                              │
└─────────────────────────────────────────────────────────────────────────┘
                                          │            │
                                          ▼            ▼
        ┌──────────────────────────┐   ┌──────────────────────────┐
   N    │  N        C      F        │   │  M            T           │
   E    │  O        O      O        │   │  A            R           │
   W    │           N      U        │   │  I            A           │
        │  R        T      N        │   │  N            N           │       H
        │  E        E      D        │   │  T            S           │       E
   M    │  L        M      E        │   │  A            M           │       I
   E    │  A        P      R        │   │  I            I           │       R
   M    │  T        O      S        │   │  N            T           │       S
   B    │  I        R                │   │  E            T           │
   E    │  V        A                │   │  R            E           │
   R    │  E        R                │   │  S            R           │
   S    │  S        I                │   │               S           │
        │           E                │   │                           │
        │           S                │   │                           │
        │  41%     2%   10%          │   │  18%         29%          │
        └──────────────────────────┘   └──────────────────────────┘
                        │                              │
                        ▼                              ▼
┌─────────────────────────────────────────────────────────────────────────┐
│                      3 DESCENDING GENERATIONS                             │
└─────────────────────────────────────────────────────────────────────────┘
```

Generational Model—U.S. Justices

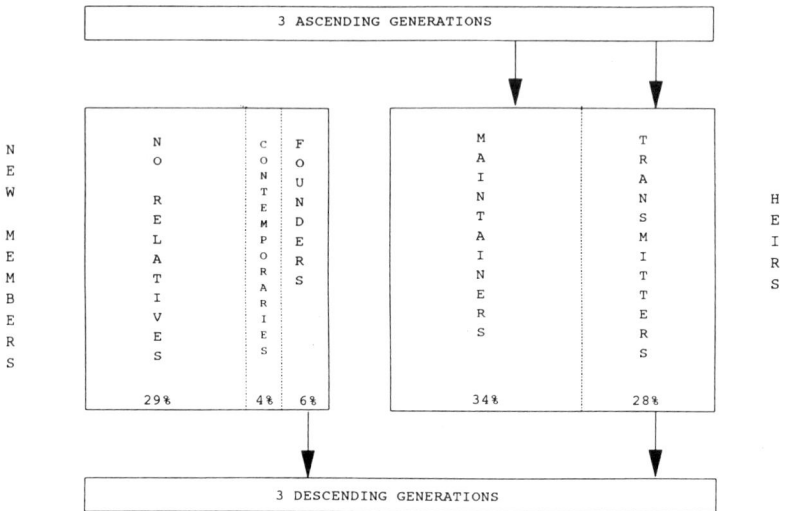

```
┌─────────────────────────────────────────────────────────────────────────┐
│                      3 ASCENDING GENERATIONS                              │
└─────────────────────────────────────────────────────────────────────────┘
                                          │            │
                                          ▼            ▼
        ┌──────────────────────────┐   ┌──────────────────────────┐
   N    │  N        C      F        │   │  M            T           │
   E    │  O        O      O        │   │  A            R           │
   W    │           N      U        │   │  I            A           │
        │  R        T      N        │   │  N            N           │       H
        │  E        E      D        │   │  T            S           │       E
   M    │  L        M      E        │   │  A            M           │       I
   E    │  A        P      R        │   │  I            I           │       R
   M    │  T        O      S        │   │  N            T           │       S
   B    │  I        R                │   │  E            T           │
   E    │  V        A                │   │  R            E           │
   R    │  E        R                │   │  S            R           │
   S    │  S        I                │   │               S           │
        │           E                │   │                           │
        │           S                │   │                           │
        │  29%     4%   6%           │   │  34%         28%          │
        └──────────────────────────┘   └──────────────────────────┘
                        │                              │
                        ▼                              ▼
┌─────────────────────────────────────────────────────────────────────────┐
│                      3 DESCENDING GENERATIONS                             │
└─────────────────────────────────────────────────────────────────────────┘
```

bers include those who are the first in their families to be politically active. These new jurists include contemporaries and founders, as well as those who had no relatives in either ascending or descending generations. New members constitute 53 percent of the Louisiana and 39 percent of the federal justices. *Heirs* claim at least one relative from an earlier generation who held office. Heirs include maintainers and transmitters, and 47 percent of the state and 62 percent of the national justices fall into this category.

As presented here, the model does not distinguish among the three ascending or descending generations. According to the definition of *relative* offered earlier, a judge could be linked to a third preceding generation if his great-grandfather held office and to a third descending generation if a great-grandson were politically active. The model could be modified to include the connections to specific generations, but at this point the presentation may be made with this simpler version.

This model is useful for three major reasons. First, while it emphasizes the distinction between those individuals who have inherited a family political tradition and those who have not, it also goes beyond this basic dichotomy by drawing attention to significant differences within these two groups. Among new members, some justices are linked to subsequent generations of relatives. They did not inherit a political career, but they did begin a pattern of family involvement that was continued by their descendants. Two groups of heirs may also be identified: those who are linked to both earlier and later generations (transmitters) and those who are connected only to the earlier generation (maintainers).

The second value of this schema is that it indicates clearly that both sets of justices are linked to earlier and to later generations of officials in two ways. Maintainers and transmitters connect the courts to one or more of three generations of ancestors, whereas founders and transmitters tie the judges to one or more generations of descendants.

The third advantage of this model is that its application is not limited to a description of the officials under consideration here. In Chapter 6 it will be employed both as a universal descriptive and as a predictive device with respect to all political leaders.

SUMMARY

Most federal and state jurists are members of political families, a characteristic that is more prevalent among the federal justices than among those on the state court. While more federal judges had kinsmen in office, the state group tended to have a larger number of relatives.

Of the fifty-nine state and seventy-five federal justices with family political connections, two-thirds of the Louisiana jurists but only half of the
federal bench had three or more relatives in politics. These politically involved relatives were closely connected to the justices; half had a parent in
office, nearly a third had a sibling, and between a fourth and a third had
children who entered politics. Many of the relatives held major offices, a
pattern that was more pronounced in the case of federal justices. A majority of members of both courts were related to at least one other judge. Judicial relatives tended to hold office in the justice's home state, but one-
fourth of the Louisiana judges and almost half of the federal judges had at
least one relative in office in another state. Most jurists were part of a two-
or three-generation sequence of public service, but the justices' position in
that sequence varied according to the court. Louisiana judges tended to be
transmitters (47%), both inheriting and passing on a family political tradition, whereas the United States judges were more likely to be maintainers,
those who inherited but did not transfer anything to the next generation.

These findings raise several questions that cannot be answered until
later in the analysis. The significance of inheriting a family political tradition and the distribution of political families throughout history will be addressed in Chapters 2 and 3, respectively. Kinship networks will be investigated more thoroughly in Chapters 4 and 5. Finally, judicial kinship
patterns were not compared with evidence from other institutional settings; that task will be undertaken in Chapter 6 along with a further application of the generational model.

❧

2

INHERITING
A POLITICAL CAREER

The concept "occupational inheritance" (or "following") has been discussed in some detail elsewhere (Kurtz 1989, 343), so only a brief definition will be offered here. An inheritance occurs when a public official has been preceded in office by any relative holding any type of position. The earlier official might even be a generational contemporary. A "succession" is a more specific type of following that occurs when the same office is held at different times by two relatives. A succession is direct if an office is filled immediately by a relative of the most recent incumbent. Intervening occupancy by a nonrelative results in an indirect succession.

Forty-three state and sixty-five federal justices inherited a political career. These jurists represent 44 percent of all the members of the state court and 63 percent of the members of the federal court. Two relevant questions must be asked. Who is the judge's closest occupational predecessor? And how many relatives held office before the justice?

To identify the closest relative, two factors—genetic or legal distance and generational distance—must be taken into account and combined to create a scale of closeness. Table 5 indicates how those two factors are treated. In this discussion, generational distance is almost as important as genetic or legal distance (according to the civil law method). An uncle is not as close a relative as a grandfather, but he is closer in generational terms, being one generation removed rather than two. The same principle applies to great-grandparents and granduncles. The great-grandparent is closer in civil law, but the granduncle is given preference because he is nearer in the generational scheme.

TABLE 5

Occupational Predecessors of Supreme Court Justices

Predecessors	Louisiana	United States
Closest		
Father	65%	58%
Uncle	12	8
Grandfather	7	12
Granduncle	2	6
Great-grandfather	2	0
Father-in-law	12	9
Other	0	6
Total	100%	100%
Number		
1	37%	49%
2	19	20
3	21	14
4	9	3
5	9	6
6+	5	8
Total	100%	100%
(N)	(43)	(65)

A majority of both sets of family-connected jurists were preceded in office by their fathers, and over three-fourths of the state and two-thirds of the federal judges followed office-holding relatives from the immediately preceding generation (father or uncle). For most justices, the political activity of relatives was not a distant experience but something that probably took place during the judges' youth.

Not only do justices usually follow a close relative, father or uncle, but most have followed several kinsmen. This is particularly true of the state judges, over 60 percent of whom have had two or more occupational predecessors. Seven justices have followed six or more relatives into political office. Five of these (Barbour, Marshall, Fuller, Washington, and Livingston) were on the federal bench, and two (Todd and Fournet) were from Louisiana. Washington with eight and Livingston with nine predecessors inherited the most firmly established tradition of family political involvement.

Ten justices are successors; that is, they are related to an earlier member of the court (see Table 6). All but one of those successions (the Voorhies) were indirect. These ten judicial successors represent 7.5 percent of those with relatives in politics or 5 percent of all state and national jus-

TABLE 6

Successions

Louisiana Court
Frank Adair Monroe (1899–1922), brother-in-law of Joshua G. Baker (1921–1922)
George R. King (1846–1850), granduncle of Winston Overton (1921–1934)
Thomas T. Land (1858–1865), father of Alfred D. Land (1902–1917) and John
R. Land (1921–1941)
Florent E. Simon (1840–1849), great-grandfather of James D. Simon (1955–1960)
Cornelius Voorhies (1854–1859), father of Albert Voorhies (1859–1865)

United States Court
Stephen J. Field (1863–1897), uncle of David J. Brewer (1889–1910)
John A. Campbell (1853–1861), first cousin once removed of L. Q. C. Lamar
(1888–1893)
John M. Harlan (1877–1911), grandfather of John M. Harlan (1955–1971)
John Jay (1789–1795), brother-in-law of Brockholst Livingston (1806–1823)

Note: Dates indicate years in office.

tices. In one instance, relatives served simultaneously. Justices Field and
Brewer (uncle-nephew) sat together from 1889 until 1897.

Two additional observations should be made. First, the author found
higher rates of succession in his study of state and local officials in
Louisiana in 1983. Twenty-eight percent of the family-connected leaders, or
7.5 percent of the total, were successors, and 73 percent of those were direct
(Kurtz 1989, 343). Second, in four instances justices are linked though
somewhat indirectly. At the federal level, Joseph Rucker Lamar and L. Q. C.
Lamar were fourth cousins, Justice Curtis' brother married a daughter of
Justice Story, and Justice Grey married the daughter of Justice Matthews
after the latter's death. At the state level, children of Justices Bullard and
Garland married. These connections contribute to the formation of kinship
networks.

To fully appreciate the significance of these findings on inheritance,
they must be compared with data from other professions. Many critics have
suggested that the patterns of occupational following identified here would
also be found in other professions. They cite anecdotal evidence to the
effect that doctors' children become doctors and plumbers' children become plumbers.

To make valid comparisons, one must focus on the percentage of *all*
justices who followed a father into politics because most other studies deal
with the parent-child transfer of an occupation. Historically, of the ninety-
eight members of the Louisiana Supreme Court, 29 percent had fathers

TABLE 7

Occupational Following in Various Professions

Profession	% Who Followed Parent
University faculty	5%
Protestant clergy	13
Women lawyers	11
Lawyers	11
Doctors	8
Accountants	4
Biological scientists	.34

Sources: Faculty: "Who faculty members are, and what they think" (1985, 26); clergy: Smith and Sjoberg (1961, 292); women lawyers: Epstein (1983, 25); all others: Laband and Lentz (1992, 183, 198)

who were also public officials; the comparable figure for the federal court is 36.5 percent. For purposes of comparison with other professions, the justices from only the most recent period, 1961–1988, should be used. During these years four justices (18%) have been followers, but only two (Tate of Louisiana and White of the federal bench) followed their fathers into public life.

Table 7 contains information on parent-child occupational transfers from other professions. The rate of following is significantly lower in all categories than it is for politics in general; among most groups of political figures, between one-fourth and one-half inherited a family political tradition (Kurtz 1995, 447–48). The exception to this generalization is that recent judges are atypical of other political figures. In fact, they are fairly typical of other occupations in this regard, particularly lawyers.

Even if it were appropriate to conclude that the incidence of occupational inheritance among all types of political leaders was statistically no different than for other professions, one would have to acknowledge the greater importance of inheriting a political career. Politics is a qualitatively different occupation in that the decision to pursue a political career is not one that an individual can act on alone. One can decide to try to enter the political arena, but to be successful, voters or appointing authorities must confirm that decision. In other professions, career choices are largely made and realized by the person involved.

IMPACT OF OCCUPATIONAL INHERITANCE

Both political leaders and scholars have commented on the impact and advantages of being the product of a politically active family. The recollections of public officials from Georgia, Louisiana, Pennsylvania, and California represent a consistent theme concerning their youthful political involvement.

Georgia congressional candidate Barbara Christmas, the daughter of a longtime warden of the state penitentiary, in speaking of the old boy network she inherited, remarked that she frequently met people in her campaigning who said, "Your daddy gave me my first job" (Clines 1992).

Louisiana treasurer Mary Landrieu, daughter of a New Orleans mayor and cabinet secretary and wife of a school board member, noted that her family took only one nonpolitical vacation while she was young. "All other trips revolved around things like the mayors' conference. Politics was in every aspect of life." Her brother, state legislator Mitch Landrieu, said he did not think he could get out of politics even if he wanted to: "It's in my blood" (Price 1989, 13).

In her first bid for office, Lynn Hardy Yeakel won the Democratic nomination for a Senate seat from Pennsylvania. Although lacking formal political experience, she felt she "was as good as anybody else." As the daughter of an eleven-term congressman, she had gone to school with Eisenhower's grandchildren, met Queen Elizabeth and Lyndon Johnson, and danced with John F. Kennedy (Hinds 1992).

Even those children of politicians who at one time felt that a political career was out of the question may eventually find themselves drawn into the public arena. California legislator Lucille Roybal-Allard did not want to marry a politician and did not like growing up in a political family. By 1992, however, her congressman-father was managing her campaign for a seat in the House of Representatives (Hasson 1992).

Those who have studied the family backgrounds of political leaders generally agree that having parents and other relatives in politics while one is young is advantageous. Matthews (1960, 49), Hess (1966, 7), Prewitt (1970, 68), and Moore, Lace, and Wagner (1985, 201) have noted the value of name recognition, the early acquisition of political skills and information, access to useful political contacts, and the development of a greater sense of political efficacy.

These observations are substantiated by a number of studies that rely on a more systematic analysis of recall data, the ability of adults to remember the political circumstances in which they were reared. For example, members of Congress who were socialized early by their families were elected at an earlier age than those whose political socialization came later through other agents (Kornberg and Thomas 1965, 773).

In their study of state legislators and city council members, Prewitt, Eulau, and Zisk found that those who grew up in politically active families reported an early interest in politics. Early exposure to politics differentiates some officials from others in terms of personal contacts, images, and predispositions, but it is "apparently unrelated to major aspects of incumbent orientation" (1966–67, 573, 581).

Browning's study of businessmen, some of whom were politically active, revealed that about half the businessmen-politicians had fathers who had been active politically, whereas none of the nonpolitical business leaders had fathers in public affairs (1968, 98). Browning suggested that a father's political experience made the son visible to party leaders, increasing the probability that they would recruit the son, and it created in the son a generally favorable attitude toward politics (1968, 98).

The nature of family political activity is also related to adult ambitions and attitudes toward the political process. Among Michigan state legislators, the more ambitious tended to be those who became interested in politics early, and "the agent of socialization most closely associated with high ambitions was the family" followed by the school (Soule 1969, 446).

The authors of a study of Oregon legislative candidates expected to find "that winning candidates might have had more politicized family backgrounds than losing candidates." Overall that was not the case, but far more successful Democrats had politically active families than did the winning Republicans (Seligman *et al.* 1974, 124).

Interviewing delegates to the 1968 Democratic National Convention, Soule and Clarke made a distinction between amateurs and professionals. Amateurs emphasized issues of intraparty democracy and were reluctant to compromise, whereas professionals were preoccupied with winning elections and were oriented toward compromise. These differences in orientations were at least partially related to the delegate's family situation. Almost two-thirds of the amateurs came from families who were not politically active, whereas the professionals and semiprofessionals were about evenly divided in that regard (1970, 888, 891–92).

Studies of both the U.S. Supreme Court and Congress suggest clearly that parental political activity is related to behavior in office and to the structure of one's career. Sidney Ulmer investigated the impact of three social background variables—birth order, father's political experience, and party affiliation—on the decisions of U.S. Supreme Court justices from 1903 to 1968. He hypothesized that justices whose fathers had held office would be more pro-government in their decisions. That proved to be the case for the period 1936–1968 but not for the years 1903–1935 (Ulmer 1986, 964). The most elaborate effort to assess the impact of family political activity employed data from several different sessions of Congress and concluded that members who were preceded in the House or Senate by a relative did in fact have certain measurable advantages over nonfollowers (Laband and Lentz 1985). In general, members who followed their fathers into Congress were more successful.

It is beyond the scope of this research to address the issue of the influence of social background characteristics on judicial decision making, nor is it possible to apply all the Laband and Lentz analysis to the courts. However, two of the comparisons between followers and nonfollowers in Congress may be replicated here, and a different approach may be used to evaluate the impact of occupational inheritance on judicial success.

The data used are as follows:

> Louisiana Supreme Court
>> Followers   43
>> Nonfollowers   39
>> Total   82
>
> United States Supreme Court
>> Followers   65
>> Nonfollowers   29
>> Total   94

This analysis omits sixteen Louisiana and ten federal justices who were not followers but who did have contemporaries or descendants in office. These are omitted on the assumption that their careers may have been influenced, even indirectly, by the existence (at that time or in the future) of politically active kinsmen (see Kurtz 1995, 450, for further details). A final methodological note is to reiterate that justices may have followed a variety of relatives, not just fathers, in contrast to the Laband and Lentz and the Ulmer data, both of which deal with parent-child following only.

The first variable to be considered is the age at which an individual first became a member of Congress or the U.S. Supreme Court. Data from all Congresses (1789–1979) and from the Eighty-ninth Congress (1965) revealed that followers entered on the average of two or three years earlier than nonfollowers (see Table 8). Similarly, federal judicial heirs reached the bench at about fifty-three years of age as compared to fifty-five for nonfollowers (see Table 9). On the Louisiana court, however, followers were somewhat older.

A second issue is the number of years that individuals remained in office. Followers in the Eighty-ninth Congress averaged twenty-three years of service compared with less than nineteen for nonfollowers. Congressional data for the longer period (1789–1979) revealed a slight tendency in

Laband and Lentz's Findings

	1965 Congress		1789–1979	
	Followers	Nonfollowers	Followers	Nonfollowers
Average age first elected to Congress	39.85	42.37	40.85	44.43
(N)	(20)	(485)	(393)	(10,188)
Average years in Congress	23.0	18.44	6.42	6.65
(N)	(20)	(485)	(393)	(10,188)

Source: Laband and Lentz (1985, 404, 405, Tables 2 and 3)

Characteristics of Followers and Nonfollowers on State and U.S. Supreme Courts

	Louisiana		United States	
	Followers	Nonfollowers	Followers	Nonfollowers
Ages when elected/appointed				
0–29	0 %	0 %	0%	0%
30–39	12.5	18.5	5	0
40–49	37.5	37	23	14
50–59	32.5	30	54	69
60+	17.5	15	18	17
Total	100 %	100.5%	100%	100%
(N)	(40)	(27)	(64)	(29)
Average age	50.33	48.29	52.95	55.03
Years on Supreme Court				
1–4	19%	38 %	5%	24%
5–9	35	20.5	28	21
10–14	21	26	14	7
15–19	2	10	17	24
20–24	16	2.5	14	10
25–29	2	0	8	14
30+	5	2.5	15	0
Total	100%	99.5%	101%	100%
(N)	(43)	(39)	(65)	(29)
Average years	11.67	8.256	16.5	13.1

the opposite direction. The authors point out that the distribution was bi-modal: some followers served only one term and others continued in office much longer than average (Laband and Lentz 1985, 402). The findings from the courts conform to the more recent congressional data. Heirs on both courts served an average of three years longer than those with no family political background.

Laband and Lentz used four sets of data and a variety of indicators to measure the relationship between political inheritance and electoral success, which is the third variable considered here. Based on 1965 data, they concluded that followers are more likely to gain renomination and less likely to be defeated for reelection (402). In 1980 candidates who opposed followers spent more money in their unsuccessful efforts than those who ran against nonfollowers (407). They found that heirs (1981–1982) were less frequently opposed for reelection (405), and historically (1789–1979) followers had a better record of securing renomination and reelection (403).

Judicial success cannot be measured in terms of performance at the polls, especially in the case of the federal court. That might be an indicator for the state judges, many of whom came to the bench during periods when justices were elected. However, judicial elections in Louisiana have never been analogous to elections to any other offices. Many judges were initially appointed to fill vacancies, then they ran as incumbents for the full term, and generally judges do not face opposition to the same extent that other officials do (Vines and Jacob 1963, 113–19). Consequently, judicial success must be measured in some other way. This will be done by examining a previously published subjective rating of all federal justices.

Albert P. Blaustein and Roy P. Mersky (1972) surveyed sixty-five students of the judiciary, requesting that they rate the ninety-six justices of the U.S. Supreme Court who had served between 1789 and 1969. The results of that survey are subjective and do not include the eight justices who came to the bench between 1970 and 1988 who are part of this study (see Table 10). Even with these deficiencies, the Blaustein and Mersky rating is valuable because it is the only one that evaluates all the justices rather than just the "great" jurists, and it is a ranking independent of this research project.

The data displayed in Table 10 reveal only slight differences between followers and nonfollowers in terms of their success on the bench. A larger percentage of followers (33%) were above average than are nonfollowers (24%), and those with a family political legacy were less likely to be in one of the two below-average categories (11% in contrast to 24% for nonfollow-

TABLE 10

Success Rating of U.S. Justices: Followers vs. Nonfollowers

Rating	Followers (N)	%	Nonfollowers (N)	%
Great	(10)	16%	(2)	9.5%
Near great	(11)	17	(3)	14
Average	(35)	55.5	(11)	52
Below average	(5)	8	(0)	0
Failure	(2)	3	(5)	24
Total	(63)	99.5%	(21)	99.5%

ers). At best, inheriting a political career results in modest differences in judicial performance.[1]

An additional line of investigation that was not pursued in other studies may further illuminate the impact of occupational following. If occupational followers did inherit the advantages noted earlier, then they would be in a position to begin their political careers earlier. This is a logical expectation given that followers in Congress and on the federal bench reached their primary positions at a younger age.

An analysis of both courts confirms this expectation. Followers held their first political office one and a half years earlier (Louisiana) and more than six years earlier (federal) than nonfollowers. Nearly half of both groups of inheritors entered politics before the age of thirty, whereas less than one-fifth of the state and one-fourth of the federal nonfollowers became active that young (see Table 11).

SUMMARY

The greater rate of occupational inheritance on the federal bench (63% to 44%) is the most notable difference between the two courts. This finding is consistent with the overall pattern noted in Chapter 1 that federal judges

1. The appropriate measure of correlation for these data would usually be Lambda b were it not for the fact that the modal category is the same for both independent variables. This problem is discussed by Welch and Comer (1988, 161). For those readers inclined to use Chi square as a measure of association (the author is not so inclined), it is 10.78 and is significant at the .05 level. Other tests of association are as follows: Cramer's V = .128; and Pearson's contingency coefficient = .114. I am indebted to Robert K. Goidel of the University of Southwestern Louisiana Department of Political Science for his assistance in this analysis.

TABLE 11

Age at Which Supreme Court Justices First Held Any Political Office

Age	% of Louisiana Justices		% of United States Justices	
	Followers	Nonfollowers	Followers	Nonfollowers
0–29	46%	17%	48%	22%
30–39	37	52	26	30
40–49	11	30	21	22
50–59	6	0	5	26
60+	0	0	0	0
Total	100%	99%	100%	100%
(*N*)	(35)	(23)	(58)	(27)
Average	33.2	34.69	33.1	39.9

generally have more relatives in politics than do the Louisiana justices. Beyond this one difference, the two courts are fairly similar. Federal and state heirs were preceded by close relatives, usually fathers or uncles, and usually by more than one relative.

Political figures, and justices historically, are far more likely to have followed a relative into the political arena than is the case for individuals in other occupational categories. However, recent jurists are more similar to other professions in this regard. The implications of this finding will be explored further in Chapters 3 and 6.

The research also indicates that there are differences between judges who are heirs and those who are not. Both sets of jurists held their first public position at a younger age and remained on the bench longer than did colleagues who did not inherit a family political tradition. The federal judges, but not the state, also reached the high court at a younger age than did nonfollowers. However, only minimal differences were found when assessing the impact of a family political background on success as a jurist.

An evaluation of all the evidence bearing on the issue of the impact of being the product of a political family leads to the conclusion that such a legacy does make a difference. Almost all the studies cited earlier in this section, as well as the judicial data, support the observation that those who have politically active kinsmen predecessors exhibit an earlier interest in politics, begin their political careers earlier, reach high office at a younger age, and remain in those positions longer than nonfollowers. In addition, heirs are more successful in their electoral careers where they face less opposition and are more likely to win.

Only three major pieces of evidence contradict this conclusion. First, among Republican legislators in Oregon, family political experience was not a factor related to winning (Seligman *et al.* 1974, 124). Second, from 1903 to 1935 supreme court justices did not differ in their decisions based on their fathers' political activity (Ulmer 1986, 964). Finally, Louisiana justices who followed relatives into politics did not reach the supreme court at a younger age. This minimal negative evidence cannot detract seriously from the generalization that coming from a politically active family is an advantage for a political figure.

Less can be said about the impact of a family political legacy on behavior once in office. The earlier discussion of other studies indicated that followers were more ambitious and more pragmatic. In addition, Ulmer's analysis of the supreme court from 1936 to 1968 revealed a relationship between father's political experience and the justice's decisions for or against the government (1986, 964). These findings suggest that followers have somewhat different orientations toward their careers and toward the political process. The present study contributes modestly to our understanding of the impact of family political activity. Only one indicator of the behavior of one court could be analyzed, and that investigation revealed that success on the bench is but weakly related to a justice's family political activity.

Although the differences between followers and nonfollowers are small, their general direction is the same: previous family political activity confers advantages that may affect some aspects of one's career. This intangible inheritance can be termed a "political legacy." Others have referred it as "human capital" (Laband and Lentz 1983, 1985) or a "symbolic family estate" (Farber 1971, 97–119). Regardless of the terminology, the idea is the same. In politics a father, or other predecessor, creates goodwill, voter loyalty, a recognizable name, contacts, and a family environment in which his children learn about politics and develop skills early in life. In some instances, a family might even create a kinship myth (Musto 1979; see also Shaw 1985). These intangible goods are transferred to the next generation, the effect of which is to make the recipients "more equal than others at the political starting gate" (Hess 1966, 1).

❖

3

HISTORICAL TRENDS

The two preceding chapters described aspects of judicial families without regard to when the judges sat on the bench. The purpose of this chapter is to develop a chronological perspective by analyzing the distribution of kin-connected jurists through seven historical periods. Others have examined public officials from a similar point of view, and that literature will be summarized first, followed by a discussion of the data on the Louisiana and United States courts.

OTHER HISTORICAL STUDIES

John Schmidhauser investigated the kinship political connections of the members of two levels of the federal judiciary. In 1959 he concentrated on the ninety-one members of the U.S. Supreme Court who served between 1789 and 1957. Twenty years later he focused on 430 judges of the U.S. Courts of Appeal from 1789 through 1976 (1979). His findings are summarized in Table 12 and are presented in graphs at the end of this chapter. Similar graphical presentations of other studies are also to be found at the end of the chapter.

According to Schmidhauser, family political linkages on the part of supreme court justices declined from a high of 85 percent in the period 1789–1828 to a low of 31 percent between 1933 and 1957, though the changes were not unidirectional over all periods (Table 12). The number of kin-connected appellate court judges declined precipitously beginning with the Jackson administration in 1829. These findings are, however, suspect in view of the work of Kermit Hall.[1]

---

1. I have chosen to follow Schmidhauser's article (1959) rather than his later book (1979). The book includes data on the courts of appeal as well as on more recent justices. The presen-

TABLE 12

Judges and Presidents with Relatives in Politics

	1789–1828	1829–1861	1862–1888	1889–1919	1920–1932	1933–1960	1961–1993	Total
U.S. justices[1]								
%	85	57	50	60	72	31[2]	NA	59
(N)	(20)	(14)	(11)	(18)	(7)	(16)		(91)
U.S. courts of appeal[3]								
%	73	33	18	17	11	6[4]	NA	15
(N)	(30)	(3)	(33)	(78)	(47)	(239)		(430)
Presidents[5]								
%	100	89	71	80	33	33	62.5	73
(N)	(6)	(9)	(7)	(5)	(3)	(3)	(8)	(41)

[1] Schmidhauser (1959, 8)

[2] Through 1957

[3] Schmidhauser (1979, 56)

[4] 1933–1976

[5] Author's analysis of Pessen (1984, 11–54) and others

TABLE 13

District, Appellate, and Territorial Judges with Relatives in Politics, 1789–1899

	1789–1800	1801–1828	1829–1860	1861–1876	1877–1899	Total
District and appellate judges						
%	93.5%	94%	82%	74%	67%	78%
(N)	(46)	(49)	(67)	(70)	(131)	(363)
Territorial judges						
%	85%	86%	65%	55%	50%	61%
(N)	(13)	(57)	(74)	(88)	(143)	(375)

Source: Hall (1980, 441)

Nineteenth-century lower federal court judges (district and appellate) and territorial judges form the database of Hall's historical analysis (1980). In both instances he documents fewer family-connected judges over the course of the century (see Table 13). Two other observations on these data are relevant. First, judges on the regular federal courts were more likely than the territorial judges to have had relatives in politics. Second, Hall found far more nineteenth-century judges with such linkages than did Schmidhauser, especially from 1829 to 1900. The databases are different: Hall focused on both district and appellate courts whereas Schmidhauser examined only the courts of appeal. It seems doubtful that the district judges included in Hall's study account for all this variance. This inconsistency is the source of my skepticism with regard to the new data included in Schmidhauser's 1979 book.

Changes in kinship connections among members of Congress from 1789 to 1960 are displayed in Tables 14 and 15. The two studies from which the data are drawn cover the same period and use the same data source, the *Biographical Directory of the American Congress, 1789–1961* (1961). That source identifies congressmen and senators who are related, thus implicitly defining political families as consisting only of members of Congress.

The two papers differ in their databases. Clubok and his colleagues (1969) examine the membership of the House and the Senate; Bogue and his associates deal only with the House. Both found a decline in kinship connections from 1789 through 1960. That change was from 24 to 5 percent

---

tation in the article is clearer and somewhat more elaborate, and I have little confidence in the appellate court data in the book for reasons to be indicated below.

TABLE 14

Percentage of Members of Congress Whose Relatives Also Served in Congress

	1789	1829	1861	1889	1921	1933	1960
%	24%	18%	15%	10%	12%	8.5%	5%
(*N*)	(95)	(284)	(265)	(451)	(563)	(553)	(559)

Source: Adapted from Clubok, Wilensky, and Berghorn (1969, 1043–44)

TABLE 15

Percentage of Members of U.S. House of Representatives
Whose Relatives Also Served in Congress

	1789– 1800	1831– 1840	1861– 1870	1891– 1900	1921– 1930	1951– 1960
% with congressional relatives of all types	34%	21%	12%	12%	12.5%	8%
% who were followers	4%	8%	5%	5.5%	7.6%	5%
(*N*)	(286)	(553)	(506)	(757)	(457)	(351)

Source: Adapted from Bogue, Clubb, McKibbin, and Traugott (1976, 287, Table 4)

in the case of both chambers (Table 14) and from 34 to 8 percent in the House of Representatives alone (Table 15). This suggests differences between the two chambers that are obscured in the Clubok paper.

Bogue and associates (1976) also make generational distinctions by dividing the members into three groups: those with congressional relatives in the same generation, those with relatives in earlier generations, and those whose descendants served in Congress. This approach is similar to the generational analysis in Chapter 1. Most interesting is their observation that "changes in the proportion of representatives who were descendants of earlier representatives are less clear" (1976, 288). In 1789, 4.2 percent of the members followed a relative into the House, whereas between 1951 and 1960 that figure was 5.1 percent. Those figures do obscure an overall decrease in political inheritance, but it is not particularly dramatic nor unidirectional. The highest and lowest rates of following are not shown in Table 15; those extremes were 9 percent in 1841–1850 and 3.6 percent in 1931–1940 (1976, 287). These rates have not varied nearly as much as the more general incidence of all types of kinship connections.

Both studies concentrated on kinship connections within Congress; relationships to officials outside of Congress were not investigated for the entire periods under consideration. However, Clubok, Wilensky, and Berghorn do offer one other useful item of information. On the basis of a questionnaire sent to two hundred members of the Ninetieth Congress (1967) and returned by eighty-five, they found that 54 percent had relatives elected to office (1040–41). Nothing more is said about this survey, but it suggests that when connections to noncongressional officials are taken into account, the proportion of such links rises significantly. Congressional relationships have decreased, but that may not be true of all kinship connections.

A final study bearing on this discussion of historical trends is provided by Edward Pessen (1984), who examined the backgrounds of all the presidents from Washington through Reagan. His findings are summarized at the bottom of Table 12. (President Bush has been added to that tabulation.) The most notable observation to be drawn from these data is that there has been a significant resurgence in kinship connections and occupational following among presidents in the last generation after a forty-year period (1920–1960) in which those phenomena characterized only one-third of the chief executives.

In summary, five of these sets of data indicate a clear decline in the percentage of kin-connected officials from 1789 through either the end of the nineteenth century or the second half of the twentieth century. Two other studies are less clear. The percentage of U.S. Supreme Court justices with relatives in politics has generally declined since 1789 (see Table 12), but that trend was interrupted between 1889 and 1932. The least consistent pattern occurs among presidents. Since 1960, more than twice as many chief executives have come from political families than in the preceding sixty years. The percentage for 1960–1989 is the same as that of a century ago. Only two of the studies discussed here addressed the more specific issue of occupational inheritance. Within the U.S. House of Representatives, following remained low and stable throughout all periods. Most presidents followed a relative into politics, and the rate of following rose and fell along with the rate of all kinship connections.

HISTORICAL PERIODS

In presenting the data on federal and state justices from a historical perspective, the discussion will follow Schmidhauser's scheme of periods with the addition of a seventh, 1961–1988. In each period, information on all kin-connected judges and on inheritors will be provided (see Table 16). Unique characteristics of the periods will be identified, and comparisons will be made to related studies.

TABLE 16

Distribution of Justices by Historical Period

	1789–1828	1829–1861	1862–1888	1889–1919	1920–1932	1933–1960	1961–1988	Total
Justices with office-holding relatives								
Louisiana	60%	59%	61%	80%	89%	57%	20%	60%
United States	95%	93%	88%	67%	57%	59%	25%	72%
Justices who were occupational followers								
Louisiana	60%	32%	39%	70%	67%	57%	10%	44%
United States	75%	77%	71%	61%	57%	59%	25%	63%
Number of justices (N)								
Louisiana	(5)	(22)	(28)	(10)	(9)	(14)	(10)	(98)
United States	(20)	(14)	(16)	(18)	(7)	(17)	(12)	(104)

Source: Adapted from Schmidhauser (1959, 7)

1789–1828.   Differences existed between the federal and state courts during these years, but little can be said about the significance of those variations because Louisiana did not become a state until 1812. Only five men came to the state court in those years in contrast with twenty federal justices.

1829–1861.   Several studies have dealt with the impact of the Jacksonian revolution on patterns of personnel selection with particular reference to changes in the class composition of the elite. Schmidhauser concluded that appointments to the court were "but lightly affected" by changes during the Jacksonian period (1959, 11–12). Changes in the class origins of nominees to the lower federal judiciary were also small, but judges began coming from more modest backgrounds (Hall 1979, 155–56). The territorial judiciary appeared to be more strongly influenced by different standards of selection. Hall found that there was "a significant but transitory effect" on the types of people chosen (Hall 1981, 279). Finally, a comparison of the appointments of Presidents Adams, Jefferson, and Jackson revealed that Jackson appointed more "men of the middle range of the class structure than did Adams or Jefferson" (Aronson 1964, 82).

Significant differences between the courts emerged during the Jacksonian period (1829–1861). The federal court had its highest percentage of followers and its second highest percentage of family-connected judges, whereas just the opposite was the case in Louisiana. The gap between the two is particularly noticeable in terms of followers: the national bench had twice as many (77%) as the state court (32%). Compared with the previous era, following remained stable on the U.S. Supreme Court but declined at the state level. However, that change in Louisiana was in relation to the first period when only five justices came to the bench.

To the extent that occupational following is an indicator of continuity, the Jacksonian period brought "new men" (Pessen's term 1969, 180) to the state court but not to the federal. It is doubtful, however, that the low rate of political inheritance in Louisiana after 1829 was a direct result of Jacksonian reforms. While there had been some Jacksonian type changes in the Constitution of 1845, they were largely undone in 1852 (see Shugg 1939, 121–43). Thus, political reform was not a factor. It seems more likely that the relative newness of the state as a political system explains the federal-state differences. Louisiana's political families, like the state, were in their formative stages. Five of the ten state jurists who were "founders" came to the court between 1829 and 1861, and they constituted over one-third of the justices in this period. Family political traditions were being created rather than maintained before the Civil War.

1862–1888. Followers as a percentage of entrants continued to decline somewhat on the federal court, but there was a slight increase on the state court from 32 to 39 percent. The figures for state judges from 1862 to 1888 are misleading because those dates do not correspond to the realities of Louisiana political developments at the time. It is more sensible to divide this period into two subperiods: 1862–1877 and 1877–1888.[2] The first sub-period corresponds to the disruptive years of the Civil War and Recon-struction, and 1877 ushered in the lengthy era of the "Bourbon Ascendancy" (see Howard 1971, Chap. 6) or "One Party Oligarchy" (Havard, Heberle, and Howard 1963, 23–27) in Louisiana politics. As one historian has com-mented, "When the long years of war and Reconstruction were over, the same class of men that had controlled the state before the war, the planters in the country and the merchants, bankers, and brokers of New Orleans, was back in control. That class would not relax its hold until well into the twentieth century" (Wall 1984, 208). Whether that control reached its "Clas-sical" phase between 1881 and 1888 (Taylor 1976, 135) or was "Triumphant" by 1900 (Hair 1969, 268–79) is not as important as the fact that the group dominated an entire period and that the data on occupational inheritance continuing into the 1930s confirm that dominance.[3]

Fourteen justices came to the state supreme court from the beginning of the Civil War through the end of Reconstruction, and another fourteen had joined the bench by the end of 1888. During the first period only five (38%) of the fourteen judges were from political families and only two (14%) were followers. After Reconstruction twelve of the fourteen (86%) had relatives in politics, and nine (64%) were inheritors. The five kin-connected pre-Reconstruction judges were Hyman and Labauve, who served from 1865 to 1868; Taliaferro, 1866–1876; Morgan, 1873–1877; and Leonard, November, 1876, to January, 1877. Leonard and Morgan were the two follow-ers. Four of the five were far from being typical Louisiana politicians.

Philip H. Morgan was a Unionist, even though four of his half brothers joined the Confederacy. John E. Leonard moved to Louisiana in 1870 and served on the court less than three months. The nature of William B. Hy-man's political loyalties was ambiguous, but he was eventually appointed to

2. In identifying historical periods I have generally followed Havard, Heberle, and Howard (1963, 18–27). They summarize and adapt a longer discussion by Howard (1957).

3. For a discussion of this entire period, see Hair (1969, 107–40). On the composition of the Bourbon elite, see Taylor (1974, 508), Sindler (1956, 25–26), Key (1949, 159), and Howard (1971, 153–54). See Taylor (1976, 135–37) on the sources of Bourbon power and Wall (1984, 214) on Bourbon attitudes. Dethloff and Jones (1968, 301–23) provide a contrasting interpretation of Bourbon power.

the court by Unionist governor Wells (Lathrop 1958, 308–18). James G. Taliaferro served in the Secession Convention and was a Cooperationist voting
against secession (Shugg 1936, 199–203). Only Justice Zenon LaBauve seems
to have supported the Confederate cause. He helped finance a Confederate
company in Iberville Parish, a group which eventually became known as
the Labauve Guards (Riffel 1985, 85).

The Civil War and Reconstruction was an unusual time in Louisiana
history, and the composition of the court reflects that situation. With the
end of Reconstruction in 1877, politics and the court began to take on the
characteristics that were to last for more than two generations.

1889–1919.   Among state judges the percentage with family political connections increased to 80 percent. That was, however, a slight decrease from
the 86 percent with such connections during the post-Reconstruction
decade of 1877–1888. The percentage of federal justices from political families continued to decline during the 1890s and into the next century. The
Louisiana court had its highest percentage of heirs (70%), somewhat more
than the 64 percent from 1877 to 1888. Followers on the federal bench fell to
just over three-fifths of the total.

1920–1932.   After the First World War, the two courts continued to move
in different directions. Louisiana had more kin-linked judges than at any
other time, whereas federal justices had fewer such connections than in any
previous period. The two courts did remain similar in terms of inheriting a
political tradition. Both recorded slight decreases in the number of members following a relative into politics.

1933–1960.   By the penultimate period in this analysis both courts had
virtually the same percentage of justices from political families, and all were
heirs. This represents little change in the case of the federal bench, whereas
in Louisiana there was a notable drop in all family-connected judges and a
modest decline in occupational inheritance.

This period corresponds generally to the Long era of 1928 to about
1960 (see Havard *et al.* 1963, 27–33). The data correspond to the 1928–1960
division even better. Fifteen judges came to the state court during the Long
era, and fourteen of them joined the court after 1932. In other words,
changing the starting date of this period from 1933 to 1928 involves the
shifting of only one justice. The data can be further rearranged to compare
the Long era with the years of "One Party Oligarchy" (Havard *et al.* 1963,

23–27), which began after Reconstruction in 1877 and ended with the Long ascent in 1928. These recalculations reveal the following:

1877–1927	66 percent heirs (21 of 32)
1928–1960	60 percent heirs (9 of 15)

Overall following decreased by only 6 percent during the entire Long era compared with the preceding period. However, during the three decades of Long power, the rate of inheritance was as low as 50 percent in the early years and then rose in the late 1940s and 1950s to 67 percent, or nearly what it had been in the 1920s. The Long era marked some change in the composition of the court at the outset, but that change was being reversed well before the end of the period. This is not to suggest that the Louisiana justices were the same types of people as in the earlier period, but in terms of family political connections the difference was not lasting.

In at least one case, however, the Longs did associate themselves with elements of earlier periods. One of Huey Long's allies was Senator John H. Overton, a brother of Winston Overton, who had come to the Louisiana Supreme Court in 1921 (Sindler 1956, 46, 80). Thomas Overton Moore was an earlier member of the Overton family. He led the secession movement as governor in 1861, whereas the Long family's Winn Parish had generally opposed breaking away from the Union (Williams 1970, 11–12). One of the more surprising aspects of this study is that other than these brief comments about the Longs, the state's most renowned family, they are not relevant to this analysis. They had no members on the court and did not marry into any judicial families.

1961–1988.   In the final period both courts were characterized by the lowest rates of family-connected judges and followers. The justices who came to the bench were White, Burger, and Powell of the federal court and Lemmon and Tate of the Louisiana court. An additional Louisiana judge was almost included in this period. Frank Summers was sworn in as a justice on December 12, 1960. He is considered to be in the 1933–1960 cohort but just barely. There is probably one more follower among the Louisiana justices in the final period. Justice Lemmon's father-in-law was in office, but his dates of public service are not known. The justice could not be considered an heir because of the possibility that their careers were contemporaneous. Taking those cases into account would increase the rate of following to 30 percent, still lower than the 57 percent of the previous period.

There are several possible explanations for these changes since 1961. First, as noted in Chapter 1, there are problems with the data for the more recent judges. Some of them may have kinship political connections, but information to that effect is not available. Second, some appointees had unusual backgrounds. According to *Current Biography* (1986, 502) and *Guide to the U.S. Supreme Court* (1979, 861–63), three justices (Goldberg, Fortas, and Scalia) were sons of immigrants. In addition, the first African American (Thurgood Marshall) and the first woman (O'Connor) came to the court after 1960. These "nontraditional" appointees constituted five of the twelve of this period who were less likely to have come from established political families.

Another explanation that must be explored is that changes in the courts in the last generation may reflect the fact that family political connections are generally no longer significant in any institutional context. An examination of the literature on recent political elites will consider that possibility, as well as afford an opportunity to compare and contrast the judiciary with other levels of the political system, a task that could not be undertaken until information on this most recent period was presented.

The findings of other scholars who have documented family political activity in the modern era are summarized in Table 17 and were discussed in two earlier works (Kurtz 1989, 332–35, and 1993, 2–6). These studies vary in their definitions of political activity and kinship, but they will serve as a basis for comparison. Regardless of these variations, the table indicates that public officials from politically active families range from a low of 28 percent in the Missouri legislature (entry #4) and among a variety of Louisiana leaders (#11) to a high of 63–64 percent among Connecticut legislators (#6) and presidents (#10). Almost all of these works identify cases who had relatives in politics before the individual's career began; that is, the table indicates the extent of occupational following among various types of political figures. Supreme court justices who inherited a political legacy in the modern period actually are at the lower end of that range. One-fourth of the federal and one-tenth of the state judges were followers.

The combined evidence from the judicial data and from Table 17 leads to three conclusions about elite kinship connections in the late twentieth century. First, political families are less prevalent now. Second, in spite of this decline historically, family linkages are still significant and are to be found in most political institutions. Finally, the courts, and the Louisiana bench in particular, deviate from the patterns found in other institutions in the last generation. One must keep in mind that some recent justices may be similar to those state jurists who served in an earlier period (1829–1861) and who were disproportionately "founders." Eventually their descendants may hold office, but they have yet to become politically active.

TABLE 17

Percentage of Public Officials with Relatives in Politics

Institution	Dates	(N)	%	Source
Congress				
1. Senate	1947–57	(180)	*ca.* 33%	Matthews (1960, 49)
2. House and Senate	1965	(150)	30%	Laband & Lentz (1985, 395)
3. House and Senate	[90th]	(85)	54%	Clubok, Wilensky, & Berghorn (1969, 1041)
State legislatures				
4. Missouri	1955, 1957	(144)	28%	Derge (1959, 416)
5. California, New Jersey, Ohio, Tennessee	1957	(474)	*ca.* 52%	Eulau *et al.* (1959, 193)
6. Connecticut	1959	(96)	*ca.* 64%	Barber (1965, 27, 71, 121, 168)
7. Oregon	1966	(107)	43%	Seligman *et al.* (1974, 125)
Other				
8. Party officials in North Carolina and Massachussetts	1963	(138)	*ca.* 38%	Bowman & Boynton (1966, 672)
9. California campaign workers	1956	(200+)	40%	Marvick & Nixon (1961, 196, 209)
10. Presidents	1961–93	(8)	63%	Kurtz, based on Pessen (1984, 11–54)
11. State and local La.	1983	(785)	28%	Kurtz (1989, 339)

Before concluding this chapter, the findings in this study must be compared with those of John Schmidhauser. He found that 59 percent of the federal justices from 1789 to 1957 had significant family political connections (1959, 8), whereas the present study puts that figure at 72 percent. In every period except one (1920–1932), the more current research indicates a larger percentage of kinship-linked judges than Schmidhauser did. This difference is a result of two factors. First, more effort has been devoted to the kinship issue because discovering those linkages was the sole purpose, whereas Schmidhauser had additional objectives. Second, the 1959 paper did not address the incidence of office holding by contemporaries and descendants as this project does. The scope of this research is both narrower and broader than Schmidhauser's work. It is narrower because it is concerned only with kinship connections, and it is broader because it seeks to document all possible office-holding relatives.

SUMMARY

Between 1789 and 1961 most supreme court justices came from political families. Except between 1889 and 1932, the federal bench always had a larger percentage of justices with kinsmen in politics. The courts differed in the directions in which they changed between 1789 and 1932. Federal judges in the earlier periods were more likely to have had relatives active in politics, but that percentage began to decline, minimally at first and then sharply, at the time of the Civil War. In contrast, the percentage of Louisiana justices with relatives in politics increased steadily from the early nineteenth century, reaching a high of 89 percent between 1920 and 1932. Only since 1933 have the courts begun to exhibit some similarities. They had nearly identical percentages of family-connected members between 1933 and 1960, and both recorded a sharp decline in that percentage between 1961 and 1988.

The historical patterns of occupational inheritance are generally similar to those identified for all family-connected judges with the exception that on the Louisiana court there was a notable decline in following during the Jacksonian period when family political traditions were being established. The federal court had more heirs in every period except the two (1889–1919 and 1920–1932) noted above. Following declined precipitously in the final period. Generally the courts have become more similar since the New Deal with respect to both variables.

Evidence from the judiciary and from other studies indicates that the patterns of kinship connections are no longer as prevalent as they once were, but they still constitute significant characteristics of the American political elite. Compared with other institutions in the modern period, the judiciary has fewer members from political families, but that may well be a temporary phenomenon that will be reversed as the current cohort of justices begins to found politically active families.

It is too early in the analysis to draw many definitive conclusions about the most recent group of justices. The next two chapters document extensive kinship networks of which the judicial families are a part. Once that presentation is made, additional observations may be made about families in the past thirty years.

FIGURE 4

Percentage of U.S. Justices with Relatives in Politics, 1789–1957

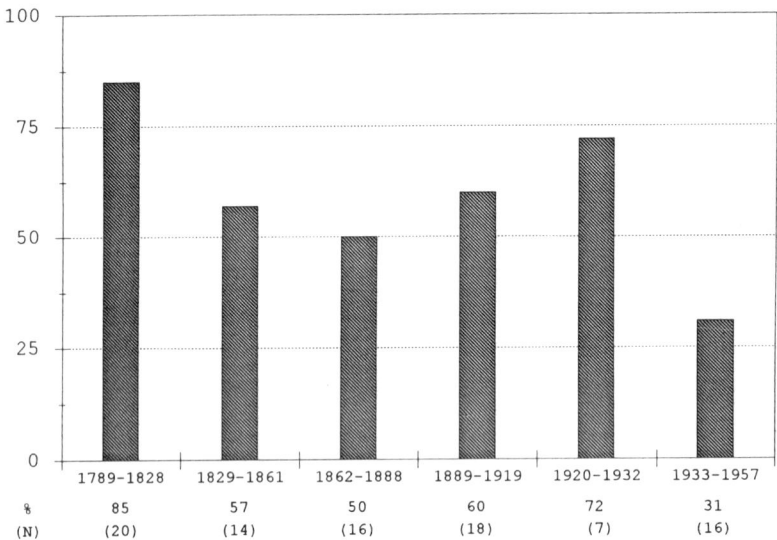

	1789-1828	1829-1861	1862-1888	1889-1919	1920-1932	1933-1957
%	85	57	50	60	72	31
(N)	(20)	(14)	(16)	(18)	(7)	(16)

Total All periods: 59% (N = 91)

Source: Schmidhauser (1959, 8)

FIGURE 5

Percentage of Members of U.S. Courts of Appeal with Relatives in Politics, 1789–1976

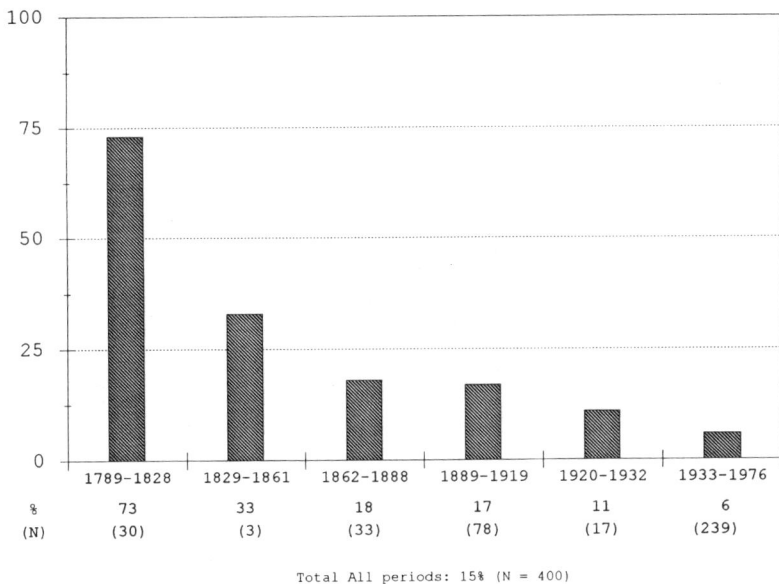

	1789–1828	1829–1861	1862–1888	1889–1919	1920–1932	1933–1976
%	73	33	18	17	11	6
(N)	(30)	(3)	(33)	(78)	(17)	(239)

Total All periods: 15% (N = 400)

Source: Schmidhauser (1979, 56)

FIGURE 6

Percentage of Judges of U.S. Courts of Appeal and District Courts
with Relatives in Politics, 1789–1899

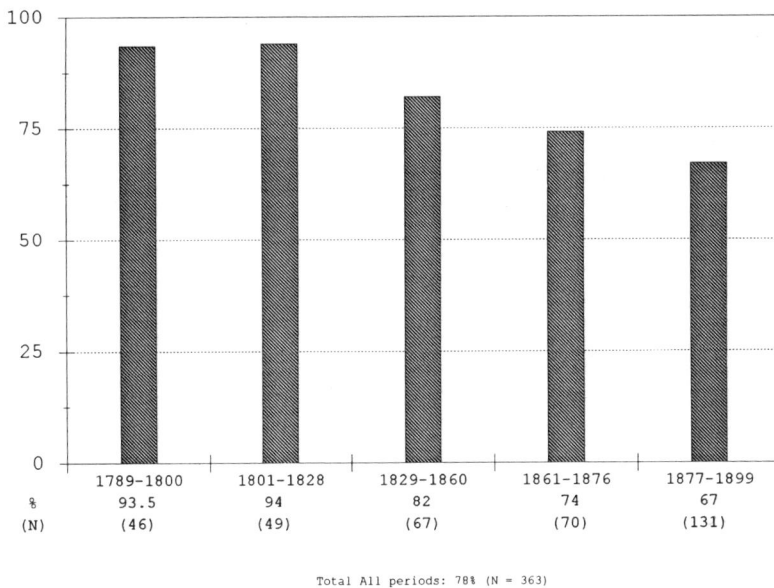

	1789–1800	1801–1828	1829–1860	1861–1876	1877–1899
%	93.5	94	82	74	67
(N)	(46)	(49)	(67)	(70)	(131)

Total All periods: 78% (N = 363)

Source: Hall (1980, 441)

Percentage of Judges of Territorial Courts with Relatives in Politics, 1789–1899

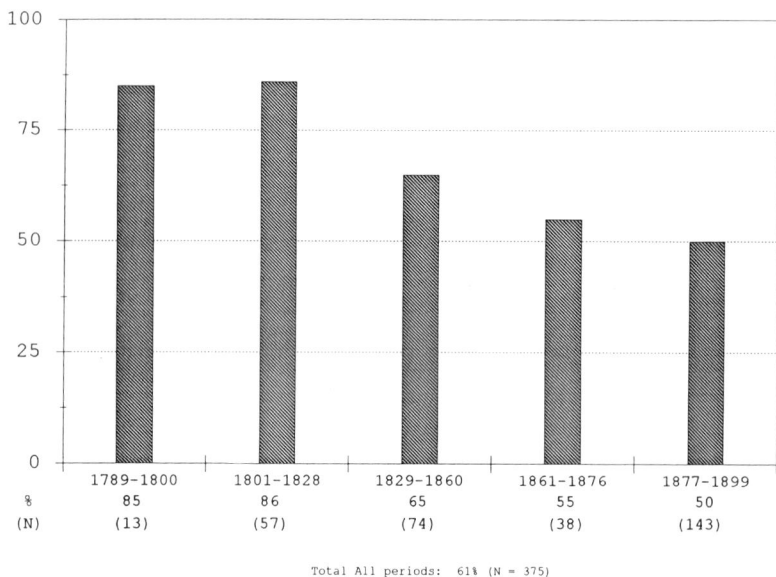

	1789–1800	1801–1828	1829–1860	1861–1876	1877–1899
%	85	86	65	55	50
(N)	(13)	(57)	(74)	(38)	(143)

Total All periods: 61% (N = 375)

Source: Hall (1980, 441)

F I G U R E   8

Percentage of Members of U.S. Senate and House of Representatives
with Relatives in Congress

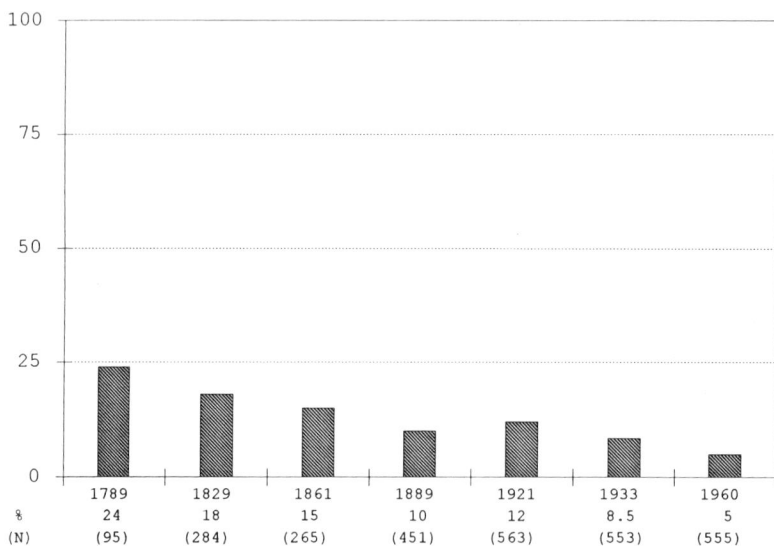

	1789	1829	1861	1889	1921	1933	1960
%	24	18	15	10	12	8.5	5
(N)	(95)	(284)	(265)	(451)	(563)	(553)	(555)

Source: Clubock, Wilensky, and Berghorn (1969, 1043–44)

FIGURE 9

Percentage of Members of U.S. House of Representatives Who Had Relatives
in Congress and Who Were Followers

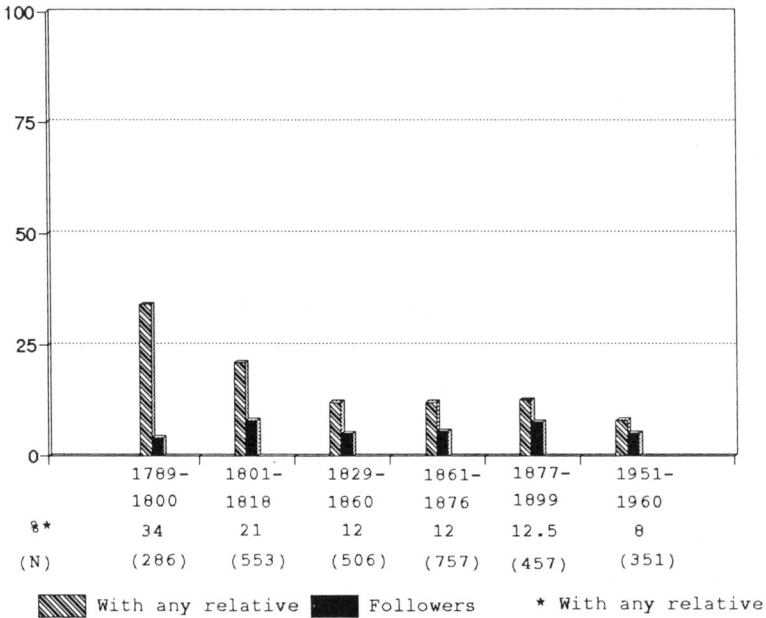

	1789–1800	1801–1818	1829–1860	1861–1876	1877–1899	1951–1960
%*	34	21	12	12	12.5	8
(N)	(286)	(553)	(506)	(757)	(457)	(351)

▨ With any relative   ■ Followers   * With any relative

Source: Bogue, Clubb, McKibbin, and Traugott (1976, 287)

FIGURE 10

Percentage of Presidents Who Had Relatives in Politics and Who Were Followers

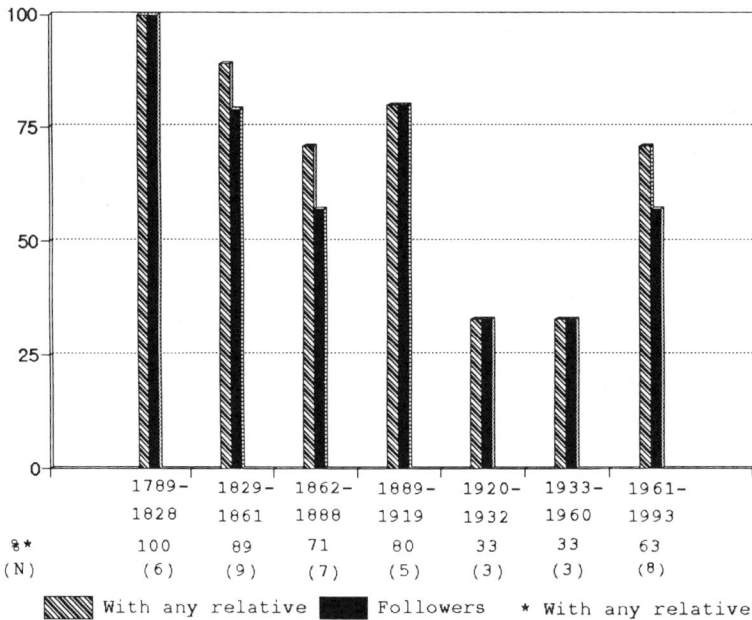

	1789–1828	1829–1861	1862–1888	1889–1919	1920–1932	1933–1960	1961–1993
%*	100	89	71	80	33	33	63
(N)	(6)	(9)	(7)	(5)	(3)	(3)	(8)

▨ With any relative   ■ Followers   * With any relative

Total all periods: 73% (N = 41)

Source: Author's analysis of Pessen (1984, 11–54) and others

FIGURE 11

Percentage of Louisiana and U.S. Justices Who Had Relatives in Politics, 1789–1988

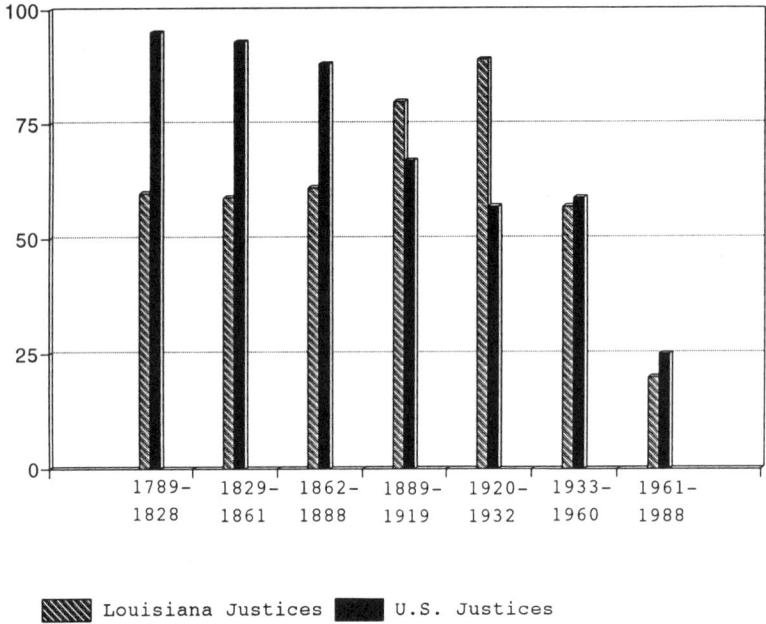

Louisiana Justices   U.S. Justices

FIGURE 12

Percentage of Louisiana and U.S. Justices Who Were Followers, 1789–1988

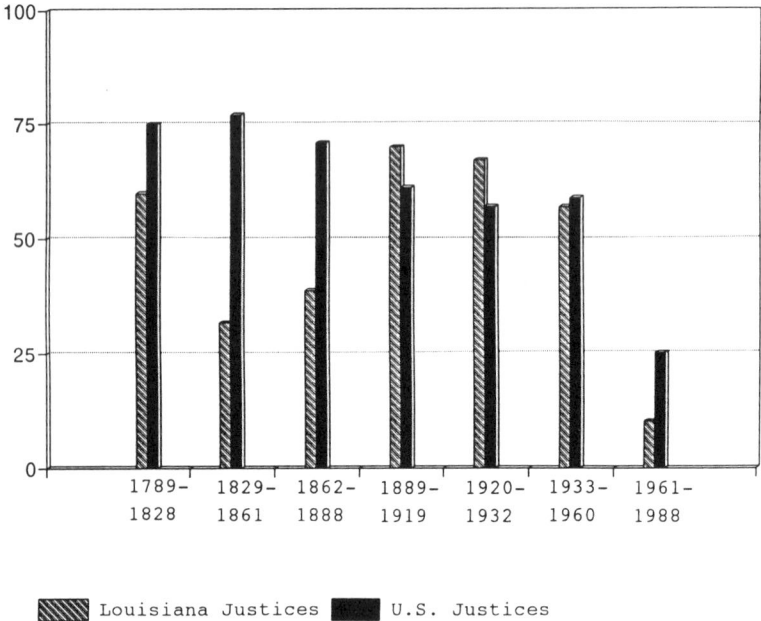

Louisiana Justices   U.S. Justices

4

THE SMALLER KINSHIP
NETWORKS

The analysis thus far has focused on the fifty-nine Louisiana and seventy-five United States justices who had relatives in public office. That approach may now be expanded to investigate the phenomenon of "kinship networks."

A kinship network exists when officeholders in two families are connected in one of three ways. First, the two could be relatives as defined in Chapter 1. For example, the two connected cases might be first cousins descended from a common grandfather. One has descended through a paternal line and the other, through a maternal line. Others in the paternal line have held office, so the cousin through that line is a member of a political family. In the case of the maternal line, the mother married into another political family, and her son bears the name and is a member of that other family. Second, officials from two families could have a common great-great-grandparent and thus be as distant as third cousins.

Third, the children, the siblings, or a sibling and a child of officials from two families could marry. Figure 1 (in Chapter 1) illustrates the possibilities. If AE and IJ constitute two families and if G, the child of E, married K, the child of J, a network would be formed.

It is important to note that these are linkages between officeholders or their children or siblings. For the purposes of this study, other relationships are not considered. In addition, the study deals only with links between the families of justices and between the family of a justice and an allied family. With one exception to be noted later, connections between allied families are not discussed, though they often exist. Documenting those linkages is beyond the scope of the research because the task is potentially endless. The result of this self-imposed limitation is that the networks do not appear to be well integrated. In a fully integrated network, every family is related to every other family (see Whitley 1974, 67, on this point). A second result is that there are more separate networks than would be the case if relationships between allied families were included. Those links would often tie two or more networks together, reducing the number of networks.

Two additional comments must be made. First, the exact nature of the connections between the various families is indicated in the entries in Appendix A for each justice. Second, those linkages may be between either the judges' "relatives" or "collateral relatives." Most of the analysis up to this point has dealt with the relatives (in a judge's family and in other families), not the more distant collateral kin. Thus, the link between the judge's family and another family may not involve a close relationship between the justice and a member of the other family, but the link is always fairly direct between officials in the two groups.

Seventy-one percent of the state judges and 59 percent of the federal judges who are members of political families are also components of political networks based on kinship. The families of these justices are connected either to each other or to 165 allied families, forming forty-five kinship networks.

These kinship networks vary considerably in size and importance, and those factors determine the method of presentation. Forty-three groups are small; the largest has only seven families. Appendix B contains a chart for each of these minor networks, and aggregate data on the groups will be discussed in the first part of this chapter. Network 44 is a larger entity, and it will be analyzed from a somewhat different perspective in the second part of this chapter. Chapter 5 continues the network analysis with a consideration of the large and complex network 45. Observations on all forty-five groups form the concluding section of Chapter 5.

NETWORKS 1–43

Twenty-two of the forty-three minor networks include twenty-nine Louisiana justices,[1] and the remaining twenty-one are centered around twenty-five federal justices (see Figure 13). The first three networks are unusual in that they consist of a single justice linked to an allied family. The case of Justice Bradley illustrates the situation. There were no other

1. Parts of three Louisiana networks (39, 41, and 43) were discussed from a different perspective in Kurtz (1989, 346–49).

Kinship Networks 1–43

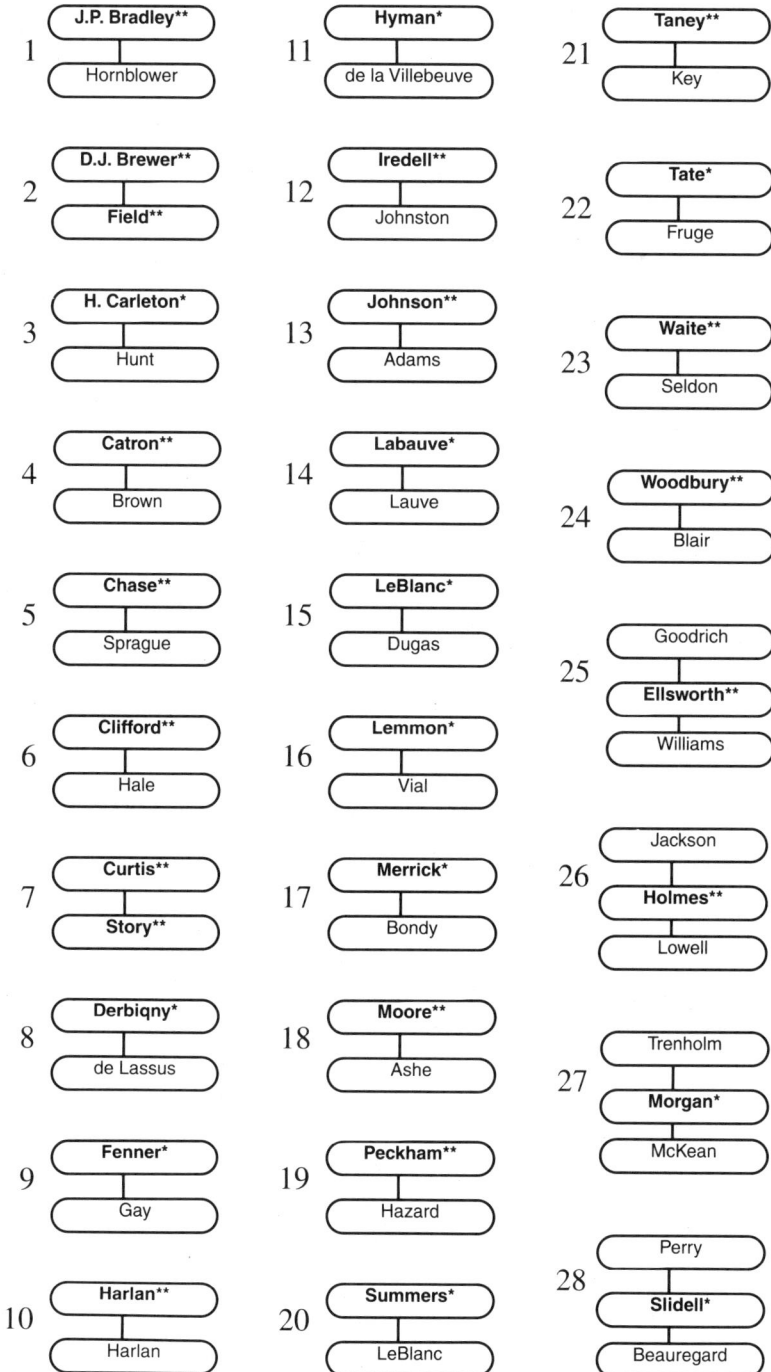

1. J.P. Bradley** — Hornblower
2. D.J. Brewer** — Field**
3. H. Carleton* — Hunt
4. Catron** — Brown
5. Chase** — Sprague
6. Clifford** — Hale
7. Curtis** — Story**
8. Derbiqny* — de Lassus
9. Fenner* — Gay
10. Harlan** — Harlan

11. Hyman* — de la Villebeuve
12. Iredell** — Johnston
13. Johnson** — Adams
14. Labauve* — Lauve
15. LeBlanc* — Dugas
16. Lemmon* — Vial
17. Merrick* — Bondy
18. Moore** — Ashe
19. Peckham** — Hazard
20. Summers* — LeBlanc

21. Taney** — Key
22. Tate* — Fruge
23. Waite** — Seldon
24. Woodbury** — Blair
25. Goodrich — Ellsworth** — Williams
26. Jackson — Holmes** — Lowell
27. Trenholm — Morgan* — McKean
28. Perry — Slidell* — Beauregard

(cont.)

FIGURE 13

(continued)

29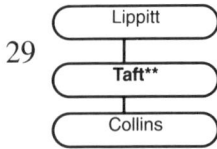

Lippitt
Taft**
Collins

30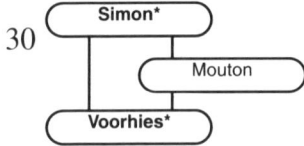

Simon*
Mouton
Voorhies*

31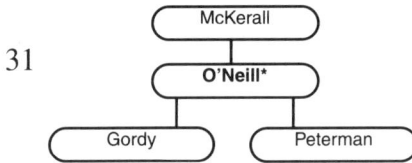

McKerall
O'Neill*
Gordy   Peterman

32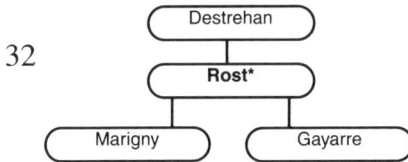

Destrehan
Rost*
Marigny   Gayarre

33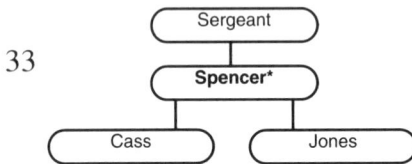

Sergeant
Spencer*
Cass   Jones

34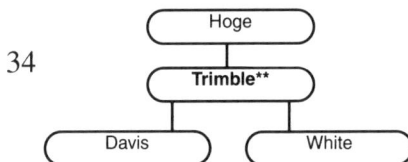

Hoge
Trimble**
Davis   White

35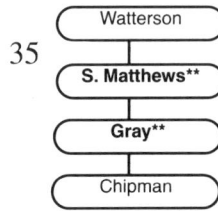

Watterson
S. Matthews**
Gray**
Chipman

36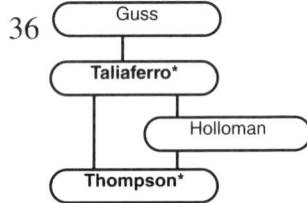

Guss
Taliaferro*
Holloman
Thompson*

37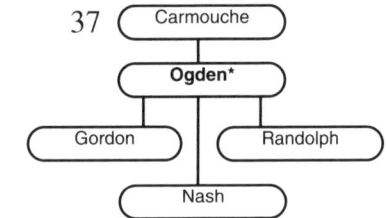

Carmouche
Ogden*
Gordon   Randolph
Nash

38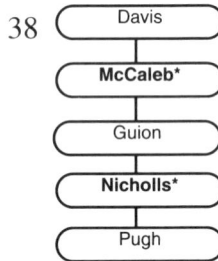

Davis
McCaleb*
Guion
Nicholls*
Pugh

39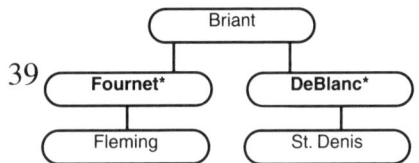

Briant
Fournet*   DeBlanc*
Fleming   St. Denis

FIGURE 13

(continued)

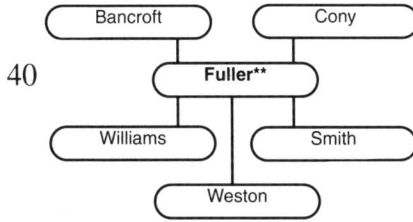

40

Bancroft — Cony
Fuller**
Williams — Smith
Weston

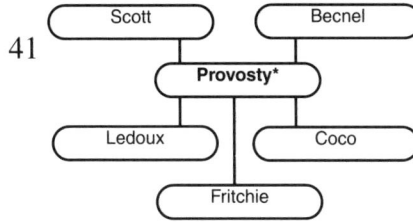

41

Scott — Becnel
Provosty*
Ledoux — Coco
Fritchie

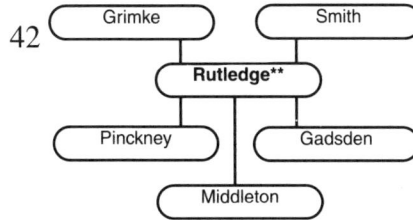

42

Grimke — Smith
Rutledge**
Pinckney — Gadsden
Middleton

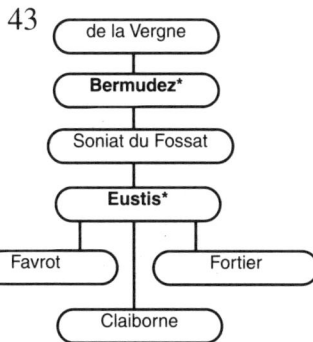

43

de la Vergne
Bermudez*
Soniat du Fossat
Eustis*
Favrot — Fortier
Claiborne

Bradley officials; his only office-holding relative was his father-in-law, Joseph C. Hornblower. If there had been no additional Hornblower officials, then there would have been a single family consisting of the justice and his father-in-law. However, there were other Hornblowers in office to whom the justice was not related. Consequently, the justice is placed in a two-component network. He alone is allied to the Hornblower family in which he has one relative, but there are others in that family to whom he is not related. This explanation applies to networks 1, 2, and 3. A somewhat similar situation was resolved differently in the case of Justice Burton and his Hitz relatives. There were only two Hitz officials, both of whom were Burton's ancestors. In that instance all three are considered to be members of the same family.

There are no instances in which a network includes both state and national justices, though one federal set (#21) does have two officials in an allied family (the Keys) who held office in Louisiana. This situation thus permits a comparing and contrasting of federal and state networks.

Table 18 indicates that there are no real differences between the state and federal networks in terms of the number of justices in each set of families. Most state and federal systems have only one justice, but one Louisiana network (#30) has four members on the high court. In that group, the Simon family had a grandfather and grandson on the court and the Voorhies family was represented by a father-son set of justices.

Fifty-five percent of the Louisiana-centered groups involve three or more families, whereas 67 percent of the United States networks involve only two families. This difference is related to the fact noted in Chapter 1 that the author had greater access to information on less prominent local families based in Louisiana. Had it been possible to examine materials in each of the states of residence of all federal judges, the number of allied families in federal networks would be far greater.

The number of officials in the various networks ranges from four to fifty-three (#43). Louisiana networks have more officials than those revolving around federal judges. Over two-thirds of the state groups boasted ten or more officeholders, while most federal networks had fewer officials. This finding is, of course, consistent with there being more families in the Louisiana-based networks.

Considerable variation exists among the networks in the extent to which members held office at or near the top of the political hierarchy (see Table 19). Here the political eminence of the networks is assessed in terms of the number of major public positions in each set of families. "Major positions" include members of the U.S. Senate or House of Representatives,

TABLE 18

Justices, Families, and Public Officials in Networks 1–43

Network Characteristics	% of Networks	
	Louisiana	United States
Justices		
1	77%	81%
2	18	19
3	0	0
4	5	0
Total	100%	100%
(N)	(22)	(21)
Families		
2	45 %	67%
3	14	14
4	18	9
5	14	5
6	4.5	5
7	4.5	0
Total	100 %	100%
(N)	(22)	(21)
Public officials		
1–9	32%	57%
10–19	41	33
20+	27	9.5
Total	100%	99.5%
(N)	(22)	(21)

the cabinet (and top assistants), governors, state supreme court justices (other than Louisiana), and ambassadors (or ministers). An "other" category includes presidents, vice presidents, members of the Continental Congress, and important foreign officers. The number of major positions in a network may exceed the number of occupants because of frequent multiple office holding.

Although the federal networks are smaller in terms of officeholders, they do have more individuals in major positions. This is the most notable difference between the two sets of networks. Forty-one percent of the Louisiana groups had no one in a major office, whereas every federal network had at least one person in one of these high offices and almost half

TABLE 19

Major Positions, States, and Years in Public Service in Networks 1–43

Network Characteristic	% of Networks	
	Louisiana	United States
Major positions		
0	41 %	0 %
1–3	36.5	24
4–6	4.5	28.5
7+	18	47.5
Total	100 %	100 %
(N)	(22)	(21)
Number of states and countries		
1	45 %	28.5%
2	23	28.5
3	9	24
4	0	9
5	4.5	5
6	4.5	0
7	14	5
Total	100 %	100 %
(N)	(22)	(21)
Range of service		
1–99	29 %	25%
100–124	14	15
125–149	9.5	25
150–174	19	20
175–199	5	5
200+	24	10
Total	100 %	100%
(N)	(21)*	(20)*

* Inadequate information for networks 7 and 8.

had seven or more major positions. The Rutledge network (#42) was the most prominent group in this respect with twenty-seven major positions. Both the Taft (#29) and a Louisiana-based network (#43) had members in twenty-two top positions.

Members of the Continental Congress were often among the "other" major positions. About one-third of the federal networks had at least one representative in that body, and again the Rutledge group led with six officials. Three presidents and two vice presidents are also included among these "other" major positions. President Taft is a part of network 29, and both Adamses are to be found in network 13. Vice President Levi P. Morton, a Eustis in-law, belongs to network 43. Jefferson Davis was the most notable member of the Davis family in network 38. Four participants in the Constitutional Convention of 1787 are also included in the "other" category; three are in network 42, and one is in network 25.

Most networks are represented by officials in more than one state, resulting in regional kinship systems. The Louisiana and United States networks are distributed differently, however. Federal groups are more likely to cross state borders (70%) than are the Louisiana networks (55%), but relatively more Louisiana groups (23% compared with 10%) list officials in five or more states. In addition, of the eight networks with leaders based in foreign countries, six are centered on a Louisiana justice's family (networks 3, 8, 30, 32, 33, and 39). France, Belgium, Canada, the Bahamas, and Honduras are the foreign countries found in the Louisiana networks. Two federal networks (2 and 35) include officials from France and Canada. Those Louisiana networks which extend outside the state usually link Louisiana to other southern or border states, but in five instances Louisiana networks (3, 27, 28, 33, and 43) include up to five northern states as well as southern and border states. Generally, it would be difficult to conclude that any significant differences exist between the state and federal groups in terms of this variable. More Louisiana networks are based in that one state alone, but multistate Louisiana networks more frequently have officeholders in five or more states.

There are two ways to assess the continuity of these political networks over time. The first is to calculate the range between the earliest and the most recent years in which a member of the group was in office. The second is to construct a time line for each network. Table 19 contains data relevant to the first approach. The figures in that table may be low because precise dates of service are often not available. For example, if it is known that someone served in a public office but not exactly when, and if that official died in 1750, then the entry "earliest office" in Appendix B will read "Ante 1750," and 1750 will be used as the date of earliest public service in all tabulations. The same problem may exist, though less frequently, with the item "latest office." In two instances it was not possible to make even an estimate in this regard, so networks 7 and 8 are omitted from this discussion.

The networks vary from a low of 50 years (#4) to a high of 367 years (#43) between first and last dates of office holding. Officials in Louisiana networks usually have served over a longer period of time than is the case

with the federal networks. Two facts support this observation. First, 29 percent of the Louisiana groups had public service spread over 175 years or
more compared with 15 percent of the federal networks. Second, the average number of years of service is 156 for the state systems compared with
132 years for those with federal judges. Even excluding network 43, which is
unusually long at 367 years, the Louisiana average is still 143 years. This
difference is once again related to the fact that Louisiana networks consist
of more families and more officials.

The figures in Table 19 do not indicate anything about the continuity
of office holding. The range of service could be great, but the network
might still be characterized by long gaps between officials. Figure 14 plots
the decades of public service for each network. In that figure an entire
decade is filled in if anyone held office during that ten-year period. Office
holding is said to be continuous if there is less than a ten-year interval between officials.

Three major observations emerge from this figure. First, a fairly large
number of networks are characterized by uninterrupted service. In fifteen
instances (37%) no gaps occur in the sequence of public service. Although
most networks did experience periods when no one was in office, the fact
that so many had continuous service is additional evidence of the continuity of family traditions of public service. A second observation is that sixteen (39%) had members in office sometime after 1950, and in five of those
cases the justice served within that latter period. Finally, one federal and
eight Louisiana networks had eleven individuals serving as recently as
1980–1988. Four of these recent incumbents left office before 1988. They
were a state district judge (#38), a federal district judge, former Louisiana
Supreme Court justice (Albert Tate, Jr.), and a member of the state legislature (#41). The other seven were still in their positions in 1988. They include
Justice Harry T. Lemmon and his wife (a district judge), two other district
judges (#39 and #43), U.S. Senator John Chafee (a member of the Lippitt
family in network 29), a mayor, and another federal district judge who is
the father of the state legislator noted above. These findings provide additional support for the assertion that the kinship factor retains relevance in
the modern era.

NETWORK 44

The first of the two major networks orbits around the family of Justice
Brockholst Livingston. It consists of five United States justices and their
families, which are connected to nineteen allied families. This kinship sys-

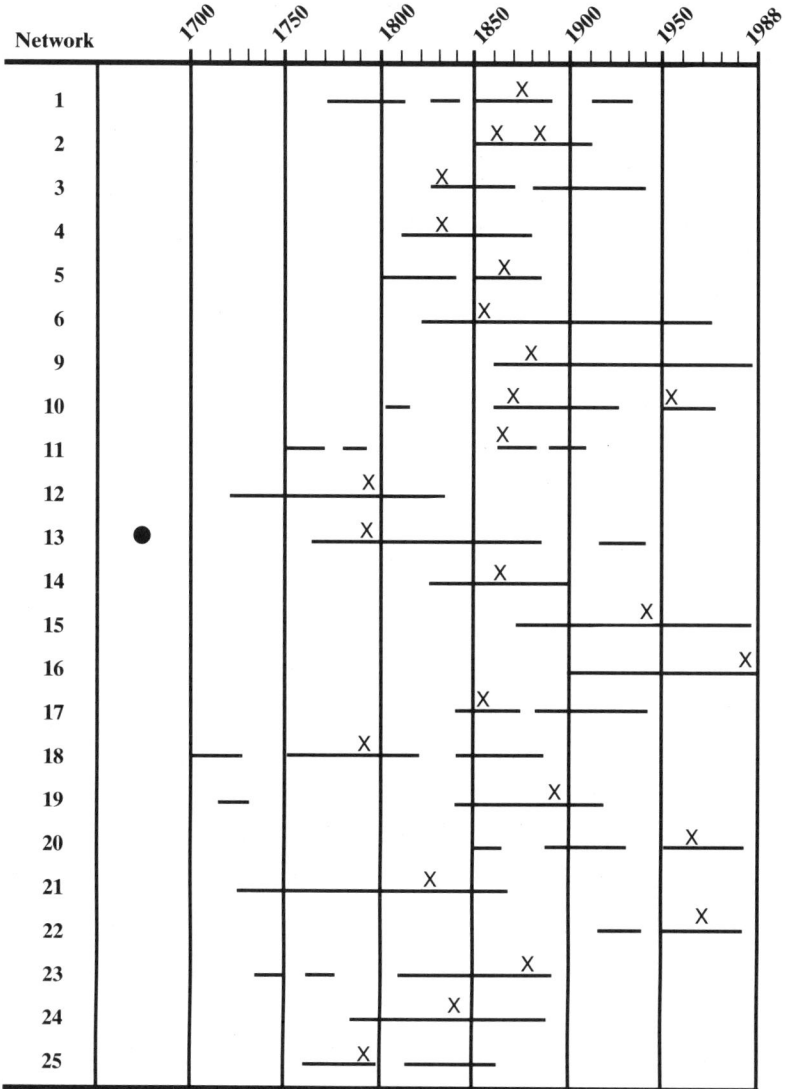

FIGURE 14

Years of Service in Networks 1–43

(cont.)

FIGURE 14

(continued)

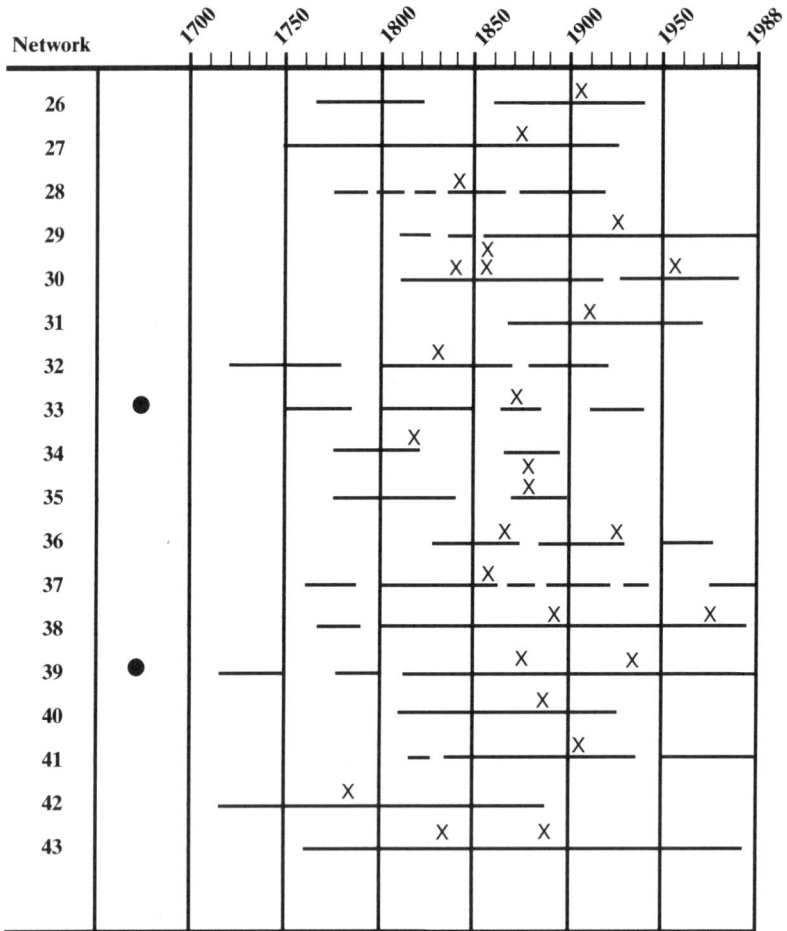

● Member of network in office prior to 1700.

tem includes 133 officials from twelve states and two foreign countries. These individuals began their public service in 1609 and still had members in office in 1988. During that 379-year period these leaders held ninety-five major offices. Geographically the group is centered in New York, New Jersey, and other northern states, but Louisiana, Virginia, and Delaware are also represented.

Kinship Network 44

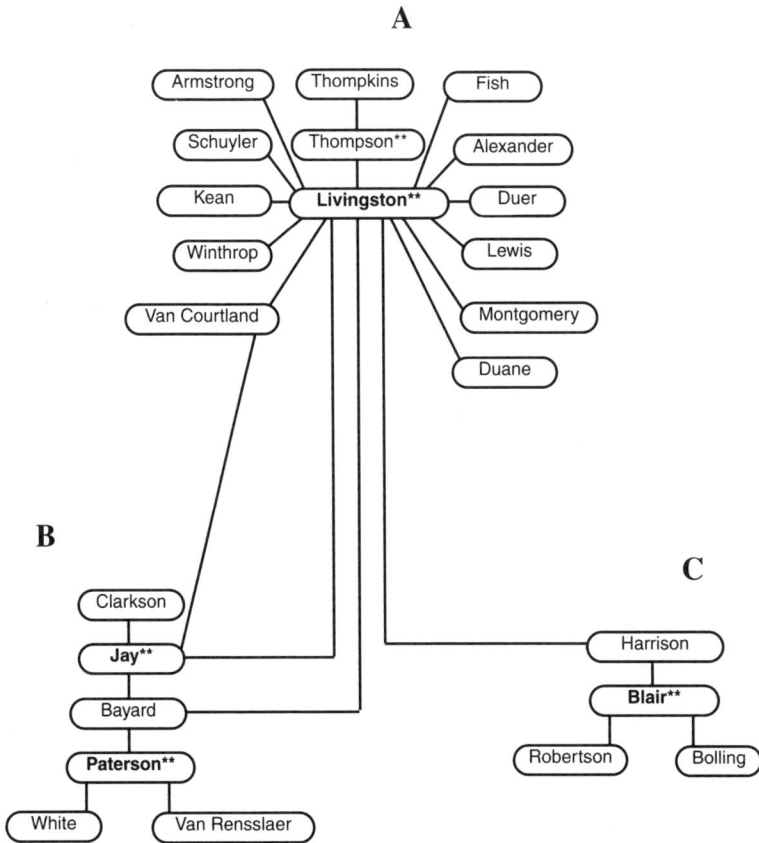

As Figure 15 suggests, this network has three somewhat independent subnetworks. The analysis that follows will deal with each part of the network, based on the data in Table 20 and Figure 16.

At the center of group A is the twenty-nine-member Livingston family, one of the largest single families in this study. It is connected to fifteen other families, second only to the Marshalls of network 45 in that regard. Livingstons account for 39 percent of the seventy-five officials, and they held over a quarter of the major positions. Livingston public service was almost continuous from about 1700 to 1850. Although based primarily in New York and New Jersey, one member of the family, Edward Livingston

Years of Service in Network 44

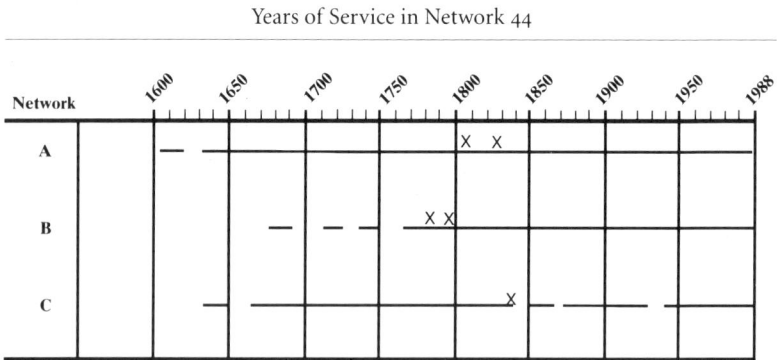

(1764–1836), became an early congressman and senator from Louisiana after having held office in New York.

An interesting note on the Livingston family's Louisiana connections is that incumbent congressman Robert L. Livingston (R-La.) is descended from the New York Livingstons and is a second cousin six times removed of Edward Livingston. Congressman Livingston is not included in the family listing in Appendix A because he is not closely enough related to any of the other officials to qualify even as a collateral relative, but he is a direct descendant of the First Lord of the Manor Robert Livingston (1654–1728). He holds the same congressional seat as did his distant kinsman.

Group A also accounts for the longest period of public service within network 44; with the exception of two decades in the early 1600s, officials served continuously from 1609 through 1988. The earliest officeholder was John Winthrop, who had been a justice of the peace in England before coming to Massachusetts where he became governor. New Jersey governor Thomas H. Kean and New York congressman Hamilton Fish, Jr., continued the public service careers of this set of families into 1988.

Members of group A held every one of the major positions in American politics. Included are twelve congressmen, eight governors (of five states), and ten members of the Continental Congress.

Group B of network 44 also has two members on the federal bench, William Paterson and Chief Justice John Jay, a brother-in-law of Justice Brockholst Livingston. Their families are connected to four others, and the total set includes twenty-nine officeholders, some of whom held eighteen major positions. The Bayard family is the largest in this group with twelve members. Their public service began in 1685 when Nicholas Bayard became mayor of New York, and it continued into the 1980s with Alexis I. DuPont

T A B L E   2 0

Selected Characteristics of Families in Network 44

Group	Justices*	Allied Families	Officials**	Earliest Office	Latest Office	Range of Years	States	Major Positions
A	2	12	75	1609	1988	380	6	59
B	2	4	29	1685	1985	301	4	18
C	1	3	29	1642	1969	328	7	18
Network total	5	19	133				12***	95

* All are federal justices, and each is from a different family.

** Includes supreme court justices.

*** Column total represents the total number of different states.

Bayard still active on the finance committee of the Democratic National Committee. Bayards can count five senators and a secretary of state among their members in New York, Pennsylvania, Delaware, and New Jersey.

The Blair-centered group C of network 44 is interesting because of its geographical concentration in Virginia, whereas the other two parts of the network are located in the northern states. Twenty, or over two-thirds, of the figures in this group held office in Virginia. All the Blairs and Bollings and four of the five Robertsons pursued their careers in that state. The Harrisons began their public service in Virginia, but only six of the fourteen members of the family served there. It was through the "northern" Harrisons that the Livingston connection was made.

There are two Harrison-Livingston linkages. Justice Livingston was a granduncle of Congressman John Scott Harrison (1804–1878) of Ohio, who in turn was the father of President Benjamin Harrison. In addition, Justice Livingston was a brother-in-law of Judge John Cleves Symmes, the grandfather of John Scott Harrison.

The Harrisons account for almost half the officials in group C and exhibit considerable longevity and geographical diversity. Benjamin Harrison I initiated the family tradition of public service as a member of the Virginia House of Burgesses in 1642. The most recent in the long line of Harrisons is William Henry Harrison, a congressman from Wyoming until 1969. Between these two kinsmen were two presidents and ten others who held office in Ohio, New Jersey, Indiana, Illinois, and Virginia.

The Robertsons were primarily a Virginia family, but in 1807 Thomas Bolling Robertson came to Louisiana, where he was appointed secretary of the Louisiana Territory by President Jefferson. Robertson became Louisiana's first congressman in 1812 and won election to the governor's office in 1820. Two of his brothers were active in Virginia politics, one in Congress and the other as governor.

❦

5

A NATIONAL ELITE NETWORK
1632–1988

The most complex of the forty-five kinship systems consists of thirteen Louisiana and fourteen United States justices from twenty-one families, which in turn are linked to eighty-six allied political families. It is a national network in that the 698 officials were active in twenty-six states, the District of Columbia, and two foreign countries. Members of these groups held 249 major positions, including the presidency. The cumulative public service of the network spans an uninterrupted 366 years beginning in 1623 and continuing into 1988 with several individuals still in office.

For analytical purposes, the network is divided into thirteen parts or groups of families (see Figure 17). These groups have no intrinsic significance other than being centered around a particular justice; the relationships among families within a group may be similar to the connections between families in two different units. The discussion that follows focuses on the notable aspects of each part of the network.[1] Some of those characteristics are presented in Table 21 and Figure 18.

GROUP A

The largest element in network 45 has fourteen families with 121 officials. At its center is the family of Chief Justice John Marshall. Although based in Virginia, members of this group have held office in thirteen other states over a period of 315 years. The extended Marshall family is the largest in this study with thirty-six members. Marshall officials are linked to fifteen allied families, eleven in group A and four in other parts of the network.

---

1. Four groups (G, H, J, and K) were discussed in Kurtz (1989, 347–49).

FIGURE 17

FIGURE 17

Kinship Network 45

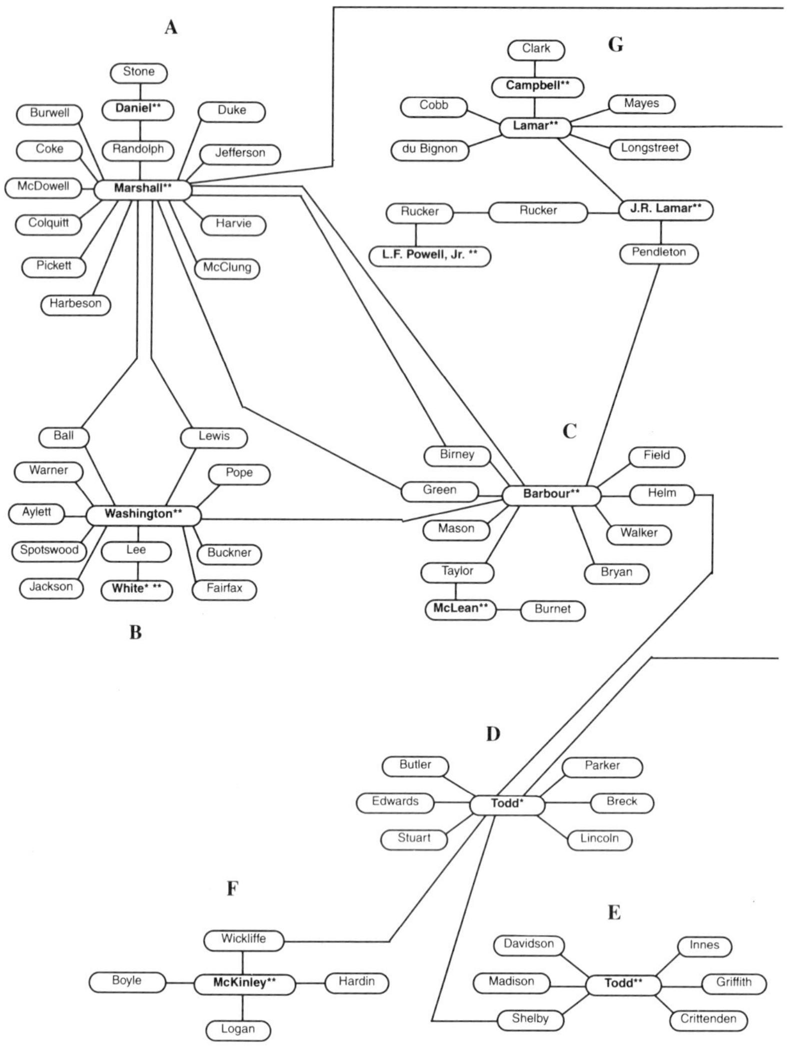

The Marshalls are also related to the families of United States Justice Philip Barbour (group C) and Justice Frank Adair Monroe of Louisiana (group H). Based almost entirely in Virginia and Kentucky, Marshalls account for eleven of the fifty-two major positions in group A including five congressmen, two senators, and three cabinet members. In addition to Chief Justice

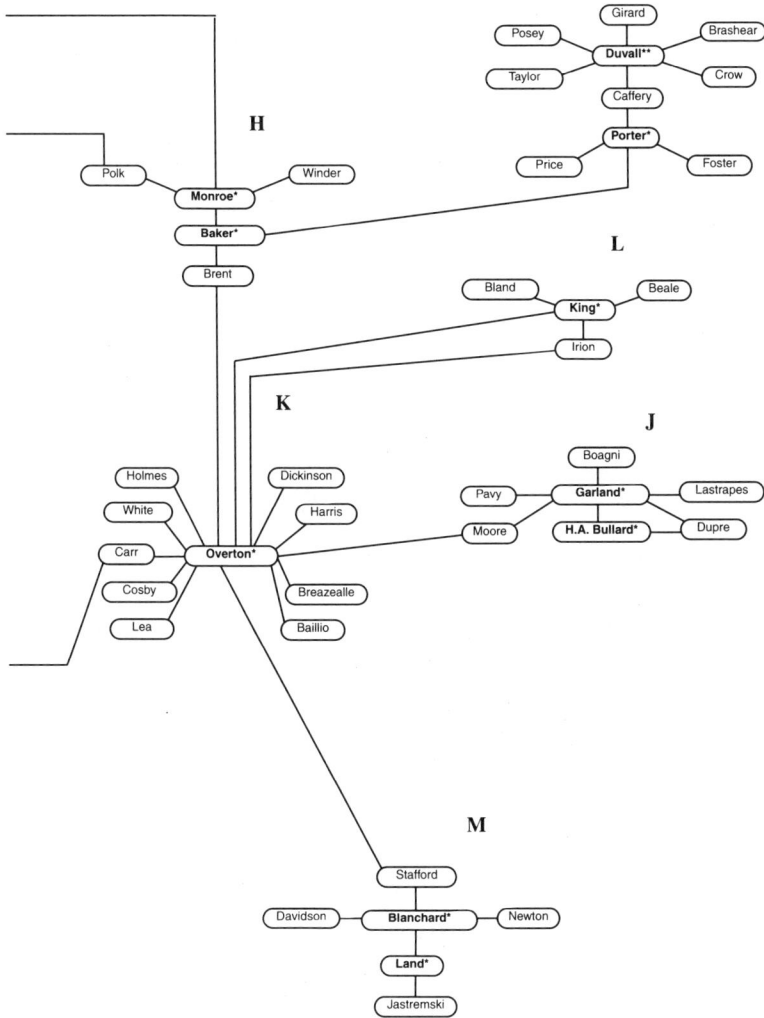

FIGURE 17

Kinship Network 45

John Marshall, the other most eminent member of the family is General George C. Marshall, a grandson of William Champe Marshall, who was a first cousin once removed of the chief justice. The public service of the group ended when General Marshall left office as secretary of defense in 1951.

TABLE 21

Selected Characteristics of Families in Network 45

Group	Justices La.	Justices U.S.	Justices' Families	Allied Families	Officials	Earliest Office	Latest Office	Range of Years	States	Major Positions
A	0	2	2	12	121	1637	1951	315	14	52
B	1	3*	3	9	99	1637	1979	343	14	34
C	0	2	2	9	62	1702	1907	206	16	26
D	1	0	1	6	46	1733	1940	208	12	20
E	0	1	1	6	40	1714	1914	201	10	15
F	0	1	1	4	25	1780	1912	133	4	13
G	0	4	2	8	70	1731	1987	257	14	29
H	2	0	2	3	41	1731	1988	258	11	17
I	1	1	2	8	40	1719	1988	270	7	9
J	2	0	1	5	29	1817	1988	172	2	5
K	1	0	1	9	67	1623	ca. 1975	353	11	22
L	1	0	1	3	24	1659	1922	264	4	3
M	4	0	2	4	34	1645	1948	304	4	~4
Total	13	14	21	86	698				27**	249

* Edward D. White is counted twice.

** Twenty-six different states and the District of Columbia.

Thomas Jefferson held a disproportionate number of the fifty-two major positions in this group, but many others also held high office: fifteen congressmen, six senators, six cabinet officers, six members of the Continental Congress, and seven governors. The governors were Beverley Randolph, Thomas Mann Randolph, Edmund Randolph, Lewis Burwell (acting), and James McDowell of Virginia, Alfred Holt Colquitt of Georgia, and Richard Coke of Texas. As one might expect to be the case in a group of prominent southern families, many held high office in the Confederacy, including at least five generals (Humphrey Marshall, Alfred Holt Colquitt, George Wythe Randolph, Basil Duke, and George Pickett).

During 315 years of public service, members of this group expanded outward from Virginia and the eastern seaboard. Maryland was the state of origin for the Stones and Dukes. Richard Duke was the earliest of the 121 officials as a member of the King's Council of Maryland in 1637. An eighth-generation descendant of that early Duke, James K. Duke was a grand-nephew of Justice Marshall. By this generation many of the Dukes were in Kentucky, but James K. Duke went to the Montana Territory and served as clerk of the territorial legislature. Virginia congressman Richard Coke, Jr., had a nephew of the same name who was a leader in Texas as a state supreme court justice, governor, and U.S. senator.

Other states represented in this group are Ohio and North Carolina (McDowells), Pennsylvania (Robert Morris), California and Louisiana (Edmund Randolph, a grandson of Governor Edmund Randolph, 1753–1813), Arkansas and Alabama (Picketts), Mississippi (Joseph P. Foree of the Marshall family), and New York (H. Snowdon Marshall).

The Randolph family deserves special note for several reasons. With twenty-six members it is one of the largest allied families. It has been described as "the leading family of colonial Virginia" (Birmingham 1987, 90). Moreover, the Randolph family of network 37 (in Chapter 4), which includes an incumbent Louisiana official, is probably related to the Virginia Randolphs, but the precise connection cannot be determined. Another set of Louisiana Randolphs consisting of William and Benjamin H., Rapides Parish officials in the nineteenth century, may be linked to the other two families (*Biographical and Historical,* 587; and Stafford 1969, 224–29). Finally, Riffel (1985, 317–18), Postell (1980, 154–56), and *Genealogies of Virginia Families* (1976, 4:226–55), offer information on a Mississippi Randolph family with several public officials who were descendants of Henry Randolph (1623–1673), probably an uncle of William Randolph of Turkey Island (1651–1711).

FIGURE 18

Years of Service in Network 45

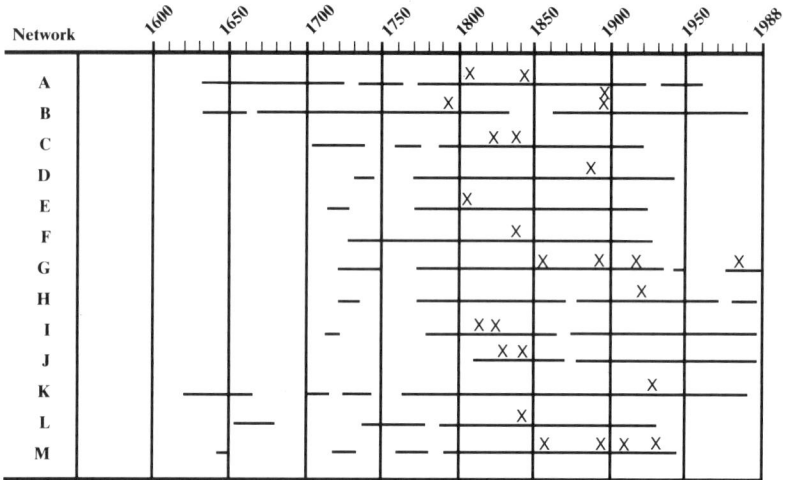

Network	1600	1650	1700	1750	1800	1850	1900	1950	1988
A					X X		X		
B					X		X		
C					X X				
D						X			
E				X					
F					X				
G						X X X		X	
H							X		
I					X X				
J					X X				
K							X		
L					X				
M					X	X X X			

GROUP B

The Washington family, at the center of this set with twenty-one members, is linked to nine allied families and the families of Justices Jackson and Barbour (in group C). Edward Douglas White's family is also included as a result of common kinship with the Lees. This part of network 45 is second only to the Marshall group in terms of political prominence with ninety-nine officials and thirty-four major offices in fourteen states.

Beginning in 1637 with Nathaniel Pope (*ca.* 1610–1660) in the Maryland Assembly and concluding in 1979 when Governor Blair Lee III left office, the group's public service is fairly continuous through 343 years except for a three-decade gap in the mid-1800s. Two other officials were in office after 1960: George Thomas Washington, on the U.S. Court of Appeals from 1949 to 1965, and P. Blair Lee, a member of the Philadelphia Housing Authority from 1955 to 1962.

Eight members (mostly Lees) served in the Continental Congress. Another eight have been governors: Simon Bolivar Buckner, Sr., of Kentucky; Alexander Spotswood, Henry Lee, and Fitzhugh Lee of Virginia; Thomas Sim Lee and Blair Lee III of Maryland; John Pope of the Arkansas Territory; and Meriwether Lewis of the Louisiana Territory.

In addition to the White family of Louisiana, there are three other connections to Louisiana. The Buckners are based in Virginia and Kentucky, but three Buckners—Louis Sr., Louis Jr., and David—held local office in Tensas Parish, Louisiana, in the late nineteenth century. Second, Governor Simon Bolivar Buckner, Sr., married Delia Hayes Claiborne, who was probably a second cousin once removed of Governor William C. C. Claiborne. Finally, the Popes were another Virginia-Kentucky family with kinsmen in Louisiana politics. Nathaniel Wells Pope was a state district judge, and his father had been a police juror and legislator from West Feliciana Parish.

Six of the fourteen states represented in this group have been noted in the preceding discussion (Virginia, Kentucky, Maryland, Louisiana, Pennsylvania, and the Arkansas Territory). More than most families, the Popes contribute to the further geographical spread of this group. In addition to members already mentioned, William Hayes Pope (b. 1870) was a New Mexico Supreme Court justice and a federal judge, Nathaniel Pope (1784–1850) was a congressional delegate from the Illinois Territory, and William Pope (1836–1874) was a Mississippi judge. Other states and their officials are North Carolina and the District of Columbia (the Whites), California (Ben Franklin Washington), and Ohio and Tennessee (the Jacksons).

GROUP C

The most distinctive characteristic of group C is the geographical dispersal of its officials over sixteen states, more than any other in network 45. Even more striking is the fact that eight of the eleven families had members in office in more than one state, and seven of those are represented in three or four states. The three single-state families are the McLeans of Ohio and the Masons and Helmses of Kentucky. Eight families have members based in Virginia and/or Kentucky, but those two states cannot be considered the center of the group, as Virginia is in the case of groups A and B. This is predominantly a southern and border state group with officials in Texas (both the state and republic), the Florida Territory, Alabama, Mississippi, West Virginia, Arkansas, Louisiana, and the District of Columbia, but the North and West are included as well (Ohio, New Jersey, Michigan, Illinois, California, and Colorado).

Group C is less prominent than A and B as measured by the number of major positions (see Table 21). The most numerous of those top positions is the U.S. Senate with six occupants including Jacob Burnet of Ohio, James David Walker of Arkansas, George Walker of Kentucky, and James Barbour, John Taylor, and John Strode Barbour, all of Virginia. There were also five members of Congress and five state supreme court justices.

James Taylor (1674–1729), a great-grandfather of President Zachary Taylor, was the earliest official, serving as a justice of King and Queen County, Virginia, in 1702. Confederate Lt. General Richard Taylor, son of the president, is the only Louisiana officeholder in the group; he was in the state legislature. The last official was John F. Rixie, a Barbour in-law, who represented Virginia in Congress from 1897 to 1907. Finally, this set of families includes one of the few female officials in this study. Emilie Todd Helm, wife of Brigadier General Ben Hardin Helm, CSA, daughter of Robert Smith Todd, and sister of Mary Todd Lincoln, was postmistress of Elizabethtown, Kentucky, from about 1883 to 1895.

GROUP D

Robert B. Todd of the Louisiana Supreme Court is the central figure in group D, but this is by no means a Louisiana-based set of families.[2] All of the families have at least one member who held office in Kentucky, the state which must be considered the central location of the group. However, Kentucky is only the starting point for movement to other areas. Every family was also active in at least one other state, and six of the seven had kinsmen in three or more states.

The Todds, Butlers, and Parkers all had some political experience in Louisiana, but only the Parkers are primarily a Louisiana family. Three of the four Parkers were based in that state, the most important of whom was John Parker, governor from 1920 to 1924. Justice Todd came to Louisiana from Missouri after the Civil War, and he, his brother-in-law J. Harvey Brigham, and his grandson Will H. Todd, Jr., were the only Louisiana Todds.

Ten members of this group served in the U.S. House of Representatives, the most frequently held major position. Representing six states, the congressmen were two Stuarts, John Todd Stuart and Alexander H. H. Stuart (of Illinois and Virginia); two Brecks, David and Samuel (of Kentucky and Pennsylvania); two Edwardses, Benjamin and his grandson Benjamin Edwards Grey (of Maryland and Kentucky); and three Butlers, William Orlando and John W. Menzies (both of Kentucky) and Thomas III (of Louisiana). The tenth member of the House was Abraham Lincoln of Illinois. Half of these congressmen served in the 1830s and 1840s.

A great-great-grandfather of President Lincoln, Mordecai Lincoln, was the first in this group to hold office; he was a justice of the peace in Penn-

---

2. Another perspective on the Todd family may be found in Kurtz and Pena (1990).

sylvania in 1733. There were no other officials until the 1770s, but from then on their service was uninterrupted until Will H. Todd, Jr., left the Louisiana legislature in 1940.

GROUP E

Some members of the Todd family of group D are related to officials in four other parts of the network, including group E, whose main figure is United States Justice Thomas Todd. His family, though not related to the family of Robert B. Todd, is also based in Kentucky as are all the families in group E. Each has at least one Kentucky official, and four of the seven have additional members in Virginia politics (Todd, Madison, Crittenden, and Innes). The Crittendens spread their political activity beyond those two states to include Missouri and the Illinois and Arkansas Territories. Somewhat similarly, the large Shelby family includes five Kentucky officeholders and another five in North Carolina, Tennessee, Alabama, and the Republic of Texas.

There may be additional Illinois officials. According to Green (1964, 206–207), Samuel Davidson, a brother of two Davidson officials, moved to Illinois in 1824 where his sons became prominent in politics. I have not been able to identify these members of the family.

One-third of the major positions represented here were governors: George Mason of Virginia, Thomas Theodore Crittenden of Missouri, John J. Crittenden and Isaac Shelby of Kentucky, and Robert Crittenden of the Arkansas Territory. The earliest official in the group was John Madison, the great-grandfather of President Madison and sheriff of King and Queen County, Virginia, in 1714. Two hundred years later, the group's public service ended when Judge David Shelby of the U.S. Court of Appeals left office in 1914.

GROUP F

Justice John McKinley was born in Virginia, but he went to Kentucky to study law. From there he moved to Alabama, the location of all his political activity. He is one of only six members of this group not from Kentucky. All the Hardins, Logans, and Boyles held office in Kentucky, as did five of the Wickliffes and the other two members of the justice's own family.

With ten members, the Wickliffes are the largest and in some ways the most interesting family in this set. Early Wickliffes located in Virginia, but Charles Wickliffe settled near Springfield, Kentucky, shortly after 1785. Two of his sons became active in Kentucky politics, one of whom was Charles Anderson Wickliffe, a member of Congress and then postmaster general from 1841 to 1845. His son Robert Charles Wickliffe (1819/20–1895) studied under Dr. Louis Marshall, a brother of the chief justice. While his father was in the cabinet, Robert Charles married a daughter of Louisiana congressman John B. Dawson in 1843. Three years later, ill health required him to leave Kentucky. He and his wife moved to Wyoming plantation, the Dawson home in West Feliciana Parish, Louisiana. Five years later, Robert Charles Wickliffe became a member of the Louisiana Senate, and in 1856 he began a four-year term as governor.

Just before the Civil War, the Wickliffes reached the height of their political influence. Between 1856 and 1861, Robert C. Wickliffe was governor of Louisiana, his brother John Crepps Wickliffe was a Kentucky legislator, a brother-in-law, David Yulee, was a U.S. senator from Florida, and another brother-in-law, Joseph Holt, was U.S. commissioner of patents and then postmaster general (1857–1859), a position previously held by his father-in-law.

As was the case with so many Kentucky families, the Civil War was a divisive event. According to the *Dictionary of American Biography* (19–20:183), Governor Wickliffe of Louisiana "disapproved of secession, but when he saw that the tide could not be stemmed, he endeavored to hasten separation." His father opposed secession and was a Union Whig in Congress from 1861 to 1863. Two of the governor's cousins died as Confederate soldiers, and David Yulee was a Confederate congressman. Another cousin was a Union cavalry officer. Wickliffes held eight of the thirteen major offices in the group, and the last official was Robert Charles Wickliffe, son of the governor, who left the U.S. House of Representatives in 1912.

GROUP G

The structure of this set of families is somewhat unusual and requires explanation. Joseph Rucker Lamar and Lewis F. Powell do not belong to "families" in the usual sense of the word. Their situations are similar to that of Justice Bradley, which was described in Chapter 4. Justice Lamar's relatives are in the Rucker (2) and Pendleton families, whereas Justice Powell's only kinsman is in the Rucker (1) family. That there are two Rucker families in this subnetwork is an exception to a basic limitation that I imposed to the effect that connections between allied families would not be considered. That rule is ignored here because both Rucker groups are branches of the same family, and the connection between them is quite clear. Tinsley White

Rucker (b. 1813) and Elbert Marion Rucker (1828–1906), both of Rucker (2), are great-great-grandsons of Thomas Rucker, of Rucker (1), as well as uncles of Justice Joseph Rucker Lamar.

Another criterion of the study is set aside in indicating a connection between Joseph Rucker Lamar and the family of Justice Lucius Q. C. Lamar. The two justices are probably fourth cousins,[3] a relationship too distant to constitute a linkage according to the definitions set forth earlier. The distance of that relationship, however, did not inhibit the two from thinking of themselves as part of the same family. A biographer of L. Q. C. Lamar contends that "he never lost interest—his letters show—in the members of his family" and that "Justice Lamar was writing encouragingly to his brilliant young cousin Joseph Rucker Lamar" (Cate 1935, 509). Given the reality of that awareness and contact, it seems appropriate to indicate a linkage that goes beyond the standards imposed earlier.

Two other Lamar leaders cannot be placed precisely in the family tree. They are Maximillian Lamar, a Revolutionary general, and James Robert Lamar, a Missouri congressman from 1903 to 1905 and from 1907 to 1909 (Cate 1935, 15, 509; *Members*, 1985, 95).

This group is one of only two in network 45 with four justices, and like the group as a whole, they are from the South. Five of the ten families are based totally or partially in Georgia. Two others are primarily from Mississippi, whereas the Pendletons and both Ruckers are spread throughout the South and parts of other regions.

Membership in the U.S. House of Representatives is the most common major position, accounting for fourteen of the twenty-nine in the group. Congressmen represented Georgia (four Lamars and two Cobbs), Missouri (two Ruckers), Ohio (two Pendletons), West Virginia (two Pendletons), Florida (Lamar), and New York (Pendleton). Five of the fourteen served during the 1840s: Nathaniel Greene Pendleton of Ohio, John Basil Lamar of Georgia, Absalom Harris Chappell (a Lamar) of Georgia, Howell Cobb of Georgia, and John Strother Pendleton of West Virginia.

The Pendletons and the two Rucker branches account for forty of seventy officials in the group. Philip Pendleton (1650–1721) founded the twenty-one-member clan when he came to Virginia from England in 1674.

3. The sources used to determine the relationship between the two Lamars are contradictory. Schmidhauser (1959, 15) says that they are cousins. Wirt Armistead Cate (1935, 13) first implies that they are third cousins, but then in tracing the lineage of L. Q. C. Lamar (13–14) he indicates that they were fourth cousins. Another source (*National Cyclopedia of American Biography*, 28:23) also indicates a fourth cousin relationship, while Virkus (1987, 1:674) suggests that they were fourth cousins once removed.

Most of the family remained in Virginia, West Virginia, or North Carolina. But Congressman Edmund Henry Pendleton represented New York, and Congressmen Nathaniel Greene Pendleton and George H. Pendleton came from Ohio. This family was prominent with eight major officials.

The Pendletons are probably connected to the Overtons of Group K through Henry Pendleton (1762–1822), a member of the Virginia House of Delegates, who married Mary B. (Overton) Burnley. The evidence as to where this Mary Overton fits into the Overton family is inconclusive.

The two branches of the Rucker family combined include nineteen public figures almost all of whom held local offices, primarily in Virginia. However, Kentucky, Montana, Missouri, Tennessee, Georgia, and South Carolina also had Rucker officials. The two more prominent Ruckers were Missouri congressmen Tinsley White Rucker (2) and William Waller Rucker (1). Peter Rucker was the first of the family in America. A French Huguenot (as were the early Lamars), he came to Virginia in 1690. John Rucker, a son of the immigrant, was the first officeholder in group G. He was a constable in Virginia in 1731. The last member of this group was Justice Lewis F. Powell, Jr., who left the bench in 1987. His father-in-law was a direct descendant of John Rucker in the sixth generation (counting John as the first).

As the discussion moves from the first seven parts of network 45 to the remaining six groups, the focus shifts. Groups A through G were centered around thirteen federal and two Louisiana justices, whereas groups H through M consist of eleven state judges but only one federal judge. The last six parts of the network are Louisiana oriented in terms of the courts, although the officials included are by no means all from that state.

GROUP H

Evidence of that observation is seen in group H. It is not really a Louisiana group in that over 70 percent of the forty-one officials held office in ten states other than Louisiana. Four of the five families had office-holding members in at least two states, the Maryland Winders being the one exception. The Polks are the most diverse in this regard with seventeen kinsmen in public positions in five states.

For seven generations Polks have held office, first in North Carolina and later in Tennessee and Louisiana. The family did not limit its political activity to the South, as evidenced by Rufus King Polk, a Pennsylvania congressman, and Frank Lyon Polk of New York, counselor of the Department of State from 1915 to 1920. The North Carolina–Tennessee branch of the family consists of near relatives of President James K. Polk. A Louisiana branch was founded by Bishop Leonidas Polk (later a major general, CSA), who came to Louisiana from North Carolina and Tennessee. Accompanying him was a nephew, William Polk, who had married Eva Lamar of group G. They had a son, grandson, and great-grandson in Louisiana politics. The great-grandson is district judge William Polk, currently on the bench. A third branch of the family, probably based in Maryland, is the one into which Victor Monroe, father of Louisiana justice Frank Adair Monroe, married.

The exact genealogy of at least two other probable members of this family cannot be determined. They are North Carolina legislator Leonidas Lafayette Polk (1837–1892) and Senator and Governor Thrusten Polk (1811–1876) of Missouri.

The Monroes, like the Polks, are not primarily a Louisiana family; only two of the eleven officials held office in this state. Virginia was the early base of Monroe political activity, and the first official in group H was Andrew Monroe, sheriff of Westmoreland County, Virginia, in 1731. He was the grandfather of President Monroe and a great-great-granduncle of Justice Frank Adair Monroe. Justice Monroe's grandfather, Thomas Bell Monroe, was born in Virginia but held office in Kentucky before moving to Pass Christian, Mississippi, toward the end of the Civil War. Frank Adair Monroe was born in Maryland and reared in Kentucky before he moved to Mississippi to join other members of his family. Admitted to the Louisiana bar in 1867, Justice Monroe pursued his judicial career in Louisiana.

Although the branch of the Brent family included here was based in Maryland, its most prominent member was Louisiana congressman William Leigh Brent. He left Maryland and went to Louisiana in 1809, having been appointed attorney general for the Western District of Orleans by President Madison (of group E). After losing a bid for reelection to Congress in 1828, he remained in Washington. Four of his sons are relevant to this network. Robert James became attorney general of Maryland; Edward married the daughter of Joshua Baker (1799–1885); Joseph Lancaster was a brigadier general in the Confederate Army; and James Fenwick settled in Rapides Parish, Louisiana, where he held office and married Laura Harriet Overton, the daughter of Walter Hampden Overton, who had defeated William Leigh Brent in the congressional election of 1828.

GROUP I

A member of the federal bench, Gabriel Duvall, and a judge on the state court, Alexander Porter, are included in group I, one of only two instances in which judges from the two courts are in the same group or network. The origins of the families in this set (in Virginia, Maryland, North Carolina, and Tennessee) as well as their descendants' political activities were documented in an earlier publication (Kurtz 1987), so only a brief discussion will be presented here.

Over 80 percent of the forty individuals in the group held office in Louisiana; only the Duvalls had no members in Louisiana politics. Five families had all their members in positions in that state, and the remaining four had but one non-Louisiana political figure. There was one Porter in Tennessee, one Caffery in-law in Mississippi, and one Taylor in South Carolina. Thomas Posey served in the Kentucky Senate, represented Louisiana in the U.S. Senate, and later became governor of the Indiana Territory.

Further evidence of the Louisiana orientation of the group is seen when examining the major positions: seven of the nine were held by Louisiana officials. The exceptions were the previously noted Thomas Posey and Justice Duvall, who had served in Congress. Two of this state's more eminent families, the Cafferys and the Fosters, account for four of the nine major offices. Two Foster brothers are currently serving in state politics, one in the state senate and the other in a parish position.

GROUP J

The families associated with Justices Garland and Bullard are even more Louisiana centered than those of group I. Twenty-eight of the twenty-nine members of this group held office in Louisiana, primarily in what is now St. Landry Parish. The one out-of-state official was Judge Lewis Moore of Virginia, the father of Congressman John Moore. The other major officials were Governor Jacques Dupre and three congressmen (Justice Bullard, Justice Garland, and Henry Garland Dupre) and a member of the Confederate Congress (also a Dupre). This is one of the more contemporary components of network 45 with four individuals in office in 1988. The incumbents are a mayor (Lastrapes), a city judge (Boagni), a district judge (Pavy), and a member of a state licensing board (another Pavy).

GROUP K

Its roots are in early colonial Virginia, but as is the case with other parts of this network, the families extended their political influence both geographically and chronologically beyond that state and era. Members of this group held office in eleven states and England beginning in 1623 with Thomas Harris in the House of Burgesses and ending in the mid 1970s when Maria

Breazeale served on the Democratic State Central Committee in Louisiana. A grandson of Senator John Holmes Overton (1875–1948), John Overton Brazelton, ran unsuccessfully for the office of Louisiana insurance commissioner in 1987.

The Overtons themselves illustrate the patterns of migration and near continuous public service over several generations typical of so many of these groups. The first of the family in America was William Overton, who came to Virginia probably in 1669. William's son and grandson, both named James, held office in Virginia. The second James Overton (1726/39–1816) had four sons in office. Two of them, Samuel (1768–1832) and Waller (1750–1827), remained in Virginia. A third son, John (1776–1837), eventually settled in Nashville, became a close associate of Andrew Jackson, and established the Tennessee branch of the family. The fourth son was Thomas (1753–1825), who went to North Carolina and held office there before moving to Tennessee to join his brother. Two sons of this fourth brother came to Louisiana and founded another branch of the family. Walter Hampden Overton was probably the first of the two to arrive in Louisiana. He came as an officer under Jackson in the Battle of New Orleans and settled in Rapides Parish. His half brother, John Holmes Overton (1797–1883), was reared in Tennessee, but he also moved to Louisiana—first to Ouachita, then to St. Landry Parish. He is the grandfather of Justice Overton.

Families in the Overton group are evenly divided between those whose political involvement was in only one state and those who were active in two or more states. The Breazeales and Baillios consist primarily of local officials, all of whom were in Louisiana. Virginia is the home state of the Harrises, none of whom held major positions. The Leas of Tennessee were more prominent; three of them served in Congress. The fifth single-state family, the Holmes of North Carolina, include two local leaders, a lieutenant general in the Confederacy, and a fourth member who was a congressman and governor.

The multistate families include the Whites, who were active in Tennessee and North Carolina; the Dickinsons, in Tennessee and Mississippi; the Cosbys, in Louisiana, Kentucky, and Pennsylvania; and the Carrs, in Virginia, Maryland, Missouri, California, and Kentucky. Overton political activity, though concentrated in the states already noted, began in England and extended to North Carolina, Florida, and Kentucky.

About 30 percent of the sixty-seven public officials served in Louisiana and a third of those were Overtons. Overtons also account for ten of the twenty-two major positions, five of which were in Louisiana. The most frequently held high office was that of congressman. At various times the House of Representatives included four Overtons, two Leas, one Carr, one

Holmes, and one Breazeale. This group also boasts governors of Louisiana (Thomas Overton Moore), North Carolina (Gabriel Holmes, Jr.), Tennessee (Hugh Lawson White), and Florida (Samuel Overton). The Baillios, Cosbys, and Harrises held no major offices.

Thomas Overton Moore, and thus the Overtons, may be linked to the family of Justice Moore (Network 18, Chapter 3) and to the family of Justice James Moore Wayne. Thomas Overton Moore is said to be a descendant of James Moore, who died in 1706 (see *DAB* 13–14:138–39). A James Moore (d. 1706) was governor of South Carolina and a great-grandfather of Justice Alfred Moore (see Moore** in Appendix A). Justice James Moore Wayne is said to be named for an early governor of South Carolina who was related to the justice's mother's family. That ancestor was probably the James Moore noted above (see Lawrence 1943, 7–8). The evidence is persuasive but ultimately inconclusive.

GROUP L

Virginia roots also characterize group L, the smallest of the components of network 45 with only two dozen officials and three major positions. All four families have some Virginia connections. Theodorick Bland (1629–1671) was the first official in the group as Speaker of the House of Burgesses in 1659. The other three members of the Bland family held office there, as did William King, Sr., great-grandfather of Justice King, and Elijah Hunt, a great-grandfather of Congressman Alfred Briggs Irion.

None of the Beales pursued political careers in Virginia, but Robert G. Beale was born into "an old Virginia family" and came to Louisiana as a young man (Fortier 1914, 593). Several Virginia Beales did hold office, but they cannot be connected to the Louisiana family. They were James Madison Hite Beale, Richard Lee Tuberville Beale, Truxton Beale, and Edward Fitzgerald Beale (*Dictionary of American Biography* 11–12:88–89; *National Cyclopedia of American Biography* 27:407–408, and 11:364–65; and du Bellet 1907, 4:348, 358).

The migrations of the Kings and Irions are similar to those of families already discussed. As noted above, Justice King's great-grandfather was a Virginia official in the mid 1700s. William King, Jr., the justice's grandfather, was a politician in Kentucky, where he had moved in 1784 (as had Charles Wickliffe of group F), and his father was active in Louisiana. Irion office holding began in Karlesruche, Baden, Germany, where Congressman Irion's great-grandfather and great-great-grandfather served under King Charles Frederic II. The great-grandfather emigrated to Culpepper County, Virginia, in the early 1760s and married into the Poindexter political family. One of their sons, George Anderson Irion I, married the daughter of Elijah Hunt and settled in Avoylles Parish, Louisiana, after the War of 1812. He was the grandfather of the Congressman Irion who married into the King family.

GROUP M

Although over 80 percent of these officials are from Louisiana, two families trace their origins to Virginia. The earliest officeholder was George Newton I, a justice of Lower Norfolk County, Virginia, in 1645. Justice Newton Crain Blanchard of the Louisiana court is a seventh-generation descendant of that George Newton. Beginning with a grandson of the first George Newton, George Newton III, four more generations of Newtons participated in Virginia politics. In 1800 Thomas Newton, Sr., Thomas Newton, Jr., and Thomas Blanchard held office in Norfolk County. Thomas Blanchard, grandfather of the justice, married Amy Wood Newton, a daughter of Thomas Newton, Jr., and a sister of Congressman Thomas Newton (the third of that name, 1768–1847). Thomas Blanchard probably moved to Mississippi with some of the Newtons and then came to central Louisiana in the 1820s.

The Lands are distinctive in being the only family with three justices. The first, Thomas T. Land, was born in Tennessee and reared in Mississippi. He attended the University of Virginia and held office in Mississippi before moving to Louisiana. The only other member of this group to serve in a state other than Louisiana or Virginia was Lynch Davidson, lieutenant governor of Texas from 1920 to 1922. The group's political activity ended with David T. Stafford in the Louisiana Senate from 1940 to 1948. He was a great-grandson of Thomas Overton Moore of group K.

There is probably another link to the Overton group. Carey H. Blanchard's first wife was Mary G. Overton (1812–1836), a daughter of James and Eliza Overton and "probably a niece of General Wade Hampden Overton" (Stafford 1947, 423). John Bennett Boddie (1967, 5:134) lists a Mary Blanchard as a daughter of James Overton and Eliza Dixon. If that source is accurate, then Mary Overton Blanchard would have been a first cousin once removed of Wade Hampden Overton.

SUMMARY

Findings based on Chapters 4 and 5 may now be summarized. In some instances, these conclusions will be phrased in terms of the forty-five networks. In other instances, the observations will relate to the forty-three minor networks, the three groups in #44, and the thirteen parts of #45, in which case the total number of units will be fifty-nine. This latter perspective is necessary because of the complexity of the two large systems. Observations about either of the two networks as a whole might not apply to more than one or two of their components.

Most generally, of those justices who have relatives in politics, 71 percent of the state and 59 percent of the federal judges are also members of kinship networks. Nearly 80 percent of the minor networks had only one justice, as did two of the groups in #44. However, of the thirteen parts of network 45, eight included two or more justices. By definition, the minimal size of a network is two families; 57 percent of the smaller sets meet only that minimal standard, whereas all the groups in the two larger networks consisted of two or more families.

The networks and their subgroups vary greatly in size as measured by the total number of officials. Forty-four percent of the minor networks have fewer than ten officeholders, but all parts of the two larger ones have twenty-four or more. That variation continues when one examines major positions; 60 percent of the minor systems have fewer than seven high offices, whereas all but three of the components of #44 and #45 had more than seven. Among the top leaders included in the judicial networks are twelve of the forty presidents who had served through 1988; seven of those presidents are in network 45.

One effect of kinship networks is to link different states and regions. Both of the larger systems are multistate in nature, and over 60 percent of the smaller sets also include officials from at least two states. Virginia and Kentucky stand out in the analysis of states and regions. Of the fifty-nine units investigated, Virginia political figures are found in seventeen and Kentucky officials are found in fifteen. Overall, twenty-one, or 36 percent, of the units have Virginia and/or Kentucky officeholders.

This is not, however, a study of the southern political elite. Over half of the small networks include officials from states other than the South and border South (defined as the eleven states of the Confederacy as well as Maryland, West Virginia, Kentucky, Missouri, and the District of Columbia). All three components of the Livingston network and nine of the thirteen parts of #45 include officials from other regions. In a few instances foreign countries are also connected to these American kinship groups. Eight of the minor networks and three groups in the two larger sets include foreign officials. Generally, over two-thirds of the fifty-nine units are not just southern in nature.

The impact of kinship networks is extensive in temporal as well as geographical terms. The average number of years between the earliest and the most recent position held in a network is as follows:

Networks 1–43	144 years[4]
Network 44	336 years
Network 45	253 years
All 57 units	179 years

Averages are sometimes misleading, so perhaps a more revealing comment is that in only eleven of the fifty-seven units was the time span less than one hundred years, and those are all minor networks. Two final perspectives focus on very early and very recent office holding. Over 50 percent of the fifty-seven units had someone in office before the American Revolution, 42 percent had an official serving between 1961 and 1988, and 18 percent had a member in office in 1988.

Three main conclusions may be drawn from these findings. First, judicial families are not isolated. Rather, most are part of a larger entity, the network, and must be viewed from that perspective. Second, the effect of being part of that larger unit is to extend connections and perhaps influence in one or more of three directions. Networks link judges' families to earlier and to subsequent generations of political leaders. To the extent that members of a network are contemporaries of the justice, generationally lateral connections are intensified. Third, a project that began as an investigation into the characteristics of 128 judicial families has now resulted in the identification of another 184 families. The existence of these allied kinship groups is further evidence of the prevalence of political families.

4. Networks 7 and 8 are omitted from this calculation.

❖

6

POLITICAL FAMILIES
IN AMERICA

Much of the analysis and many of the observations in preceding chapters were phrased in terms of a data set consisting of only the kin-connected justices. Here, however, a somewhat different approach will be adopted. Conclusions will be based on all 202 justices (98 Louisiana and 104 federal). Generalizations will be stated in terms of percentages of the total membership of both courts, as well as the combined membership of both courts. Readers who are interested in the extent to which an attribute characterized only the kin-connected judges may refer to the original analysis in the appropriate chapter. At this point, however, the concern is with descriptions and observations that apply to *all* the justices of the two courts. As a result of this different perspective, most statements will apply to a minority of the justices because they will deal with characteristics of a fraction of the 134 judges from political families (out of the total membership of 202).

The first and most obvious finding is that *a majority of supreme court justices are members of political families.* Two-thirds have at least one relative who held public office. One of the more important differences between the two courts is that *more federal justices have politically active kinsmen than do state judges.* These findings are surprising in two respects. First, the extent to which judges come from political families is greater than expected. At the beginning of the project, I thought that perhaps half of the justices might have office-holding relatives. Second, I expected to find politically active families to be more common among the state rather than the federal jurists.

Supreme court justices are members of fairly large political families consisting of close relatives whose political activity is often spread over three or

T A B L E 2 2

Major Findings

	La. %	U.S. %	All %
1. Relatives in office	60%	72%	66%
2. Three or more relatives in office	40	37	38
3. Parent in office	29	37	33
4. Sibling in office	17	22	20
5. Child in office	22	19	21
6. Ancestors in office	46	60	53
7. Contemporaries in office	33	38	35
8. Descendants in office	41	36	38
9. In-laws in office	29	38	33
10. Three or more generations of family political activity	44	38	41
11. Transmitters	29	27	28
12. Maintainers	17	33	25
13. Relatives in major office	26	44	35
14. Relative a judge	33	42	38
15. Relatives in office in more than one state	15	36	26
16. Occupational follower	44	63	53
17. Followed father	29	37	33
18. More than one occupational predecessor	28	32	30
(*N*)	(98)	(104)	(202)

more generations. Items 1 through 10 in Table 22 support this observation. Over one-third of the judges had three or more office-holding relatives, one-third had a parent in office, one-fifth had a child and or a sibling in politics, and two-fifths were part of a three-generation (or longer) family political tradition. The federal jurists were most likely to have had an ancestor in office, and more than a third of the members of both courts had contemporaries and/or descendants in public positions. The Louisiana judges were usually transmitters, while the federal justices were more evenly divided between maintainers and transmitters.

Justices are often related to major public figures. Most offices held by relatives were local in nature, an expected finding given that most public positions are at the local level. However, many judges are connected by kinship to the higher levels of state politics and to the national political scene. Over a third had at least one highly placed kinsman.

The marriages of justices and their children extend their families' political influence. One-third of the justices married the daughter or sister of a public official or had a child who married a politician. These patterns were more prevalent among federal judges (38%) than among state jurists (29%). Most of these marriages (69%) resulted in the creation of a new kinship network or in the expansion of an existing one with the state judges having a greater impact in this regard (79%) than the federal judges (62%). Another way of making this point is to say that almost one-fourth of the justices were linked to allied families directly through their own or their childrens' marriages.

Justices are related to other judicial officials. Nearly 40 percent of the justices had a relative who was also a judge. In one sense this is not surprising given that judicial positions are so numerous. When I studied 785 state and local officials in 1983, 29 percent of the offices were judgeships (Kurtz 1989, 339). However, when one considers that almost a fourth of the Supreme Court justices had two or more relatives in the judiciary, it becomes clear that some families have a distinct judicial orientation.

Kinship connections frequently cross state boundaries. Slightly over one-fourth of the members of the two courts were related to a political figure in another state. This finding suggests that many of these families are mobile and that the family political tradition is transportable from one setting to another.

Most justices are the product of an established tradition of political activity on the part of their close ancestors. Just over 50 percent of the jurists were occupational inheritors with about a third having followed their fathers into political life. Almost a third followed more than one relative into public office. One of the major differences between the two courts emerges in this context. *Federal justices come from a more firmly established family political tradition than do state justices.* They are more likely to be heirs, and more of them followed their fathers.

Many justices belong to extensive networks of interconnected political families. For the purposes of this analysis, the three parts of network 44 and the thirteen parts of network 45 are treated as distinct units for a total of 59 networks. Over 40 percent of the judges belong to a family that in turn is linked to at least one other family of public officials (see Table 23). More than one-fourth are in kinship systems that involve three or more families, link two or more states, consist of ten or more officials, or extend over 150 or more years. Generally, the state justices are in larger networks whose members are spread over a longer period, whereas federal judges are more likely to be in a multistate network. The largest network (#45) includes 13 percent of the 202 justices who served on both courts.

Historically, there were significant differences between the courts in the percentage of justices from political families, but they became more similar in

TABLE 23

Network Summary

	La. %	U.S. %	All %
In a network	42%	43%	43%
Network with 3 or more families	31	25	28
Multistate network	24	35	30
Network with 10 or more officials	36	27	31
Network with 150+ years of service	30	25	27
(N)	(98)	(104)	(202)

the mid-twentieth century. The major difference occurred between 1789 and 1932. During that time a majority of both sets of judges were members of political families, but the size of that majority varied by as much as 35 percent from 1789 to 1828 when 95 percent of federal judges but just 60 percent of the state judges were related to other officials. In addition, the lead in the number of kin-connected justices changed in the late nineteenth and early twentieth centuries. Initially, the United States court had a larger percentage (1789 through 1888), but then for the next four decades (1889–1932) the Louisiana court took the lead. From the time of the New Deal, the courts have been nearly identical in this regard.

The courts varied considerably in their rates of occupational following for a hundred years, but that difference has been minimal since 1889. The greatest divergence occurred during the Jacksonian period (1829–1861) when 77 percent of the national judges but only 32 percent of the state judges were followers.

The justices of the two supreme courts share kinship characteristics, and in some ways they are becoming more similar. The principal differences between the courts are that federal judges are more likely to (1) be members of political families, (2) be occupational followers, (3) have a relative in an ascending generation, (4) have a relative in a major office, (5) have an office-holding relative in another state, and (6) be a part of a multistate network. Of these differences, the greater tendencies of United States justices to come from political families and to be occupational followers are the most significant, and those differences have decreased over time. What strikes this observer is that the contrasts between the two sets of officials are minimal. Others will perhaps disagree as to what constitutes minimal difference, but the extent to which the two courts are parallel is more surprising and impressive than are the instances in which they diverge. An earlier comparison of federal and state courts produced much the same conclusion (Mott *et al.* 1933, 149–50).

Judicial families are a current reality with a continuing impact on elite composition. A logical first reaction to this observation would be that the data presented in Chapter 3 do not support the statement. That discussion revealed a marked decline in both general kinship connections and in political inheritance in the past thirty years. While that finding is important in understanding historical trends, it is not necessarily conclusive. Two additional aspects of the issue must be considered. This involves assessing the significance of the percentage of family-connected judges in the modern era and examining other types of linkages to that period.

First, the fact that 20–25 percent of the recent entrants to the bench came from political families is a significant statement, even though it is a much lower figure than in earlier periods. Being able to say something about 20 percent of a group of public figures is an important contribution warranting further attention.

Second, another perspective can be gained by examining the extent to which the justices who served before 1961 are linked to this latest period through their relatives, collateral relatives, and allied families. Forty-two percent of the kinship networks have had at least one official serving since 1961 and 18 percent had someone in office in 1988. This indicates the current impact of the networks of which the justices are members.

Three even more specific indicators may be developed to substantiate the point being made. Table 24 contains a tabulation of three types of connections of justices to the 1961–1988 period. The justices listed came to the court before 1961 and had one or more of those connections. Column 1 shows the justices who had a relative holding his *first* office in 1961 or later. Column 2 lists collateral relatives whose first position came within the last three decades. Finally, column 3 tabulates justices whose family was linked to an allied family that had a member reach his first office in that era.

It is important to note two points about these definitions. First, these connections involve officials who began their formal careers after 1960. This is a much more limiting criterion than simply counting those in office in the modern period. Someone in office in the 1970s may well have started his career a decade or two earlier and is in some ways a carryover from an earlier era. Second, column 3 takes note of instances in which a justice's family is linked directly to an allied group with a recent official. This is a different indicator than counting the justices who were in a network with a recent entrant into the political arena. For example, the family of Justice Nicholls (network 38, Chapter 4) is shown in Table 24 as being linked to an allied

TABLE 24

Connections of Justices Before 1961 to Latest Period (1961–1988)

Justice	Year Joined Supreme Court	First Held Public Office in 1961 or Later		
		Relative	Collateral Relative	Allied Family Member
Louisiana				
LeBlanc	(1949)	X	X	X
Moise	(1949)	X		
Fournet	(1935)	X		X
Provosty	(1922)	X		X
Monroe	(1899)			X
Parlange	(1893)	X		
Nicholls	(1892)			X
Fenner	(1880)		X	X
Voorhies, A.	(1859)		X	X
Voorhies, C.	(1854)		X	X
Ogden	(1853)			X
Garland	(1840)			X
Eustis	(1839)			X
Porter	(1821)			X
Total		5	4	12
% of 57 kin-connected justices before 1961		9%	7%	2%
United States				
Clark	(1949)	X		
Lamar, L. Q. C.	(1888)			X
Livingston	(1807)			X
Total		1	0	2
% of 72 kin-connected justices before 1961		10%	0%	3%

family (the Pughs) that had a member become politically active after 1960. Justice McCaleb was also a part of network 38, but his family was not directly linked to the Pugh family, so McCaleb is not counted.

Fifty-seven kin-connected justices came to the Louisiana court before 1961. Of that number, 9 percent had a relative who first came to office in 1961 or later. Seven percent had a collateral relative, and 21 percent were linked to an allied family, the two other types of possible connections to the modern period. The fourteen Louisiana justices in Table 24 represent 25 percent of the fifty-seven pre-1961 entrants. If the two justices who came to the court since 1961 are added to these fourteen, a total of 16 percent of all ninety-eight Louisiana justices had some connection to the most recent historical period.

The seventy-two federal justices who entered the court before 1961 and who were members of political families have far fewer links to the recent period, but they still contribute support to the argument being developed. Three of the seventy-two pre-1961 entrants (or 4%) had some connection to the contemporary era. More generally, six (or 6%) of the total membership of the court either came to the court or were connected to someone who began a career after 1960. Combining federal and state justices with some post-1960 tie indicates that 11 percent of all judges who served on the two courts have some direct or indirect link to the modern period.

BEYOND THE JUDICIARY

The discussion thus far has been restricted to observations concerning the data on supreme court justices. As valuable as those remarks may be, they have limited utility if they apply only to the judiciary and not to the broader spectrum of American political leaders. This section moves beyond the judiciary. It begins with a series of propositions about the nature of kinship in American politics, then it summarizes the evidence supporting those statements. The analysis will draw on the judicial data, but it will also incorporate other evidence to generalize about the totality of the American political elite.

Propositions

1. Political families are a current national phenomenon affecting all institutions and levels of government and all regions of the country.
2. These families are frequently linked to other families forming kinship networks.
3. Families and/or networks link public officials in one historical period to those serving in earlier and later periods.
4. The early socialization of members of political families is different than for officials who came from politically inactive families. Heirs receive a political legacy that involves real career advantages and that may be transported to a new location.
5. Political marriages are a significant component of the dynamics of political families and networks.
6. Three-fifths of American public officials are drawn from fewer than 10 percent of the country's families.

Each of these propositions will be considered in turn, and evidence in their support will be drawn from the judicial data and other sources.

Proposition 1: Political families are a current national phenomenon affecting all institutions and levels of government and all regions of the country.

The findings of other scholars who have dealt with this subject were summarized and discussed in Chapter 3. That literature included studies of a variety of institutions and levels of government in the most recent historical period and indicated that from one-fourth to nearly two-thirds of the cases came from politically active families. The conclusions reached in Chapter 3 alone would provide adequate support for proposition 1, but additional evidence is available. Earlier I noted the extent to which justices had relatives in other states and were members of interstate kinship networks, and further analysis of the judicial data will highlight the national character of political families.

Several factors might lead one to the conclusion that the patterns of family political activity described here are basically southern and not characteristic of the nation as a whole. Almost half the database, the Louisiana justices, are obviously southern as are many of the federal judges. The most extensive kinship network (#45) is based in the South. In their study of Congress, Clubok, Wilensky, and Berghorn concluded that the South has always had more members with congressional kinship connections than any other region and that change has occurred less rapidly in that area (1969, 1042, 1047). Another study of the judiciary found that inheriting a position was more common among southern trial court judges (Ryan *et al.* 1980, 130).

Closer analysis reveals, however, that the South does not have a monopoly on political families. Thirty-eight (or 36.5%) of the 104 national jurists are from the South or border South. Of those southern justices 79 percent were from political families. Of the sixty-six nonsouthern members of the federal court, 68 percent had office-holding relatives. Southern members of the federal court are therefore somewhat more likely to have come from political families than their colleagues from other regions. Balancing that finding is the fact that of the fifty-nine kin-connected state justices, 24 percent had a relative (and sometimes collateral relatives as well) who held office outside the South or were in a kinship network that included nonsouthern officials.

If different definitions had been used, the nonsouthern character of the findings would be accentuated. I define the South and border South broadly in Chapter 5 and include more states than Clubok *et al.* do in their definition (1969, 1041). A stricter definition of the region would result in there being fewer jurists categorized as southern. In addition, this study follows the methods of William J. Daniels (1978), who classified the justices according to their state of residence at the time of their appointment to the court. This approach is simple but misleading. Daniels (228) lists Chief Justice Burger as being from Virginia, his residence when appointed to the court. It is doubtful that Warren Burger considered himself to be a Virginia jurist. A better approach is that of Woodford L. Gardner, Jr. (1972, 121–42), who made distinctions among justices born and active in Kentucky, active in Kentucky, or born there but professionally active elsewhere.

Proposition 2: These families are frequently linked to other families forming kinship networks.

Proposition 3: Families and/or networks link public officials in one historical period to those serving in earlier and later periods.

Propositions 2 and 3 concern the prevalence of kinship networks and their effect of linking historical periods. Support for these assertions based on the judicial data have already been summarized above. Additional evidence of the existence of these interconnected groups and their historical impact may be found in several other studies.

Stephen Hess' appendices (1966, 623–72) list the members of his political dynasties and their collateral relatives as well as families that have had three or more members in Congress. Although he does not use the concept of network, he has in fact identified many such groups, some of which are discussed in this volume.

Merlie and Silva contend that nearly 60 percent of the first thirty-six presidents can be connected to each other through kinship, resulting in clear linkages over a long period of time (1975, 152). Aronson's study of the personnel of the Adams, Jefferson, and Jackson administrations was more limited in scope, but he also made the point that elites in one period are related to those in both earlier and later periods (1964).

The prevalence of kinship networks is one of the factors that led to the development of this volume. The author's earlier work on Louisiana families (1987, 1989, with Pena 1990), identified so many links to families outside the state that it soon became evident that an investigation of a national set of leaders was in order. One can seldom conduct any research on a set of families without discovering an expanding circle of related families.

*Proposition 4: The early socialization of members of political families is differ-
ent than for officials who come from politically inactive families. Heirs receive
a political legacy that involves real career advantages and that may be transported to a new location.*

Support for part of proposition 4 was detailed in Chapter 2 in the discussion of the impact of occupational inheritance, which indicated that
justices with such a tradition began their careers earlier, remained on the
bench longer, and in the federal case reached the high court earlier. Laband
and Lentz's study (1985) of members of Congress provides additional
confirmation of these advantages, as did the comments of numerous political leaders themselves.

The fact that so many families and networks cross state and regional
boundaries clearly indicates that the legacy resulting from earlier family
political involvement can be transported from one place to another. A child
of a public official does not need to pursue a political career in the same location as the parent because much of what the child has inherited is in no
way tied to a particular locality. This observation in turn suggests that the
political inheritance consists of two types of advantages or commodities.

The two dimensions of the legacy can be seen as the internal and the
external. Some of what a child learns or acquires from a parent can be of
political value regardless of where the child chooses to reside. Like capital,
it can be invested anywhere. This is the internal dimension, and it consists
of skills, knowledge, attitudes, and efficacy. Others need not be aware that
an aspiring politician possesses these attributes for them to be of use. In
contrast, name recognition, name loyalty, goodwill, and some types of contacts form the external dimension of the legacy because these valuables are
dependent for their utility on other actors in the political process. To the
extent that this dependence exists, the potential politician may have to in-
vest his capital in a specific place. Many families are active in local politics
only, and members of those groups make maximum use of their family
legacy by remaining near the ancestral home.

Some families are able to transcend this local or regional orientation
because of the national prominence of one or more of their members. A
few examples will illustrate this point and also demonstrate that the transportable legacy is still very much a part of our political culture.

Four recent families provide evidence in support of the point being
made. Kennedys hold or have held office in Massachusetts, New York, and
Rhode Island. Rockefellers have been major figures in New York, Arkansas,
and West Virginia. Goldwaters represented Arizona and California in the

Senate and House of Representatives. The Bush family originated in Connecticut in the first generation, moved to Texas in the second, and is active in both Texas and Florida in the third.

Proposition 5: Political marriages are a significant component of the dynamics of political families and networks.

One-third of the justices married the daughter or sister of a public official or had a child who married a political figure, and most of these marriages formed a link to another political family. That finding illustrates one of the two effects of political marriages, which is to extend the family's potential political influence by the formation of something of an alliance between the two families.

The other possible effect of marriages is internal to the family. The marriage of close cousins may result in intensifying the family's political tradition, whereas the marriage of distant cousins can reunite two branches of an extended family. The Randolph family's marriage patterns provide examples of both close and distant cousin marriages (see Appendix C). More recently, the marriage of Eleanor Roosevelt and Franklin Roosevelt, fifth cousins once removed, brought together the distinct Oyster Bay and Hyde Park branches of that family (DeGregorio 1984, 484).

Political marriages continue to characterize the American political elites. The Eisenhower-Nixon, Johnson-Robb, and Kennedy-Cuomo unions are among the more famous recent examples. One may also cite the case of Senator Howard Baker, whose father and mother served in Congress and who married the daughter of Senator Everett Dirksen. Hillary Rodham Clinton's brother and the daughter of Senator Barbara Boxer also recently announced their intention to marry.

Throughout this volume the term *political legacy* has been employed as a synonym for the concepts of "human capital" (Laband and Lentz 1983) and "symbolic family estate" (Farber 1971). Marriages have an effect on that legacy. As Bernard Farber has stated, marriages between families with similar norms and values and marriages between cousins are strategies for maintaining and enhancing the symbolic family estate (1971, 8, 9).

Proposition 6: About three-fifths of American public officials are drawn from less than 10 percent of the nation's families.

This is the broadest and most important of the six generalizations. It is both a tentative conclusion and a hypothesis for further testing. Direct and indirect evidence exists to support this statement.

Substantiating this proposition requires that one determine the following figures: (1) the percentage of the total population that holds office, (2) the percentage of the population that is intensely involved in politics just short of formal office holding, and (3) the percentage of public officials who had relatives in office in a preceding generation.

Probably about 1 percent of the United States' population holds public office. Putnam suggested that the figure is less than .5 percent (1976, 10), and Prewitt puts it at less than 2 percent (1970, 53–54). Hennessy argued that between .5 and 1 percent were "fully participant," a category including not just occupants of formal positions but others as well (1985, 48).

Data from the judiciary and other studies reported here suggest that about 30 percent of any group of political leaders will have had relatives in public positions before them. Thirty percent is a conservative figure in that it is at the lower to middle range of the reported instances of prior family political activity as detailed in Chapter 3 (Table 17).

If 1 percent of the population holds office at any time and if 30 percent of any set of officials had kinsmen in office in an earlier generation, then one may conclude that at least 30 percent of any group of leaders comes from about 1 percent of the population.

This situation is presented in Figure 19, which represents a model of the kinship dimension of political recruitment and is a variation of the two models discussed in Chapter 1. Figure 19 differs from the earlier models in that it is three-generational in scope, whereas the first two accounted for seven generations.

The next task is to identify that percentage of the citizenry which is unusually active in politics on a regular basis but does not hold formal positions. These are the people for whom politics is a serious, time-consuming avocation, bordering on a vocation. People in this category are members of *politicized families.*

Scholarly estimates in this regard are fairly similar. Prewitt argued that the politically active constitute less than 10 percent of the population (1970, 53–54), and Verba and Nie said that the "complete activists" were 11 percent of the population (1972, 79). A survey in the late 1940s indicated that 10.3 percent of a national sample of eight thousand were "very active" in public affairs (Woodward and Roper 1950, 876). Hennessy's estimate is even smaller: citizens who are "mobilizable" form from 3 to 5 percent of the community (1985, 48). Given these estimates, it seems reasonable to say the nonoffice-holding, informally active stratum consists of 10 percent or less of all citizens (see also Rosenau 1974, 21–88, on this point).

FIGURE 19

A Three-Generational Model of Political Families and Elite Recruitment

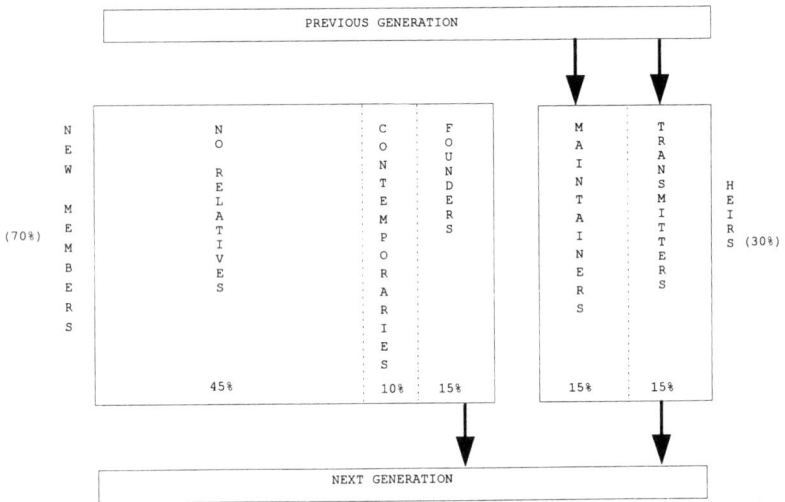

If 30 percent of political leaders, those from political families, are drawn from less than 1 percent of the population, then it is safe to assume that an additional 30 percent come from the 10 percent or so who are intensely involved. This estimate is sensible because the relationship between office holding is 30 to 1; that is, 30 percent of the officials are drawn from 1 percent of the population. *Politicized families* may be as much as ten times more numerous than *political families*, but the estimate as to the proportion of leaders from that segment is only doubled.

A generational model of politicized families is presented in Figure 20. Here the previous generation represents the 10 percent of families that are the highly active stratum and contribute 60 percent of the public officials in the next generation (the heirs). Of those heirs, some will transmit their political legacy to the next generation. The question to be answered is what percentage will be transmitters. The answer is to be found in an analysis of the features of Figure 19, which by their nature cannot change in Figure 20.

The subgroups—founders, contemporaries, and transmitters—must be the same size in Figure 20 as in Figure 19. The percentages for these groups will not change in this model because, in focusing on the link to the next generation, the analysis shifts away from politicized families back to political families. The political elite under consideration (consisting of

FIGURE 20

A Three-Generational Model of Politicized Families and Elite Recruitment

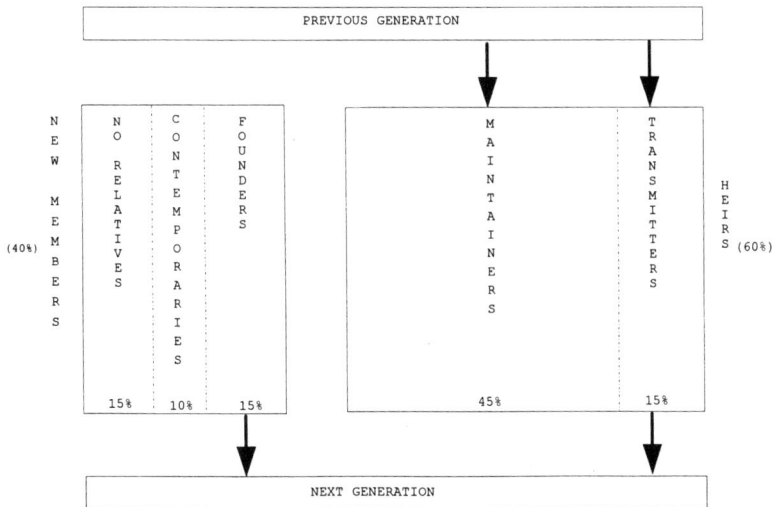

PREVIOUS GENERATION

(40%) NEW MEMBERS | NO RELATIVES (15%) | CONTEMPORARIES (10%) | FOUNDERS (15%) | MAINTAINERS (45%) | TRANSMITTERS (15%) | HEIRS (60%)

NEXT GENERATION

new members and heirs) is by definition a group of officials. Also by previous definition, founders and transmitters are officials whose descendants go into politics, and contemporaries are politicians who have kinsmen of the same generation in politics. Thus, the only two parts of the model that may change are the percentages of maintainers and those with no relatives.

A logical corollary of proposition 7 is that only a minority of American politicians, about two-fifths, are truly new to the political system. This minority corresponds to those Bay Area councilmen whom Prewitt (1970, 60–61) found to have been "mobilized" into politics (38%) or the ones who were "lateral entrants" (12%). Neither type of officials had family socialization experiences as children that eventually led them to become formally involved. Similarly, Marvick and Nixon determined that only 20 percent of the campaign workers in the Los Angeles area "came from families where the parents were neither interested nor active in public affairs" (1961, 209).

Of the 40 percent who are new members, most are connected to other political leaders through kinship through an intragenerational link (contemporaries) or connected to the next generation as founders. The American political elite, then, exhibits considerable continuity over time. It is a relatively closed group in that such a small percentage is drawn from families that did not have something of a political tradition either as formal officeholders or as highly active informal participants.

The two models presented here may, and should, be tested by other scholars using other data. As a preliminary test of the validity of the model of political families (Figure 19), I developed a small data set consisting of the nine presidents who served from 1933 through 1988, a period corresponding to the two most recent periods analyzed in Chapter 3.

Again, one must remember that these models cover three generations, so the question applied to the presidents was whether they had relatives in their father's, their children's, or their own generation.

The results with respect to the presidency are as follows:

Heirs (33%)
    Transmitters   11%
    Maintainers   22%
New members (67%)
    Founders   22%
    Contemporaries   11%
    No relatives   33%

These findings are fairly close to the expected results as predicted in Figure 19, and they provide initial support for the accuracy of the model. At the very minimum this framework offers other scholars a basis for comparing and contrasting the kinship characteristics of other groups of political leaders.

Proposition 6 is not new; rather, it is a modified version of Kenneth Prewitt's conclusion of two decades ago that "upwards of two-fifths of the politically active stratum come from approximately five percent of the nation's families" (1970, 66). His statement was based on respondents citing parental influence as a factor motivating political interest and subsequent entry into offices. By taking into account the fact that relatives other than parents may be influential in the socialization process and that each generation affects the next, Prewitt's conclusion can be made more inclusive, as reflected in proposition 6.

This argument involves a far more precise explanation of the origins of political leaders than the conventional observation that political elites are drawn from the well-educated, upper-middle-class, professional level of society. While it is probable that many political families are from the upper middle class, most may not be that high on the social ladder, particularly if they are active in local and especially rural politics. This explanation is independent of social class.

Before I draw this discussion to a close, it seems appropriate to address two criticisms or concerns that have been expressed by anonymous reviewers of this and other of my publications and by discussants at a number of conferences. I would label these reservations the "policy bias concern" and the "presidential royalty argument."

The "policy bias concern" was best expressed by a discussant several years ago in response to a paper I presented. The discussant was complimentary about the rigor of the research and quality of the style of the paper but concluded by saying, "It's too bad you did not indicate how kinship connections are related to policy outcomes." I have two responses to this observation.

First, the purpose of this and earlier research on political families is in many ways exploratory. Little work has been undertaken in this area, and my purpose is relatively modest: to document kinship connections and to offer explanations as to their prevalence and impact on the political career. Investigating the policy implications of kinship has not been and is not now an objective. The concern expressed is legitimate, but that is an issue to be explored later and perhaps by others who can build on this research and the hints in the literature.

Two studies discussed in Chapter 2 suggest that family political connections might make a difference in decisions and policy outcomes. Soule and Clarke in their analysis of 1968 convention delegates (1970, 891–92) and Ulmer in his work on the supreme court (1986, 964) found some evidence of attitudes and orientations being related to prior family political experience.

In the event that subsequent research indicates an absence of direct or obvious policy implications of kinship connections, the argument presented here remains valid: that kinship makes a difference in the structure of the political career and has an impact on who becomes a policymaker. The findings are significant even if no policy implications exist.

The "presidential royalty argument" takes two different forms, both of which seem to say that "everybody is related to everybody else." One perspective is represented by some in the academic community. They suggest that a similar investigation of another population such as corporate CEOs would yield the same results in terms of extensive family connections.

The first response to this assertion is that the evidence on occupational inheritance clearly proves that political offices are different from most other occupations in the matter of generational transfers. Corporate executives are not as likely to have inherited their position, nor are they as likely to transmit it to a later generation.

Second, this criticism is only an assertion unsupported by any evidence. If the patterns of kinship identified in the political realm are to be found elsewhere, they have yet to be documented. The findings presented here cannot be criticized because they might also be found in other contexts.

The second form of the royalty argument actually does occasionally concern royalty. For example, one very useful source of data on presidential families includes an entire appendix devoted to "Presidents of Royal Descent" and another to "Some Remarkable Kinships" (*Burke's* 1975, 607–30). One illustrative chart indicates that Richard M. Nixon is a twentieth-generation descendant of King Edward III (1312–1377) of England (624). Another source concentrates on connections between presidents, noting that Nixon and Carter are sixth cousins and Ford and Bush are seventh cousins (Roberts 1989, 207, 244).

Clearly these are inconsequential relationships of interest perhaps to the genealogist, but not to the social scientist. While ultimately everyone may be related to everyone else, the judicial kinship connections discussed here are defined very precisely and involve relationships that are close enough for those affected to be aware of the link.

CONCLUSION

The thoughts developed here are very much influenced by the argument Kenneth Prewitt articulated over twenty-five years ago (1970, 53–82). It is surprising that his provocative conclusions failed to stimulate more research into this aspect of elite socialization and recruitment. Investigations of the type presented in this volume on the judiciary are still few in number, and the prevailing wisdom is well summarized by Putnam, who concluded that "political lineage is now rarely politically significant, the Kennedy dynasty to the contrary notwithstanding" (1976, 61). The evidence assembled here suggests that this conventional point of view is not accurate. For years there have been abundant published clues as to the salience of the family in American politics, but the scholarly community, with a few exceptions (Prewitt, Hess, Schmidhauser, and Marvick and Nixon), has ignored them.

The paucity of research on political families is the result of several interrelated factors: the United States has an egalitarian political ideology, political leaders and the media perpetuate the "log cabin" myth, scholars make certain assumptions about the nature of modern society, and the research involved is both interdisciplinary and difficult.

Our egalitarian and individualistic ideology is one of the more important considerations. In the introduction to his volume on political dynasties, Stephen Hess said, "It is as if a native ethos . . . prohibits calling attention to the fact that there are some families who have more talents or more appeal to the voters; who, in short, are far more equal than others at the political starting gate" (1966, 1). Similarly, in a discussion of the patrician class Edward Saveth argued that our cultural emphasis on individualism has caused historians to overlook the family (1963, 237). Edward Pessen has made much the same point (1984, 171).

As products of that culture, political leaders contribute directly and indirectly to the process of minimizing or even obscuring prominent lineage. They and the media contribute to the perpetuation of the "log cabin" myth: the belief that presidents and other prominent political figures emerge from humble origins, overcome significant impediments, and rise to the top (Pessen 1984). Abraham Lincoln "deliberately cultivated the Jacksonian persona of the common man" (Purvis 1982, 160) in spite of the fact that many of his relatives enjoyed "economic and social status [ranging] from middle class to the lesser gentry" (Purvis 1982, 159). Theodore Roosevelt, a product of a lineage noted for both its economic and political eminence, "talked so constantly of himself as not wealthy that the actual facts are surprising" (Beale 1954, 200). George Bush preferred to emphasize his days of working in the Texas oil fields rather than his father's political prominence.

There is also an assumption among scholars, and social scientists in particular, that in a modern technological society ascriptive factors such as family ties are no longer important. Clubok, Wilensky, and Berghorn argue that "the rate of decline [in the kinship percentage] can be used as a measure of modernization" (1969, 1062). To a lesser extent Bogue and his coauthors make much the same point (1976, 288). Putnam suggested that kinship may still be a factor in elite recruitment and integration in traditional but not in advanced societies (1976, 108; see also Keller 1963, 216–18). The assertion that kinship ties and modernity are antithetical results in researchers ignoring evidence to the contrary.

The necessarily interdisciplinary nature of the study of the political family also contributes to a lack of scholarly attention. This field exists at the intersection of several disciplines with the result that everyone thinks it belongs to someone else. Historians see the subject as being too closely associated with genealogy (Saveth 1963, 237), and political scientists usually leave the study of the family to sociologists and anthropologists (Elshtain 1982, 1). There is no natural home for those interested in this subject, a situation that militates against its further development.

Finally, the research effort required to trace and identify the kinship connections of any number of public officials is daunting. As was pointed out in Chapter 1, researchers must rely on a wide variety of materials, many of which are not readily available. No single source contains all the necessary information. Evidence as to the number and variety of works that must be consulted can be seen by examining Schmidhauser's appendix (1959, 50–57), Hess's extensive footnotes (1966, 529–621), and Appendix C of this volume.

Ideology, myths, assumptions about modernity, ambiguous disciplinary identity, and research difficulties should not deter scholars from further investigations. Even modest research designs would contribute to a more accurate appreciation of the family as a significant element in elite formation, continuity, and integration. To understand fully the nature of the current generation of political leaders we must look to their ancestors, and to know something about the next generation we need only look to the children of those who lead today.

EPILOGUE

An inevitable aspect of research on families is that it never really ends. New leads and information develop almost without effort on the part of the investigator. I continued to discover interesting families and connections as I completed this analysis and wrote the text. I will be pleased to share that additional information with interested readers upon request.

Aronson, Sidney H. 1964. *Status and kinship in the higher civil service: Standards of selection in the administrations of John Adams, Thomas Jefferson, and Andrew Jackson.* Cambridge: Harvard University Press.

Barber, James David. 1965. *The lawmakers: Recruitment and adaptation to legislative life.* New Haven: Yale University Press.

Beale, Howard K. 1954. Theodore Roosevelt's ancestry: A study in heredity. *New York Genealogical and Biographical Record* 85 (October): 196–205.

Bill, James A., and Carl Leiden. 1974. *The Middle East: Politics and power.* Boston: Allyn and Bacon.

Bill, James A., and Robert L. Hardgrave. 1973. *Comparative politics: The quest for theory.* Columbus: Charles E. Merrill.

Biographical and historical memoirs of Northwest Louisiana. 1890. Chicago and Nashville: Southern (a 1976 reprint by the North Louisiana Historical Association).

Biographical directory of the American Congress, 1789–1961. 1961. Washington: Government Printing Office.

Birmingham, Stephen. 1987. *America's secret aristocracy.* New York: Berkley Books.

Blaustein, Albert P., and Roy P. Mersky. 1972. Rating supreme court justices. *American Bar Association Journal* 58 (November): 1183–89.

Blumberg, Paul M., and P. W. Paul. 1975. Continuities and discontinuities in upper-class marriages. *Journal of Marriage and the Family* 37 (February): 63–77.

Boddie, John Bennett. 1967. *Historical southern families.* Vol. 5. Baltimore: Genealogical.

Bogue, Allan G., Jerome M. Clubb, Carroll R. McKibbin, and Santa A. Traugott. 1976. Members of the House of Representatives and the process of modernization. *Journal of American History* 63 (September): 275–302.

Bowman, Lewis, and G. R. Boynton. 1966. Recruitment patterns among local party officials: A model and some preliminary findings in selected locales. *American Political Science Review* 60 (September): 667–76.

Browning, Rufus P. 1968. The interaction of personality and political system in decisions to run for office: Some data and a simulation technique. *Journal of Social Issues* 24 (July): 93–109.

Burke's presidential families of the United States of America. 1975. London: Burke's Peerage.

Cate, Wirt Armistead. 1935. *Lucius Q. C. Lamar: Secession and reunion.* Chapel Hill: University of North Carolina Press.

Centers, Richard. 1949. Marital selection and occupational strata. *American Journal of Sociology* 54 (May): 530–35.

Clines, Francis X. 1992. Showing the good ol' boys how to play their own game. New York *Times,* 25 September, 8A.

Clubok, Alfred B., Norman H. Wilensky, and Forrest J. Berghorn. 1969. Family relationships, congressional recruitment, and political modernization. *Journal of Politics* 31 (November): 1035–62.

Congressional Quarterly's guide to the U.S. Supreme Court. 1979. Washington: Congressional Quarterly.

Daniels, William J. 1978. The geographic factor in appointments to the Supreme Court. *Western Political Quarterly* 31 (June): 226–37.

DeGregorio, William A. 1984. *The complete book of U.S. presidents.* New York: Dembner Books.

Derge, David R. 1959. The lawyer as a decision-maker in the American state legislature. *Journal of Politics* 21 (August): 408–33.

Dethloff, Henry C., and Robert Jones. 1968. Race relations in Louisiana, 1877–1898. *Louisiana History* 9 (fall): 301–23.

Domhoff, G. William. 1983. *Who rules America now? A view for the eighties.* Englewood Cliffs: Prentice Hall.

du Bellet, Louise Perquet. 1907. *Some prominent Virginia families.* Vol. 4. Lynchburg, Va.: J. P. Bell.

Elshtain, Jean Bethke. 1982. *The family in political thought.* Amherst: University of Massachusetts Press.

Epstein, Cynthia Fuchs. 1983. *Women in law.* Garden City, N.Y.: Anchor Books.

Eulau, Heinz, William Buchanan, Leroy Ferguson, and John C. Wahlke. 1959. The political socialization of American state legislators. *Midwest Journal of Political Science* 3 (May): 188–206.

Farber, Bernard. 1971. *Kinship and class: A midwestern study.* New York: Basic Books.
————. 1973. *Family and kinship in modern society.* Glenville, Ill.: Scott, Foresman.
————. 1981. *Conceptions of kinship.* New York: Elsevier.

Fortier, Alcée. 1914. *History of Louisiana.* Vol. 3. Madison, Wisc.: Century Historical Association.

Gardner, Woodford L., Jr. 1972. Kentucky justices on the U.S. Supreme Court. *Register of the Kentucky Historical Society* 70 (April): 121–42.

Genealogies of Virginia families from the William and Mary College Quarterly Historical Magazine. 1982. Vol. 4. Baltimore: Genealogical.

Green, Thomas Marshall. 1964. *Historic Kentucky families.* Baltimore: Regional.

Griffith, Lucille. 1963. *The Virginia House of Burgesses, 1750–1774.* Northport, Ala.: Colonial Press.

Hair, William T. 1969. *Bourbonism and agrarian protest: Louisiana politics, 1877–1900.* Baton Rouge: Louisiana State University Press.

Hall, Kermit L. 1979. *The politics of justice: Lower federal judicial selection and the second party system.* Lincoln: University of Nebraska Press.

———. 1980. The children of the cabin: The lower federal judiciary, modernization, and the political culture, 1789–1899. *Northwestern University Law Review* 75 (October): 423–71.

———. 1981. Hacks and derelicts reunited: American territorial judiciary 1789–1959. *Western Historical Quarterly* 12 (July): 272–89.

Hansen, Edward C., and Timothy C. Parrish. 1983. Elites versus the state: Toward an anthropological contribution to the study of hegemonic power in capitalist society. In *Elites: Ethnographic issues,* ed. George E. Marcus, 257–78. Albuquerque: University of New Mexico Press.

Hareven, Tamara K. 1971. The history of the family as an interdisciplinary field. *Journal of Interdisciplinary History* 2 (autumn): 399–414.

———. 1977. *Family and kin in urban communities, 1700–1930.* New York: New Viewpoints.

Hasson, Judi. 1992. Next generation goes for votes. *USA Today,* 1 June, 2A.

Hatch, David L., and Mary A. Hatch. 1947. Criteria of social status as derived from marriage announcements in the New York *Times. American Sociological Review* 12 (August): 396–403.

Hatcher, John Henry. 1974. Fred Vinson: Boyhood and education in the Big Sandy Valley. *Register of the Kentucky Historical Society* 72 (July): 243–61.

Havard, William C., Rudolph Heberle, and Perry H. Howard. 1963. *The Louisiana elections of 1960.* Baton Rouge: Louisiana State University Press.

Heiberg, Robert A. 1969. Social backgrounds of the Minnesota Supreme Court justices, 1858–1968. *Minnesota Law Review* 53: 901–37.

Hennessy, Bernard. 1985. *Public opinion.* 5th ed. Monterey, Calif.: Brooks/Cole.

Hess, Stephen. 1966. *America's political dynasties: From Adams to Kennedy.* Garden City, N.Y.: Doubleday.

Hinds, Michael deCourcy. 1992. Skillful political novice. New York *Times,* 4 April, 11A.

Hollingshead, August B. 1950. Cultural factors in the selection of marriage mates. *American Sociological Review* 15 (October): 619–27.

Howard, Perry H. 1957. *Political tendencies in Louisiana, 1812–1952.* Baton Rouge: Louisiana State University Press.

———. 1971. *Political tendencies in Louisiana.* Rev. ed. Baton Rouge: Louisiana State University Press.

Hunt, Thomas C. 1940. Occupational status and marriage selection. *American Sociological Review* 5 (August): 495–504.

Keller, Suzanne. 1963. *Beyond the ruling class.* New York: Random House.

Key, V. O., Jr. 1949. *Southern politics.* New York: Vintage Books.

Kornberg, Allan, and Norman Thomas. 1965. The political socialization of national legislative elites in the United States and Canada. *Journal of Politics* 27 (November): 761–75.

Kurtz, Donn M. 1986. Politics as a family business: Preliminary observations on the case of Louisiana. Presented at the annual meeting of the Louisiana Political Science Association, March, Lafayette, La.

―――. 1987. Kinship and politics: The public service careers of three early Louisiana families and their descendants. *Louisiana Genealogical Register* 34 (September): 201–12.

―――. 1989. The political family: A contemporary view. *Sociological Perspectives* 32 (fall): 331–52.

―――. 1993. Introduction: The family in politics. In *The American political family,* ed. Donn M. Kurtz II, 1–11. Lanham, Md.: University Press of America.

―――. 1995. Inheriting a political career: The justices of the United States and Louisiana Supreme Courts. *Social Science Journal* 32(4): 441–57.

Kurtz, Donn M. II, and Pamela Pena. 1990. The political genealogy of the Todd family: A Kentucky-based national elite network. *Journal of Kentucky Studies* 7 (September): 87–106.

Laband, David N., and Bernard F. Lentz. 1983. Like father, like son: Toward an economic theory of occupational following. *Southern Economic Journal* 50 (October): 474–93.

―――. 1985. Favorite sons: Intergenerational wealth transfers among politicians. *Economic Inquiry* 23 (July): 395–414.

―――. 1992. Self-recruitment in the legal profession. *Journal of Labor Economics* 10 (April): 182–201.

Lathrop, Barnes F. 1958. Disaffection in Confederate Louisiana: The case of William Hyman. *Journal of Southern History* 24 (August): 308–18.

Lawrence, Alexander A. 1943. *James Moore Wayne, southern Unionist.* Chapel Hill: University of North Carolina Press.

McGoldrick, Monica, and Randy Gerson. 1985. *Genograms in family assessment.* New York: W. W. Norton.

Marvick, Dwaine, and Charles Nixon. 1961. Recruitment contrasts in rival campaign groups. In *Political decision makers,* ed. Dwaine Marvick, 193–217. Glencoe, Ill.: Free Press.

Matthews, Donald R. 1960. *U.S. senators and their world.* Chapel Hill: University of North Carolina Press.

Members of Congress since 1789. 1985. Washington: Congressional Quarterly.

Merlie, Michael P., and Edward T. Silva. 1975. The first family: Presidential kinship and its theoretical implications. *Insurgent Sociologist* 5 (spring): 149–70.

Mills, C. Wright. 1959. *The power elite.* New York: Oxford University Press.

Moore, Stanley W., James Lace, and Kenneth A. Wagner. 1985. *The child's political world: A longitudinal perspective.* New York: Praeger.

Mott, Rodney L., Spencer D. Albright, and Helen R. Semmerling. 1933. Judicial personnel. *Annals of the American Academy of Political and Social Science* 167 (May): 141–55.

Musto, David. 1979. Continuity across generations: The Adams family myth. In *Kin and communities: Families in America*, ed. Allan J. Lichtman and Joan R. Challinor, 77–94. Washington: Smithsonian Institution.

Pessen, Edward. 1969. *Jacksonian America: Society, personality, and politics*. Homewood, Ill.: Dorsey Press.

———. 1984. *The log cabin myth*. New Haven: Yale University Press.

Postell, William Dosite. 1980. *They came to Iberville: A saga of the Kleinpeters, Schlatres, Dardennes, and Desobrys*. New Orleans: privately printed.

Prewitt, Kenneth. 1970. *The recruitment of political leaders: A study of citizen-politicians*. Indianapolis: Bobbs-Merrill.

Prewitt, Kenneth, Heinz Eulau, and Betty Zisk. 1966–67. Political socialization and political roles. *Public Opinion Quarterly* 30 (winter): 569–82.

Price, Anne. 1989. The next generation. *Baton Rouge Sunday Advocate Magazine*, 9 July, 12–13.

Purvis, Thomas L. 1980. High-born, long-recorded families: Social origins of New Jersey assemblymen. *William and Mary Quarterly*, 3d ser., 37 (October): 592–615.

———. 1982. The making of a myth: Abraham Lincoln's family background in the perspective of Jacksonian politics. *Journal of the Illinois State Historical Society* 75 (spring): 148–60.

Putnam, Robert D. 1976. *The comparative study of political elites*. Englewood Cliffs, N.J.: Prentice Hall.

Riffel, Judy. 1985. *Iberville Parish history*. Baton Rouge: Le Comité des Archives de la Louisiane.

Roberts, Gary Boyd. 1989. *The ancestors of American presidents*. Santa Clarita, Calif.: Carl Boyer, 3d.

Rosenau, James N. 1974. *Citizenship between elections*. New York: Free Press.

Ryan, John, Paul Allan Ashman, Bruce D. Sales, and Sandra Shane-DuBow. 1980. *American trial judges: Their work styles and performance*. New York: Free Press.

Saveth, Edward. 1963. The American patrician class: A field of research. *American Quarterly* 15 (summer): 235–52.

Schmidhauser, John R. 1959. The justices of the Supreme Court. *Midwest Journal of Political Science* 3 (February): 1–57.

———. 1979. *Judges and justices: The federal appellate judiciary*. Boston: Little, Brown.

Seligman, Lester G., Michael R. King, Chong Lim Kim, and Roland E. Smith. 1974. *Patterns of recruitment: A state chooses its lawmakers*. Chicago: Rand McNally.

Shaw, Peter. 1985. All in the family: A psychobiography of the Adamses. *American Scholar* 54 (autumn): 501–16.

Shugg, Roger W. 1936. A supressed co-operationist protest against secession. *Louisiana Historical Quarterly* 19 (January): 199–203.

———. 1939. *The origins of the class struggle in Louisiana*. Baton Rouge: Louisiana State University Press.

Sindler, Allan P. 1956. *Huey Long's Louisiana: State politics, 1920–1956.* Baltimore: Johns Hopkins University Press.

Smith, James Otis, and Gideon Sjoberg. 1961. Origins and career patterns of leading Protestant clergyman. *Social Forces* 39 (May): 290–96.

Soule, John W. 1969. Future political ambitions and the behavior of incumbent state legislators. *Midwest Journal of Political Science* 13 (August): 439–54.

Soule, John W., and James W. Clarke. 1970. Amateurs and professionals: A study of delegates to the 1968 Democratic national convention. *American Political Science Review* 64 (September): 888–98.

Stafford, George Mason Graham. 1947. *General George Mason Graham of Tyrone plantation and his people.* New Orleans: Pelican.

———. 1969. *General Leroy Augustus Stafford.* Baton Rouge: Claitor's.

Stevenson, Noel C. 1979. *Genealogical evidence.* Laguna Hills, Calif.: Aegean Park Press.

Stone, Lawrence. 1971. Prosopography. *Daedalus* 100 (winter): 46–79.

Taylor, Joe Gray. 1974. *Louisiana reconstructed, 1863–1877.* Baton Rouge: Louisiana State University Press.

———. 1976. *Louisiana: A bicentennial history.* New York: W. W. Norton.

Ulmer, Sidney. 1986. Are social background models time-bound? *American Political Science Review* 80 (September): 957–67.

Verba, Sidney, and Norman H. Nie. 1972. *Participation in America: Political democracy and social equality.* New York: Harper and Row.

Vines, Kenneth N., and Herbert Jacob. 1963. *Studies in judicial politics.* New Orleans: Tulane University.

Virkus, Frederick A., ed. 1987. *The compendium of American genealogy.* Vol. 1. Baltimore: Genealogical.

Wall, Bennett H., ed. 1984. *Louisiana: A history.* Arlington Heights, Ill.: Forum Press.

Welch, Susan, and John Comer. 1988. In *Quantitative methods for public administration.* Homewood, Ill.: Dorsey Press.

Whitley, Richard. 1973. Commonalities and connections among directors of large financial institutions. *Sociological Review* 21 (November): 613–32.

———. 1974. The city and industry: The directors of large companies, their characteristics and connections. In *Elites and power in British society,* ed. Philip Stanworth and Anthony Giddens, 65–80. London: Cambridge University Press.

Williams, T. Harry. 1970. *Huey Long.* New York: Bantam Books.

Who faculty members are, and what they think. 1985. *Chronicle of Higher Education,* 18 December, 24–28.

Woodward, Julian L., and Elmo Roper. 1950. Political activity of American citizens. *American Political Science Review* 44 (December): 872–85.

THE JUSTICES AND THEIR FAMILIES

The types of entries in this appendix were explained in Chapter 1, but they will be discussed in more detail here for the sake of convenience and clarity. Each set of entries begins with the surname of the justice followed by ** for United States justices and by * for Louisiana justices.

The first entry in the set is that of the justice, and his full name is capitalized. Immediately following the justice and with no further heading are the relatives of the judge who are in his family. In the case of Justice John Marshall, the Marshall relatives are Thomas Marshall through William Lewis Marshall. "Relatives from other families" are listed second and include additional relatives of Justice Marshall who are members of other political families (based on the surname), such as Duff Green. Other members of Duff Green's family held public office, but he is the only one related to Justice Marshall. The Greens are one component of the Marshall-centered kinship network (number 45, group A in Chapter 5). A third group of officials, "collateral relatives," consists of other members of the extended Marshall clan who are not relatives of the justice (as relatives were defined in Chapter 1).

The final set of entries for Justice Marshall, "other connections," indicates how the Marshall family is linked to other families in network 45. The range of possible connections was discussed in Chapter 4. Individual entries in this section begin with the name of Martin Pickett Marshall, a member of the extended Marshall family, followed by a statement about his relationship to Martin Pickett, a member of another political family. The Picketts are thus an allied family in the Marshall network.

Members of allied families are not listed in their entirety in this or any other appendix. Only their links to the family of a justice are indicated. However, Appendix C does include the biographical sources for all allied families.

BAKER*

JOSHUA G. BAKER* (b. 1852). Judge, criminal district court, New Orleans, 1898–1921. Louisiana Supreme Court, 1921–1922.

Joshua Baker (1799–1885). Judge, St. Mary Parish, 1829–1832. Military governor, 1868. State board of public works. Senate. Grandfather.

Joshua G. Baker (1763–1816). Kentucky constitutional convention, 1799. Mississippi Territorial Legislative Council, 1805–1808. Great-grandfather.

Relatives from Other Families

Frank Adair Monroe*. Brother-in-law. See **MONROE***.

Other Connections

Joshua G. Baker (1763–1816) was the father-in-law of **Alexander Porter**.

A daughter of **Joshua Baker** (1799–1885) married a son of **William Leigh Brent**.

BALDWIN**

HENRY BALDWIN* (1780–1844). U.S. House of Representatives, Pennsylvania, 1817–1822. Supreme Court, 1830–1844.

Abraham Baldwin (1754–1807). Continental Congress, Georgia, 1785–1788. U.S. constitutional convention, 1787. U.S. Senate, 1799–1807. Half brother.

Joel Barlow (1754–1812). Consul to Algeria, 1795–? Minister to France, 1811–1812. Brother-in-law.

BARBOUR**

PHILIP PENDLETON BARBOUR* (1783–1841). Virginia House of Delegates, 1812–1814. U.S. House of Representatives, 1814–1825, 1827–1830. Judge, general court, 1825–1827. Constitutional convention, 1829. U.S. circuit court, 1830–1836. Supreme Court, 1836–1841.

Thomas Barbour. House of Burgesses and justice of the peace. Father.

James Barbour (d. 1775). Presiding justice, Culpepper County Court, Virginia, 1764. Grandfather.

James Barbour. Virginia House of Burgesses, Culpepper County, 1765. Uncle.

James Barbour (1775–1842). Virginia House of Delegates, 1796–1812. Governor, 1812–1814. U.S. Senate, 1815–1825. Secretary of war, 1825–1828. Minister to England, 1828–1829. Brother.

John Strode Barbour, Sr. (1790–1855). Virginia House of Delegates, 1813–1816, 1820–1823, 1833–1834. U.S. House of Representatives, 1823–1833. Constitutional convention, 1829, 1830. First cousin once removed.

James Barbour (1820–1896). Auditor, Kentucky, 1850–1851. First cousin once removed.

Benjamin Johnson Barbour (1821–1897?). Virginia legislature, Orange County. Nephew.

Relatives from Other Families

John Pendleton (1719–1799). Clerk, Virginia House of Burgesses. First cousin.

Edmund Pendleton (1721–1803). Continental Congress, 1774, 1775. Constitutional ratification convention, Virginia. Judge, Supreme Court of Appeals. First cousin.

James Barbour Mason. Kentucky legislature. First cousin once removed.

George Keith Walker. Secretary, Florida Territory. U.S. attorney, Florida. Second cousin.

David Shelby Walker (1815–1891). Florida Senate, 1845. House of Representatives, 1848, 1849. Florida Supreme Court, 1858–1865. Governor, 1866–1868. Judge, circuit court, 1877–1891. Second cousin.

Thomas Barbour Bryan (1828–1906). Commissioner, District of Columbia, 1875–1878. Nephew.

Charles Page Bryan (b. 1855). Colorado legislature, 1880. Illinois General Assembly, 1890–1897. Minister to Brazil (1898–1902), to Switzerland (1902–1903), to Portugal (1904–?). Grandnephew.

R. H. Field. Judge, general court, Virginia. Son-in-law.

Collateral Relatives

James Foster. Postmaster, Natchez. Father-in-law of James Barbour (1820–1896).

J. B. Hogan. Collector, Port of Mobile. Brother-in-law of John S. Barbour, Sr.

Henry Minor. Alabama Supreme Court. Brother-in-law of John S. Barbour, Sr.

James Barbour (d. 1895). Virginia legislature. Constitutional convention, 1849. Secession convention, 1861. Son of John S. Barbour, Sr.

John Strode Barbour, Jr. (1820–1892). Virginia legislature, 1847–1851. U.S. House of Representatives, 1881–1887. U.S. Senate, 1889–1892. Son of John S. Barbour, Sr.

John F. Rixie (1854–1907). Commonwealth attorney, Virginia, 1879–1891. U.S. House of Representatives, 1897–1907. Son-in-law of James Barbour (d. 1895).

Other Connections

James Barbour (1820–1896) was

a second cousin once removed of **Bushrod Washington**** (see **WASHINGTON****);

a nephew of **John Green;**

a first cousin once removed of **James C. Birney** (1792–1857);

a second cousin of **Humphrey Marshall** (1812–1872). See **MARSHALL****.

A son of **James Barbour** (no dates, uncle of Justice Barbour) married a daughter of **James Taylor.**

BERMUDEZ*

EDWARD EDMOND BERMUDEZ* (1832–1892). Secession convention, 1861. President, board of school directors, New Orleans, after Civil War. City attorney, New Orleans, 1865–1867. Chief justice, Supreme Court, 1880–1892.

Joaquim Bermudez (1796–1866). Justice of the peace. City judge, New Orleans. Judge, probate court. Father.

Relatives from Other Families

Gui Soniat Du Fossat (1726–1794). Alcalde, Louisiana, 1772–1778, 1786–*ca.* 1794. Great-grandfather.

Gustave V. Soniat Du Fossat (1856–1903). Police jury, Jefferson Parish. Second cousin.

Charles T. Soniat Du Fossat (b. 1847). Louisiana Senate, 1888–1890. School board, 1912. Second cousin.

Jules de la Vergne (1818–1887). Louisiana House of Representatives, 1844. Senate, 1856. Brother-in-law.

BLACK**

HUGO L. BLACK** (1886–1971). Judge, police court, Birmingham, Alabama, 1907–1927. U.S. Senate, 1927–1937. Supreme Court, 1937–1971.

Martha Toland Black. Postmistress, Harlan, Alabama. Mother.

BLAIR**

JOHN BLAIR, JR.** (1732–1800). Virginia House of Burgesses, 1765–1770. Clerk, Virginia Council, 1770–1775. Judge, general court, 1778–1780. U.S. constitutional convention, 1787. Judge, court of appeals, 1780–1789. Supreme Court, 1790–1796.

John Blair, Sr. (1687–1771). Virginia House of Burgesses, 1734–1740. Governor's Council, 1745–1770. Acting governor, 1758, 1768. Father.

Archibald Blair. Virginia House of Burgesses, 1718–1734. Grandfather.

James Blair (1655–1743). President, Virginia Council. Acting governor, 1740–1741. Granduncle.

Relatives from Other Families

Robert Bolling (1738–1769). Virginia House of Burgesses, 1769. First cousin.

Thomas Bolling (1735–1814). Justice, Chesterfield County, Virginia. First cousin.

William Bolling (1777–1845). Virginia legislature. First cousin once removed.

Other Connections

James Blair was a son-in-law of **Benjamin Harrison II** (1645–1712).

John Blair, Jr.** was a first cousin twice removed of **Thomas Bolling Robertson.**

BLANCHARD*

NEWTON CRAIN BLANCHARD* (1849–1922). Democratic committee, Caddo Parish, 1876. Constitutional convention, 1879. U.S. House of Representatives, 1880–1893. U.S. Senate, 1893–1897. Supreme Court, 1897–1904. Governor, 1904–1908. President, constitutional convention, 1913.

Carey Hansford Blanchard (1805–1861). House of Representatives, Rapides Parish, 1840–? Father.

Thomas Blanchard. Borough council, Norfolk County, Virginia, 1800. Grandfather.

James Ashton Blanchard (b. 1874). President, Shreveport Board of Health, *ca.* 1905. Son.

Lawrence Crain Blanchard (b. 1886). Judge, city court, Shreveport, 1910–1916. District attorney, Caddo Parish, 1916–1930. Nephew.

William Payne (b. 1877). Sheriff, Natchitoches Parish, Grandnephew.

Relatives from Other Families

Thomas Newton, Jr. Borough council, Norfolk, Virginia, 1800. Board of commissioners, Virginia Navy, 1776. Great-grandfather.

Thomas Newton (1768–1847). Virginia House of Delegates, 1796–1799. U.S. House of Representatives, 1801–1830, 1831–1833. Granduncle.

Other Connections

Lawrence Crain Blanchard's brother married a daughter of **David T. Stafford.**

James Ashton Blanchard was a son-in-law of **Alfred D. Land***. See **LAND***.

Carey H. Blanchard's son married a daughter of **Neal Davidson.**

BLATCHFORD**

SAMUEL BLATCHFORD* (1820–1893). U.S. district judge, New York, 1867–1872. U.S. court of appeals, 1872–1882. Supreme Court, 1882–1893.

Richard Milford Blatchford (1798–1875). New York legislature, 1855. Minister to the Papal States, 1862–1863. Public parks commissioner, New York City, 1872. Father.

Richard Milford Blatchford (1859–1934). Major general, U.S., *ca.* 1917. First cousin once removed.

BOND*

NAT W. BOND* (1892–1948). House of Representatives, 1914–1918. Judge, civil district court, Orleans Parish, 1934–1947. Supreme Court, 1947–1948 (less than a year).

Martin Behrman (1864–1926). Clerk, city council, New Orleans, 1892–1896. Board of education, 1892–1906. Senate, 1904. Mayor, New Orleans, 1904–1920, 1925. Father-in-law.

BRADLEY**

JOSEPH P. BRADLEY* (1813–1892). Supreme Court, 1870–1892.

Relatives from Other Families

Joseph Coerten Hornblower (1777–1864). New Jersey legislature, 1829. Chief justice, New Jersey Supreme Court, 1832–*ca.* 1846. Father-in-law.

BRANDEIS**

LOUIS D. BRANDEIS****** (1856–1941). Supreme Court, 1916–1939.

Charles Nagel (1849–1940). Missouri House of Representatives, 1881. President, city council, St. Louis, 1893–1897. U.S. secretary of commerce and labor, 1909–1913. Republican national committee, 1908–1912. Brother-in-law.

BRENNAN**

WILLIAM JOSEPH BRENNAN, JR.****** (b. 1906). Judge, superior court, New Jersey, 1949–1950. Judge, Appellate Division, 1950–1952. New Jersey Supreme Court, 1952–1956. Supreme Court, 1956–1990.

William Joseph Brennan, Sr. (d. 1930). Police board, Newark. Public safety commissioner, Newark, ?–1930. Father.

BREWER**

DAVID J. BREWER****** (1837–1910). Judge, probate and criminal court, Leavenworth, Kansas, 1863–1864. District judge, 1865–1869. County attorney, 1869–1870. Kansas Supreme Court, 1870–1874. U.S. circuit court, 1884–1889. Supreme Court, 1889–1910.

Relatives from Other Families

Stephen J. Field******. Uncle. See **FIELD****.
David Dudley Field. Uncle. See **FIELD****.

BULLARD*

HENRY ADAMS BULLARD***** (1788–1851). Parish judge, 1819–1821, 1826–1830. Louisiana House of Representatives, 1820–? President, board of trustees, Alexandria, 1823. U.S. House of Representatives, 1831–1834, 1850–1851. Supreme Court, 1834–1836.

Relatives from Other Families

Henry L. Garland. Son-in-law. See **GARLAND***.
Robert Lee Garland. Grandson. See **GARLAND***.

Other Connections

Henry Adams Bullard* was a great-great-grandfather of **Henry Garland Dupre.**

BURGER**

WARREN BURGER****** (b. 1907). Assistant attorney general, 1953–1956. U.S. court of appeals, 1956–1959. Chief justice, Supreme Court, 1969–1986.

Joseph Burger. Minnesota legislature after Civil War. Grandfather.

BURTON**

HAROLD HITZ BURTON** (1888–1964). Ohio House of Representatives. Mayor, Cleveland, 1935–1940. U.S. Senate, 1941–1945. Supreme Court, 1945–1958.

John Hitz (b. 1828). Swiss consul to the United States, 1864–1881. Grandfather.

John Hitz. Swiss consul to the United States, 1853–1864. Great-grandfather.

Note: The two Hitz officials could be considered "Relatives from other families" as is the case with Justices Bradley**, Brewer**, and Carleton*. In those three cases the "other" family includes officials to whom the justice is not related, so they are treated as networks. Here there are no other Hitz officeholders, so all three are considered a single family.

CAMPBELL**

JOHN A. CAMPBELL** (1811–1880/89). Alabama legislature. Supreme Court, 1853–1861. Assistant secretary of war, CSA, 1862–1865.

Duncan G. Campbell. Legislator. Indian commissioner. Father.

John A. Campbell. Judge, court of admiralty, North Carolina. Grandfather.

Relatives from Other Families

Lucius Q. C. Lamar**. First cousin once removed. See **LAMAR****.

Lucius Q. C. Lamar. First cousin. See **LAMAR****.

Other Connections

Duncan G. Campbell and **John Clark** married sisters.

CARDOZO**

BENJAMIN CARDOZO** (1870–1938). New York Supreme Court, 1914–1928. U.S. Court of appeals, New York, 1928–1932. Supreme Court, 1932–1938.

Albert Cardozo. New York Court of Common Pleas. New York Supreme Court, ?–1872. Father.

CARLETON*

HENRY CARLETON* (1785?–1863). U.S. attorney, 1832. Supreme Court, 1837–1839.

Relatives from Other Families

Carleton Hunt (1836–1921). U.S. House of Representatives, Louisiana, 1883–1885. City attorney, New Orleans, 1888–1892. Grandson.

CATRON**

JOHN CATRON** (1778/81–1865). State's attorney, third circuit, Tennessee, 1815–1817. Tennessee Supreme Court, 1824–1836 (chief justice, 1830–1836). Supreme Court, 1837–1865.

John Childress. U.S. marshall, Western District, Tennessee. (May also have been a judge.) Father-in-law.

Other Connections

John Catron** and **Morgan Brown** married sisters.

CHASE**

SALMON P. CHASE** (1808–1873). U.S. Senate, Ohio, 1849–1855. Governor, 1855–1859. Secretary of the treasury, 1861–1864. Chief justice, Supreme Court, 1864–1873.

Ithamar Chase (d. 1817?). Held various unspecified state and local offices. Father.

Dudley Chase (1771–1846). State's attorney, 1803–1811. Vermont legislature, 1805–1812. U.S. Senate, 1813–1817, 1825–1831. Chief justice, Vermont Supreme Court. Uncle.

Dudley Chase Denison (1819–1905). U.S. House of Representatives, Vermont, 1875–1879. First cousin.

Relatives from Other Families

William Sprague (1830–1915). Governor, Rhode Island, 1859–1863. U.S. Senate, 1863–1875. Son-in-law.

CLARK**

THOMAS C. CLARK** (1899–1977). Civil district attorney, Dallas County, Texas, 1927–1932. U.S. attorney general, 1945–1949. Supreme Court, 1949–1967.

William Franklin Ramsey (1855–1922). Justice, criminal court of appeals, 1908–1911. Texas Supreme Court, 1911–1912. Father-in-law.

William Henry Clark. Chancery judge, Mississippi. Grandfather.

William Henry Clark. Judge, Vicksburg, Mississippi. State treasurer. Great-grand-father.

William Ramsey Clark (b. 1927). U.S. attorney general, 1967–1969. Son.

CLARKE**

JOHN H. CLARKE** (1857–1945). U.S. district judge, Ohio, 1914–1916. Supreme Court, 1916–1922.

John Clarke (1814?–1884). Prosecuting attorney. Judge, court of common pleas, New Lisbon, Ohio. Father.

CLIFFORD**

NATHAN CLIFFORD** (1803–1881). Maine legislature, 1830–1834. Attorney general, Maine, 1834–1838. U.S. House of Representatives, 1839–1843. U.S. attorney general, 1846–1848. Supreme Court, 1858–1881.

Nathaniel Clifford (1750–1824). Town tax collector. Grandfather.

William Henry Clifford (1839–1901). U.S. circuit court commissioner. Son.

Other Connections

William Henry Clifford's son married a daughter of **Clarence Hale.**

CURTIS**

BENJAMIN R. CURTIS** (1809–1874). Massachusetts House of Representatives, 1851. Supreme Court, 1851–1857.

George Ticknor Curtis (1812–1894). Massachusetts House of Representatives, 1840–1843. Brother.

Other Connections

George Ticknor Curtis was a son-in-law of **Joseph Story****. See **STORY****.

CUSHING**

WILLIAM CUSHING** (1732–1810). Judge, probate court, Lincoln County, Massachusetts, 1760–1761. Superior court, Massachusetts, 1772–1789. Constitutional convention, 1779. Constitutional ratification convention, 1788. Supreme Court, 1790–1810.

John Cushing. Governor's Council. Judge, superior court, Massachusetts Bay, *ca.* 1749–1772. Father.

John Cushing. Governor's Council. Judge, superior court, Massachusetts Bay. Grandfather.

Josiah Cotton. County judge. Member, general court, Massachusetts Bay. Grandfather.

John Cushing (1627–1708). Selectman, 1674–1686. Deputy, general court, 1692. Governor's Council, 1706–1707. Great-grandfather.

Matthew Cushing (1665–1715). Selectman. Granduncle.

Charles Cushing. Sheriff, Lincoln County, Massachusetts, *ca.* 1760. Brother.

Thomas Cushing, Sr. Member, general court, Massachusetts, 1731–1746 (Speaker, 1742–1746). First cousin once removed.

Thomas Cushing, Jr. (1725–1788). General court, Massachusetts, 1761–1774 (Speaker, 1767–1774). Continental Congress, 1774, 1775. Judge, court of common pleas and probate, 1776–1777. Lt. governor, 1780–1788. Constitutional ratification convention, 1788. Second cousin.

Collateral Relatives

Edmund Cushing. Representative, general court, Massachusetts. Senate. Governor's Council. Great-grandson of Matthew Cushing.

Luther Stearns Cushing (1803–1856). Clerk, Massachusetts House of Representatives, 1832–1844. Representative, general court, 1844. Judge, court of common pleas, 1844–1848. Reporter, Massachusetts Supreme Court, 1850–1856. Son of Edmund Cushing.

Edmund Lambert Cushing (1807–1883). New Hampshire House of Representatives, 1850, 1852, 1853. Judge, court of common pleas, 1855. Chief justice, New Hampshire Supreme Judicial Court, 1874–1876. Son of Edmund Cushing.

DANIEL**

PETER V. DANIEL** (1784–1860). Virginia legislature, 1809–1810. Lt. governor. U.S. district judge, 1836–1840. Supreme Court, 1841–1860.

Peter Daniel. Justice of the peace, Stafford County, Virginia. Grandfather.

William Daniel, Sr. Judge, general court, Virginia. Second cousin.

Raleigh Travers Daniel (1805–1877). Commonwealth attorney, Henrico County, Virginia. ?–1852. Legislature, 1842–? Lt. governor. Nephew.

John Moncure Daniel (1825–1861). U.S. Representative to Sardinia, 1853–1861. Grandnephew.

Collateral Relatives

William Daniel, Jr. Judge, Virginia Supreme Court of Appeals. Son of William Daniel, Sr.

John Warwick Daniel (1842–1910). Virginia House of Delegates, 1869–1872. Senate, 1875–1881. U.S. House of Representatives, 1885. U.S. Senate, 1887–1910. Son of William Daniel, Jr.

Relatives from Other Families

Edmund Randolph (1753–1812). Virginia convention, 1776. Attorney general, Virginia, 1776–1782. Continental Congress, 1779–1782. Governor, 1786–1788. Constitutional convention, 1787. Constitutional ratification convention, Virginia, 1788. U.S. attorney general, 1790–1794. Secretary of state, 1794–1795. Father-in-law.

Peyton Randolph (d. 1828). Clerk, Virginia Supreme Court. Brother-in-law.

Other Connections

Raleigh T. Daniel was a grandson of **Thomas Stone.**

DAVIS**

DAVID DAVIS** (1815–1886). Illinois legislature, 1844. Constitutional convention, 1847. Judge, circuit court, 1848–1862. Supreme Court, 1862–1877. U.S. Senate, Illinois, 1877–1883.

William P. Walker. Judge, probate court, Berkshire, Massachusetts. Father-in-law.

Henry Winter Davis (1817–1865). U.S. House of Representatives, Maryland, 1855–1864. First cousin.

DAWKINS*

BENJAMIN CORNWELL DAWKINS* (1881–1966). District judge, Ouachita Parish, 1912–1918. Supreme Court, 1918–1924. U.S. district judge, 1924–1953.

Benjamin Cornwell Dawkins, Jr. (b. 1911). U.S. district judge, Louisiana, 1953 into 1980s (Ret.). Son.

Robert Brooks Dawkins. District judge, Louisiana, 1898–1917. Judge, court of appeals, 1917–1923. Uncle.

James Monroe Dawkins (1854–1925). House of Representatives, Union Parish, 1902–1905. Parish treasurer, 1906–1909. Clerk of court, 1914–1925. Uncle.

James Robert Dawkins (b. 1901). Mayor, Farmerville, *ca.* 1930s. City attorney. District judge, 1953–1971. First cousin.

DAY**

WILLIAMS RUFUS DAY** (1849–1923). Judge, court of common pleas, Ohio, 1886–1890. Secretary of state, 1898. U.S. court of appeals, 1899–1903. Supreme Court, 1903–1922.

Luther Day. Ohio Supreme Court, 1874–? Father.

Rufus Spalding (1798–1886). Ohio legislature, 1839–1842. Ohio Supreme Court, 1849–1852. U.S. House of Representatives, 1863–1869. Grandfather.

Zephaniah Swift (1759–1823). Connecticut General Assembly, 1787–1793. U.S. House of Representatives, 1893–1897. Connecticut Supreme Court, 1801–1819. Great-grandfather.

DE BLANC*

ALCIBIADES DE BLANC* (1821–1883). Supreme Court, 1877–1883.

Louis Charles de Blanc (1753–1826). Commandant, Natchitoches Post, 1787–1795. Commandant, Attakapas Post, 1795. Grandfather.

Bertrand F. de Blanc (b. 1911). District attorney, Lafayette Parish, 1954–1972. Grandson.

Césaire de Blanc (1683?–1783). Commandant, Illinois Territory. Commandant, Natchitoches Post, 1746. Great-grandfather.

Relatives from Other Families

Pierre Paul Briant, Sr. (1776–1853). Sheriff, St. Martin Parish, 1810–1816. Parish judge, 1816–1845. Constitutional convention, 1845. Senate. Parish recorder, ?–1853. Father-in-law.

Pierre Paul Briant, Jr. (b. 1833). Judge, St. Martin Parish, 1845–? Son. Brother-in-law.

Other Connections

Louis Charles de Blanc was a grandson of **Louis St. Denis.**

DERBIGNY*

PIERRE AUGUSTE DERBIGNY* (1769–1829). Secretary, Municipality of New Orleans. Clerk, court of common pleas. Secretary, Legislative Council. House of

Representatives, Orleans Parish, 1812. Supreme Court, 1813–1820. Secretary of state, 1820–1827. Governor, 1828–1829.

Charles Derbigny (1794–1875). Louisiana House of Representatives and Senate. Son.

Augustin B. Derbigny. Mayor, Laon, France. Father.

Relatives from Other Families

Don Carlos (or Charles August) de Lassus (1764?–1842). Commandant of New Madrid, Illinois District of Spanish Louisiana, 1797–1799. Lt. governor, Upper Louisiana, 1799–1804. Governor of West Florida, 1807. Brother-in-law.

Pierre Charles de Hault de Lassus (1739–1806). Commandant of New Bourbon, Upper Louisiana, *ca.* 1795. Father-in-law.

DOUGLAS**

WILLIAM O. DOUGLAS★★ (1898–1980). Chairman, Securities and Exchange Commission, 1936–1939. Supreme Court, 1939–1975.

Orville Fisk (1844?–1885). County clerk, school board, Maine, Minnesota. Grandfather.

Clifton Eugene Hester (b. 1891). Sheriff, Madison Parish, Louisiana. Father-in-law.

DUVALL**

GABRIEL DUVALL★★ (1752–1844). Governor's Council, Maryland, 1783, 1784. House of Delegates, 1787–1794. U.S. House of Representatives, 1794–1796. Chief justice, general court, 1796–1802. Comptroller, U.S. Treasury, 1802–1811. Supreme Court, 1811–1835.

Benjamin Duvall (1692?–1774). Constable, 1719. Granduncle.

Charles Duvall (1729–1814?). Constable, Maryland. First cousin once removed.

Other Connections

Charles Duvall was

a great-great-grandfather of **Lloyd Posey, Felix** and **Eloi Girard,** and **Charles Duvall Caffery;**

a great-grandfather of **Edward Sumpter Taylor** and **William C. Crow;**

a grandfather of **Charles Duvall Brashear.**

Note: There were many other Duvall officials, but their precise relationship to Justice Duvall could not be determined.

ELLSWORTH**

OLIVER ELLSWORTH★★ (1745–1807). Connecticut General Assembly, 1775. State's attorney, 1777. Continental Congress, 1777–1783. Governor's Council, 1780–1784, 1801–1807. Judge, superior court, 1784–1789. U.S. constitutional convention, 1787. U.S. Senate, 1789–1796. Chief justice, Supreme Court, 1796–1800. Commissioner to France, 1799.

William Wolcott Ellsworth (1791–1868). U.S. House of Representatives, Connecticut, 1829–1834. Governor, 1838–1842. Connecticut Supreme Court, 1847–1861. Son.

Henry Leavitt Ellsworth (1791–1858). Indian Agent, 1828–1836. Mayor, Hartford, Connecticut, 1835. U.S. commissioner of patents, 1836–1848. Son.

Henry William Ellsworth (1814–1864). Chargé to Sweden and Norway, 1845–1849. Grandson.

Relatives from Other Families

Thomas Scott Williams (1777–1861). Connecticut General Assembly, 1813, 1815, 1816, 1819, 1825. U.S. House of Representatives, 1817–1819. Supreme Court of Errors, 1829–1847. Son-in-law.

Other Connections

Henry William Ellsworth was a grandson of **Elizur Goodrich.**

Note: According to Aronson (1964, 223–24, 228–29), Oliver Ellsworth** is a distant relative of Oliver Wolcott and is linked to Roger Griswold. He also says that Henry L. Ellsworth was a sixth cousin of Henry Baldwin. All these relationships are too distant to be considered here.

EUSTIS*

GEORGE EUSTIS* (1796–1858). House of Representatives, Orleans Parish. Attorney general, 1830–1832. Secretary of state, 1832–1834. Supreme Court, 1839. Constitutional convention, 1845. Chief justice, Supreme Court, 1846–1852.

William Eustis (1753–1825). General court, Massachusetts, 1788–1794. U.S. House of Representatives, 1801–1805, 1820–1823. Secretary of war, 1809–1813. Minister to Holland, 1814–1818. Governor, Massachusetts, 1823–1825. Uncle.

Abraham Eustis. Brigadier general. First cousin.

Henry Lawrence Eustis (1819–1885). Brigadier general, Massachusetts Volunteers, 1863–1864. First cousin once removed.

George Eustis, Jr. (1828–1872). U.S. House of Representatives, Louisiana, 1855–1859. Son.

James B. Eustis (1834–1899). Louisiana House of Representatives, 1866–1868, 1872–1874. Senate, 1874–1877. U.S. Senate, 1877–1879, 1885–1891. Ambassador to France, 1893–1897. Son.

William C. Eustis (1862–1921). Secretary, U.S. embassy, London, 1901. Grandson.

Charles Eustis Bohlen (1904–1974). Counselor, Department of State, 1947. Ambassador to Soviet Union (1953–1957), Philippines (1957–1959), France (1962–1968). Deputy undersecretary of state, 1968–1969. Great-grandson.

Collateral Relatives

Levi Parsons Morton (1824–1920). U.S. House of Representatives, New York, 1877–1881. Minister to France, 1881–1885. Vice president, 1889–1893. Governor, New York, 1895–1897. Father-in-law of William C. Eustis.

Thomas Corcoran. Magistrate, postmaster, and mayor, Georgetown, District of Columbia. Great-grandfather of William C. Eustis.

Martin Duralde (1737?–1822). Commandant, Opelousas Post, 1795–1803. Great-grandfather of James Eustis and George Eustis, Jr.

Other Connections

George Eustis, Jr., and his brother **James B. Eustis** were
first cousins once removed of **William C. C. Claiborne II** (and a number of other Claibornes);
second cousins of **Gustave** and **Charles T. Soniat du Fossat;**
first cousins once removed of **Leo M. Favrot** (and to other Favrots);
second cousins once removed of **James J. A. Fortier.**

FENNER*

CHARLES E. FENNER* (1834–1911). Louisiana House of Representatives, 1865. Supreme Court, 1880–1893.

Charles Payne Fenner (1867–1927). Louisiana Senate, 1896–1900. Son.

Jacob Usher Payne. High sheriff, Kentucky. Father-in-law.

Darwin Ponton Fenner (1841–1888). U.S. consul to Guatamala. First cousin.

Relatives from Other Families

Edward James Gay II (1878–1952). House of Representatives, Iberville, 1904–1918. U.S. Senate, 1918–1921. Louisiana State University Board, *ca.* 1922. State director, National Recovery Act, 1934–1935. Director, National Emergency Council for Louisiana, 1935–1936. President, Louisiana Board of Finance, 1940–1944. Atchafalaya Basin Levee Board, 1946–1948. President, Lake Long Drainage District. Son-in-law.

Andrew Price Gay (b. 1917). Police jury, Iberville Parish, three terms, *ca.* 1960. Louisiana Soil Conservation Board. Grandson.

Collateral Relatives

Darwin S. Fenner (1908–1979). Member, Health Education Authority of Louisiana, 1968–1979. Grandson of Darwin Ponton Fenner.

FIELD**

STEPHEN J. FIELD** (1816–1899). California legislature. California Supreme Court, 1857–1863 (chief justice, 1859–1863). Supreme Court, 1863–1897.

David Dudley Field (1805–1894). Delegate to New York Democratic convention, 1847. U.S. House of Representatives, 1876 (for two months). Brother.

Relatives from Other Families

David J. Brewer**. Nephew. See **BREWER****.

Collateral Relatives

Sir Anthony Musgrave. Governor, British Columbia. Son-in-law of David Dudley Field.

FOURNET*

JOHN B. FOURNET* (1895–1984). House of Representatives, Jefferson Davis Parish, 1928–1932. Lt. governor, 1932–1935. Supreme Court, 1935–1970 (chief justice, 1949–1970).

L. Paul Fournet (b. 1841/43). Police jury, secretary, treasurer, St. Martin Parish. Grandfather.

Valsin A. Fournet (b. 1817). President, police jury, St. Martin Parish. Clerk of court, 1846–1870. Great-grandfather.

Edmund Monge. Judge, St. Martin Parish. Great-grandfather.

Alexander V. Fournet (b. 1849). Assessor, St. Martin Parish, 1871–1879. Clerk of court, 1883–1895. State treasurer, 1896–1900. Granduncle.

Gabriel Antoine Fournet. Judge, St. Martin Parish. District judge, Calcasieu Parish, 1892–? Granduncle.

Charles Fournet. State fire marshall. Uncle.

Kenneth L. Fournet. Coroner, St. Martin Parish, 1980s. Nephew.

Collateral Relatives

Gustave Fournet (b. 1821). Sheriff, St. Martin Parish, 1865–1869. Brother of Valsin A. Fournet.

Fred Gerard Fournet (b. 1904). City council, St. Martinville, 1951–1960s. Grandson of Gustave Fournet.

Other Connections

F. G. Fournet was a grandson of **A. V. Fleming.**

L. Paul Fournet is a grandson of **Pierre Paul Briant, Sr.**

Valsin A. Fournet and **Alcibiades de Blanc*** married sisters.

FULLER**

MELVILLE W. FULLER** (1833–1910). Common council president and city attorney, Augusta, Maine, 1856. Illinois constitutional convention, 1861. Illinois House of Representatives, 1863–1865. Chief justice, Supreme Court, 1888–1910.

Frederick Augustus Fuller (1806–1849). Chairman, board of commissioners, Penobscot, Maine. Father.

Henry Weld Fuller (1784–1841). Probate judge, Kennebec County, Maine, 1828–1841. County attorney, 1826. Grandfather.

Hugh Campbell Wallace (1863–1931). Receiver of public monies, Salt Lake City, Utah, 1885–1887. Democratic national committee, 1892–1896, 1916–1920. Ambassador to France, 1919–1921. Son-in-law.

Relatives from Other Families

Nathan Weston (1782–1859). Representative, general court, Maine, 1808. Judge, circuit court. Chief justice, Maine Supreme Court, 1820–1841. Grandfather.

Daniel Cony. Representative, general court, Massachusetts. Senate. Judge, court of common pleas. Probate judge, Kennebec County, Maine. Maine constitutional convention, 1820. Great-grandfather.

Nathan Weston. Clerk, Maine Supreme Court. Uncle.

George Melville Weston. County attorney, Kennebec County, Maine. Uncle.

Samuel Cony (b. 1775). Adjutant general, Maine. Uncle.

Joseph Emerson Smith. Delegate, Democratic national convention, 1864. First cousin.

Samuel Cony (1811–1870). Maine legislature, 1835–1836, 1862–1863. Governor's Council, 1839. Probate judge, Kennebec County, Maine, 1840–1846. First cousin.

Joseph Hartwell Williams (1814–1896). Maine Senate, 1856. Acting governor, 1857–1858. House of Representatives, 1864–1866, 1874–1876. First cousin once removed.

Other Connections

Melville Fuller** was a first cousin twice removed of **George Bancroft.**

GARLAND*

RICE GARLAND* (1795–1861). U.S. House of Representatives, Louisiana, 1834–1840. Supreme Court, 1840–1846.

Henry L. Garland (1826–1908). Senate, St. Landry Parish, 1876–? Son.

Robert Lee Garland (1869–1939). District attorney, St. Landry Parish, 1896–1936. Grandson.

Collateral Relatives

Charles S. Thompson. Clerk of court, St. Landry Parish, 1888–1904. Son-in-law of Robert Lee Garland.

Other Connections

Rice Garland* was a great-great-grandfather of **Henry Garland Dupre.**

Robert Lee Garland was a grandson of **Henry Adams Bullard***. See BULLARD*.

Henry L. Garland was

first cousin of **Henry Lastrapes, Jr.;**

great-grandfather of **Ben Boagni** and **Kenneth Boagni, Jr.;**

great-grandfather of **Henry Garland Pavy;**
son-in-law of **Henry Adams Bullard*.** See **BULLARD*.**
Henry L. Garland's son married a daughter of **Joseph M. Moore.**

GRAY**

HORACE GRAY** (1828–1902). Massachusetts Supreme Court, 1864–1882. Supreme Court, 1882–1902.
Francis Calley Gray (1790–1856). Massachusetts legislature, 1822–1836. Senate, 1825–1826, 1828–1829, 1831, 1843. Uncle.
William Gray (1750–1825). Selectman. Constitutional ratification convention, 1788. Massachusetts Senate, 1807–1808. Lt. governor, 1810–1812. Constitutional convention, 1820. Grandfather.

Relatives from Other Families

Stanley Matthews**. Father-in-law. See **MATTHEWS**.**
Ward Chipmen (1754–1824). Solicitor general, New Brunswick, Canada. House of Assembly, 1785, 1793, 1802. New Brunswick Supreme Court, 1809. President and commander in chief, New Brunswick. Granduncle.
Ward Chipman, Jr. Chief justice, New Brunswick Supreme Court. First cousin once removed.

HARLAN**

JOHN MARSHALL HARLAN** (1833–1911). Attorney general, Kentucky, 1863. Supreme Court, 1877–1911.
JOHN MARSHALL HARLAN** (1899–1971). U.S. court of appeals, 1954–1955. Supreme Court, 1955–1971. Grandson.
James Harlan (1800–1863). U.S. House of Representatives, Kentucky, 1835–1839. Secretary of state, Kentucky, 1840–? Attorney general, Kentucky, 1851–1854. U.S. attorney. Father.
James Harlan. Vice chancellor, chancery court, Louisville, Kentucky. Brother.
John Maynard Harlan (1864–1934). Alderman, Chicago. Son.
James Shanklin Harlan (b. 1861). Attorney general, Puerto Rico, 1901–1903. Interstate Commerce Commission, 1906–1918. Son.

Note: All relationships are to the first Justice Harlan unless otherwise indicated.

Other Connections

James Harlan (1800–1863) was a third cousin of **George Harlan** (who represents a family from a related line of Harlans).

HOLMES**

OLIVER WENDELL HOLMES** (1841–1935). Supreme Judicial Court, Massachusetts, 1883–1902. Supreme Court, 1902–1932.

Oliver Wendell. Massachusetts Senate. Council of the Commonwealth. Judge. Great-grandfather.

Relatives from Other Families

Charles Jackson (1775–1855). Supreme Judicial Court, Massachusetts, 1813–? Constitutional convention, 1820. Grandfather.

Jonathan Jackson (1743–1810). Provincial Congress, 1775. Massachusetts legislature, 1777. Continental Congress, 1782. Senate, 1789. U.S. marshall, 1789–1791. State treasurer, 1802–1806. Great-grandfather.

John Lowell (1799–1836). City council, Boston. Massachusetts legislature. First cousin once removed.

HUGHES**

CHARLES EVANS HUGHES** (1862–1948). Governor, New York, 1907–1910. Supreme Court, 1910–1916. Secretary of state, 1921–1925. Hague Tribunal, 1926–1930. Permanent Court of International Justice, The Hague, 1928–1930. Chief justice, Supreme Court, 1930–1941.

Charles Evans Hughes, Jr. (b. 1899). U.S. solicitor general, 1929–1930. Son.

Henry Connelly. New York Senate, 1874–1875, 1886–1887. Uncle.

Samuel Jones. Magistrate, Wales. First cousin.

Walter Steuben Carter (1833–1904). U.S. commissioner and master in chancery, U.S. court, Wisconsin. Father-in-law.

HYMAN*

WILLIAM B. HYMAN* (1814–1884). Chief justice, Supreme Court, 1865–1868. Judge, Jefferson Parish, 1871–1880.

Thomas McCabe Hyman (1848–1909). City attorney, New Orleans. Clerk, Louisiana Supreme Court, 1891–1909. Son.

William Mithoff, Jr. (1843–1886). Adjutant general of Louisiana, 1865–? Son-in-law.

Other Connections

Thomas McCabe Hyman is a brother-in-law of **Charles F. de la Villebeuvre.**

IREDELL**

JAMES IREDELL** (1751–1799). Collector, Port of Edenton, North Carolina, 1774–1776. Judge, superior court, 1778. Attorney general, North Carolina, 1779–1781. Supreme Court, 1790–1799.

James Iredell (1778–1853). House of Commons, North Carolina, 1813, 1816–1820, 1823–1828. Governor, 1827–1828. U.S. Senate, 1828–1831. Son.

Relatives from Other Families

Samuel Johnston (1733–1816). North Carolina Assembly, 1759–1775. Provincial Congress. Senate, 1779, 1783, 1784. Continental Congress, 1780–1782. Governor,

1787–1789. Constitutional ratification convention, 1788. U.S. Senate, 1789–1793. Judge, superior court, 1800–1803. Brother-in-law.

JACKSON**

HOWELL E. JACKSON** (1832–1895). Judge, court of arbitration for western Tennessee. Tennessee legislature, 1880. U.S. Senate, 1881–1886. U.S. court of appeals, 1886–1893. Supreme Court, 1893–1895.

Alexander Jackson. Tennessee legislature. Father.

William Hicks Jackson (1835–1903). Brigadier general, CSA, 1862–? Brother.

William H. Jackson. Judge, superior court, Cincinnati. Son.

Other Connections

Howell E. Jackson was a second cousin once removed of President **George Washington**. See **WASHINGTON****.

Note: Justice Jackson's father-in-law was General William Giles Harding (b. 1808) of Tennessee. His precise rank is not known. One source indicates that Justice Jackson was a kinsman of A. W. O. Totten of the Tennessee Supreme Court (1850–1855). No verification of this connection to Justice Totten or other officials in his family can be found.

JACKSON**

ROBERT H. JACKSON** (1892–1954). Assistant U.S. attorney general, 1936–1938. Solicitor general, 1938–1939. U.S. attorney general, 1940–1941. Supreme Court, 1941–1954.

William Jackson (d. 1899). Justice of the peace (and other unspecified local offices) Granduncle.

JAY**

JOHN JAY** (1745–1829). Continental Congress, 1774–1779. Provincial Congress, New York, 1776. Chief justice, New York Supreme Court, 1776–1778. Minister to Spain, 1779. Secretary of foreign affairs, 1784–1789. Chief justice, Supreme Court, 1789–1795.

Peter Jay (1704–1782). Alderman, New York City. Father.

James Jay (1732–1815). New York Senate, 1778–1782. Brother.

Peter Augustus Jay (1776–1843). New York Assembly, 1816. Recorder (criminal court judge) 1820. Constitutional convention, 1821. Son.

William Jay (1789–1858). Judge, Westchester County Court, New York, 1818–1843. Son.

John Jay (1817–1894). Minister to Austria, 1869–1874. New York Civil Service Commission, 1884–1887. Grandson.

Augustus Jay (1850–1919). Secretary, American embasssy, Paris. Great-grandson.

Relatives from Other Families

Henry Brockholst Livingston**. Brother-in-law. See **LIVINGSTON****.

William Livingston. Father-in-law. See **LIVINGSTON****.

Jacobus Van Cortland (1658–1739). Assembly of William and Mary for New York, 1691–?, 1702–1709, 1710–1715. Mayor, New York City, *ca.* 1719. Grandfather.

Oloff Van Cortland (1600–1684). Burgomaster, New Amsterdam, 1655–1664. Alderman, various years between 1665–1672. Great-grandfather.

Pierre Van Cortland, Sr. (1721–1814). New York Assembly, 1777–1795. Provincial Congress. Constitutional convention, 1777. Lt. governor, 1777–1795. Second cousin.

Collateral Relatives

Peter Augustus Jay (b. 1877). Minister to Romania, 1921. Son of Augustus Jay.

Other Connections

Peter Jay was a grandnephew of **Nicholas Bayard** (1644–1707).

Peter Augustus Jay (1776–1843) was a son-in-law of **Matthew Clarkson.**

JOHNSON**

THOMAS JOHNSON** (1732–1819). Maryland Provincial Assembly, 1762. Continental Congress, 1774–1775. Governor, Maryland, 1777–1779. House of Delegates, 1780–1781, 1786–1787. Constitutional ratification convention, 1788. Chief judge, general court, Maryland, 1790–1791. Supreme Court, 1792–1793.

Thomas Jennings. Clerk, provincial court, Maryland. Registrar, state land office. Father-in-law.

Thomas Johnson (1702–1777). Delegate, Lower House, Maryland Assembly, Post 1725. Father.

Joshua Johnson (b. 1742). U.S. consul to London, 1790–1797. Superintendent of Stamps, *ca.* 1797–death. Brother.

Bradley T. Johnson (1829–1903). Chairman, state Democratic committee, Maryland, 1859–1860. Brigadier general, CSA, 1864–1865. Virginia Senate, 1875–1879. President, electoral college, Maryland, 1884. Grandnephew.

Relatives from Other Families

Charles Francis Adams (1807–1886). Massachusetts House of Representatives, 1840–1843. Senate, 1843–1845. U.S. House of Representatives, 1859–1861. Minister to England, 1861–1868. Grandnephew.

Collateral Relatives

Sir James Johnson. Member of Parliament, 1681. Great-grandfather of Thomas Johnson (1702–1777).

Thomas Johnson, Jr. Bailiff, Norfolk, England, 1644, 1661. Father of Sir James Johnson.

Thomas Johnson. Bailiff, Norfolk, England. Member of Parliament, 1625. Grandfather of Sir James Johnson.

James Johnson. Bailiff, Norfolk, England, Post 1588. Great-grandfather of Sir James Johnson.

JOHNSON**

WILLIAM JOHNSON** (1771–1834). South Carolina legislature, 1794–1798. Judge, court of common pleas, 1798–1804. Supreme Court, 1804–1834.

William Johnson (b. 1741). Legislature, South Carolina, for two decades after 1775. Father.

Joseph Johnson (1776–1862). Commissioner of public schools, Charleston, South Carolina. Brother.

Thomas Bennett (1781–1865). South Carolina House of Representatives, 1814–1818. Senate, 1819–1820, 1837–1840. Governor, 1820–1822. Brother-in-law.

KING*

GEORGE ROGERS KING* (1807–1871). Louisiana House of Representatives. District attorney. District judge. Supreme Court, 1846–1850.

George King (1769–1850). Clerk of court, Opelousas, 1805–1807. Judge, St. Landry Parish, 1807–1842. Father.

John Edwards King (1). Judge, St. Landry Parish. Son.

William King, Sr. Justice of the peace and clerk of court, Stafford County, Virginia, 1742–1760. Great-grandfather.

William King, Jr. (b. 1745). Kentucky constitutional convention, 1792. Kentucky Senate, 1792. Grandfather.

John Edwards King (2) (1757–1828). General in command of Kentucky troops, War of 1812. Clerk, county and circuit courts. Granduncle.

Valentine King (d. 1835). Land office registrar, Opelousas. President, police board, Opelousas. Second cousin and son-in-law.

Milton King (b. 1799). Clerk, county and circuit courts, Cumberland County, Kentucky, ?–1850. First cousin once removed.

John Quincy Adams King (b. 1825). Kentucky House of Representatives, Cumberland County, 1840–1849. Senate, 1852, 1855–1863. Second cousin.

William Woodson King. Judge, San Antonio, Texas. Second cousin.

Relatives from Other Families

John Holmes Overton-1. Brother-in-law. See **OVERTON***.
Thomas Overton-1. Nephew. See **OVERTON***.
Winston Overton*. Grandnephew. See **OVERTON***.
John Holmes Overton-2. Grandnephew. See **OVERTON***.

Theodorick Bland, Jr. (1742–1790). Continental Congress, 1780–1783. Constitutional ratification convention, Virginia, 1788. U.S. House of Representatives, 1789–1790. House of Delegates, 1786–1788. Granduncle.

Valentine King Irion (b. 1862). School superintendent, St. Landry Parish. Board of the Louisiana State Normal School. Louisiana State Board of Dentistry, *ca.* 1913. Grandnephew.

Clifford Hill Irion. President, Louisiana State Board of Health, 1904–1908. Grandnephew.

Other Connections

John Edwards King (2) was the father-in-law of **Lindsay D. Beale.**

LABAUVE*

ZENON LABAUVE* (1801–1870). Senate, Iberville Parish, 1834–1836, 1842–1843, 1851. Mayor, Plaquemine, 1843–1844. City council, 1846, 1858, 1862. Constitutional convention, 1845. Supreme Court, 1865–1868.

Thomas W. LaBauve. City council, Plaquemine, 1880. Grandson.

Andre Caneza (1844?–1898). Mayor, Plaquemine, 1877, 1879–1882, 1890–1891, 1892–1893, 1894–1895. Son-in-law.

Relatives from Other Families

Charles Oscar Lauve (b. 1835). Mayor, Plaquemine, 1878. Police jury, Iberville Parish, 1882. Son-in-law.

LAMAR**

LUCIUS Q. C. LAMAR* (1825–1893). Georgia legislature, 1853. U.S. House of Representatives, 1857–1860, 1872–1877. U.S. Senate, 1877–1885. Secretary of the interior, 1885–1888. Supreme Court, 1888–1893.

Lucius Q. C. Lamar (1797?–1834). Judge, superior court, Georgia, 1830. Father.

William Bailey Lamar (1853–1928). U.S. House of Representatives, Florida, 1903–1909. Nephew.

Mirabeau Bonaparte Lamar (1798–1859). Georgia Senate, 1829. Vice president, Republic of Texas. President, Republic of Texas, 1838–1841. Minister to Nicaragua and Costa Rica. Uncle.

Thomas B. Lamar. Delegate, Democratic national convention, 1860. Brother.

John Basil Lamar (1812–1862). Georgia House of Representatives, 1837–1838. U.S. House of Representatives, 1843. Succession convention, 1861. First cousin once removed.

Henry G. Lamar (1798–1861). Judge, superior court, Georgia. House of Representatives. U.S. House of Representatives, 1829–1833. Georgia Supreme Court. First cousin once removed.

Charles A. Lamar (1824–1865). Alderman, Savannah. Second cousin.

Relatives from Other Families

William Polk, Jr. Police jury, Rapides Parish. House of Representatives, 1900–1904, 1908–1912. First cousin once removed.

A. B. Longstreet (1790–1869). Judge, Mississippi. Legislature. Father-in-law.

John A. Campbell**. First cousin once removed. See **CAMPBELL****.

Collateral Relatives

Absalom Harris Chappell (1801–1878). U.S. House of Representatives, Georgia, 1843–1845. Brother-in-law of M. B. Lamar.

Other Connections

Charles A. Lamar was the father-in-law of **Fleming Grantland du Bignon.**

John Basil Lamar was a brother-in-law of **Howell Cobb** (1815–1868).

Note: Lucius Q. C. Lamar** and **Joseph Rucker Lamar**** were fourth cousins.

LAMAR**

JOSEPH RUCKER LAMAR** (1857–1916). Georgia House of Representatives, 1886–1889. Georgia Supreme Court, 1901–1905. Supreme Court, 1910–1916.

Relatives from Other Families

Tinsley White Rucker (b. 1813). Georgia legislature. Uncle.

Elbert Marion Rucker (1828–1906). Secession convention, 1861. Judge, South Carolina. Uncle.

Tinsley White Rucker (1848–1926). U.S. House of Representatives, Missouri, 1917. First cousin.

Elbert Marion Rucker (1866–1926). South Carolina General Assembly, 1900–1910. Special associate justice, South Carolina Supreme Court. First cousin.

William Kimbrough Pendleton (1817–1899). President, West Virginia constitutional convention, 1872. Father-in-law.

Note: Joseph Rucker Lamar** and **Lucius Q. C. Lamar**** were fourth cousins.

LAND*

THOMAS T. LAND* (1815–1893). Mississippi legislature, 1839–1843. Judge, Caddo, De Soto, and Bossier Parishes, 1854–1858. Supreme Court, 1858–1865. Constitutional convention, 1879.

ALFRED DILLINGHAM LAND* (b. 1842). District judge, Caddo, 1894–1903. Supreme Court, 1903–1917. Son of Thomas T. Land*.

JOHN R. LAND* (b. 1862). House of Representatives, Caddo Parish, 1888–1890. District attorney, 1892–1904. District judge, 1913, 1916, 1920. Supreme Court, 1921–1941. Son of Thomas T. Land*.

John R. Land, Jr. Clerk, Supreme Court, 1934–? Son of John R. Land*.

Thomas T. Land (2) (b. 1874). Mayor, Benton. District attorney, Bossier and Webster Parishes, 1900–1905. District attorney, Bienville and Claiborne Parishes, 1912–? Grandson of Thomas T. Land* and nephew of Alfred D. and John R. Land*.

Tiley H. Scovell (b. 1869). Board of education, Caddo Parish, 1908–1910, President, 1912–? Son-in-law of Alfred D. Land*.

Relatives from Other Families

Henry Jastremski (b. 1871). Secretary and vice president, board of the state school for the deaf. Secretary, state board of appraisers. Secretary, state railroad commission, *ca.* 1910. Nephew of Alfred D. and John R. Land and grandson of Thomas T. Land*.

Leon Jastremski (1843–1911). Mayor, Baton Rouge, 1876–1882. Commissioner of agriculture, 1899–1900. Constitutional convention, 1879. Consul general to Callao, Peru. Brigadier general, Louisiana Militia. Chairman, state Democratic central committee. Brother-in-law of Alfred D. and John R. Land and son-in-law of Thomas T. Land*.

Eugene Jastremski. Secretary, state board of agriculture, *ca.* 1910. Nephew of Alfred D. and John T. Land and grandson of Thomas T. Land*.

James Ashton Blanchard. Son-in-law of Alfred D. Land*. See **BLANCHARD***.

Collateral Relatives

Matthew Watson. Sheriff, Caddo Parish, 1846–1857. Grandfather of Thomas T. Land (b. 1874).

LEBLANC*

SAM A. LEBLANC* (b. 1886). Louisiana House of Representatives, 1912–1916. District judge, 1921–1930. Court of appeals, 1930–1949. Supreme Court, 1949–1954.

Joseph E. LeBlanc (1842–1902). School board, Assumption Parish. Clerk of court, 1880–1884. House of Representatives, 1888–1892, 1900–1902. Senate, 1894–1896. Father.

Robert E. LeBlanc (1870–1937). School board, Assumption Parish, 1905–1937. Brother.

Henry A. LeBlanc (b. 1874). House of Representatives, Assumption Parish, 1908–1912. Brother.

George Etienne LeBlanc (b. 1903). School board, Assumption Parish, 1937–1960s. Nephew.

Henry Arthur Folse (1899–1951). Mayor, Donaldsonville, 1933–1941. Nephew.

Sam A. LeBlanc III. House of Representatives, Jefferson Parish, 1972–1980. Grandson.

Relatives from Other Families

Eloi F. X. Dugas (d. 1879). House of Representatives, Assumption Parish, 1874–1875, 1886–1887. Grandfather.

Claiborne Dugas (b. 1848). Clerk of court, Assumption Parish, 1886–? Uncle.

Honoré Dugas (b. 1844). Police jury, Assumption Parish, 1888–? House of Representatives, Assumption Parish, 1896–? Atchafalaya Basin Levee Board. Uncle.

Collateral Relatives

Noelle Engler LeBlanc. Secretary, Department of Culture, 1984– . Wife of Sam A. LeBlanc III.

LEMMON*

HARRY T. LEMMON* (b. 1930). Judge, court of appeals, 1970–1980. Supreme Court, 1980– .

Mary Ann Vial Lemmon (b. 1941). District judge, St. Charles Parish, 1983– . Wife.

Relatives from Other Families

James P. Vial (b. 1909). Board of public welfare. Board of election supervisors, St. Charles Parish. Father-in-law.

LEONARD*

JOHN E. LEONARD* (1845–1878). District attorney, Ouachita Parish, 1871–1872. Supreme Court, November, 1876–January, 1877. U.S. House of Representatives, 1877–1878.

John Edwards (1786–1843). Deputy attorney general, Delaware County, Pennsylvania, 1811. U.S. House of Representatives, 1839–1843. Granduncle.

LEVY*

WILLIAM M. LEVY* (1827–1882). House of Representatives, Natchitoches Parish, 1859–1861. U.S. House of Representatives, 1875–1877. Supreme Court, 1879–1882.

Charles H. Levy (b. 1837). Justice of the peace, Natchitoches Parish, 1879 to at least 1890. Brother of William M. Levy.

LIVINGSTON**

HENRY BROCKHOLST LIVINGSTON** (1757–1823). Judge, New York Supreme Court, 1802–1806. Supreme Court, 1807–1823.

William Livingston (1723–1790). New York General Assembly, 1759–1761. Continental Congress, New Jersey, 1774–1776. Governor, New Jersey, 1776–1790. U.S. constitutional convention, 1787. Father.

Philip Livingston (1686–1749). New York Council. Grandfather.

Peter Van Brugh (1666–1740). Mayor, Albany, New York, 1699, 1721–1723. Great-grandfather.

Philip Livingston (1716–1778). Board of aldermen, New York City, 1754–1762. General Assembly, 1763–1769. Continental Congress, 1774–1778. New York Senate, 1777. Uncle.

Robert Livingston (1708–1790). New York General Assembly, 1737–1758. Uncle.

Peter Van Brugh Livingston (1710–1792). Speaker, Provincial Congress, New York, 1775. Uncle.

John Livingston (1680–1720). Connecticut Assembly and Council. Granduncle.

Gilbert Livingston (1690–1746). General Assembly, 1728–1737. Granduncle.

Robert Livingston (1688–1775). New York General Assembly, 1726–1727. Granduncle.

Peter R. Livingston (1737–1794). New York General Assembly, 1761–1769. First cousin.

Walter Livingston (1740–1797). New York Assembly, 1777–1779. Continental Congress, 1784–1785. Commissioner, U.S. Treasury, 1785. First cousin.

James Livingston (b. 1728). Provincial Congress, New York, 1776–1777. High sheriff, Dutchess County, 1761. First cousin once removed.

Robert R. Livingston (1718–1775). Judge, court of admiralty, New York, 1760–1763. Justice, New York Supreme Court, 1763–1775. General Assembly, 1769–1775. First cousin once removed.

Henry Walter Livingston (1768–1810). New York Assembly, 1802, 1810. U.S. House of Representatives, 1803–1807. First cousin once removed.

Robert LeRoy Livingston (b. 1784). U.S. House of Representatives, New York, 1809–1812. First cousin once removed.

Edward Philip Livingston (1779–1843). New York Senate, 1808–1812, 1822–1824, 1838–1839. Lt. governor, New York, 1830. First cousin once removed.

Peter Van Brugh Livingston (1792–1868). Minister to Ecuador, 1848. First cousin once removed.

Charles Ludlow Livingston (d. 1873). Speaker, New York Assembly, 1832–1833. New York Senate, 1834–1837. First cousin once removed.

Henry Livingston (1714–1799). New York General Assembly, 1759–1768. First cousin once removed.

Gilbert Livingston (1742–1800/06). Provincial Congress, New York, 1775–1777. New York Assembly, 1777–1778, 1788. Second cousin.

Edward Livingston (1764–1836). U.S. House of Representatives, New York, 1795–1801. U.S. attorney, 1801–1803. Mayor, New York City, 1801–1803. Louisiana House of Representatives, 1820. U.S. House of Representatives, Louisiana, 1823–1829. U.S. Senate, 1829–1831. Secretary of state, Louisiana, 1831–1833. Minister to France, 1833–1835. Second cousin.

Robert R. Livingston (1746–1813). Recorder, New York City, 1773. General Assembly, 1775. Continental Congress, 1775–1777, 1779–1781. Chancellor, New York, 1777–1801. Secretary of foreign affairs, 1781–1783. Minister to France, 1801–1804. Second cousin.

Robert G. Livingston, Jr. (1749–1787). Provincial Congress, New York, 1775–1776. Second cousin.

Matthew Ridley. Diplomat. Brother-in-law.

Relatives from Other Families

Pierre Van Cortland, Jr. (1762–1828). New York Assembly, 1811–1812. U.S. House of Representatives, 1811–1813. Second cousin.

Philip Van Cortland (1749–1831). Provincial Congress, New York, 1775. Brigadier (brevet), 1783. Constitutional ratification convention, 1788. New York Assembly, 1788–1790. Senate, 1791–1793. U.S. House of Representatives, 1793–1809. Second cousin.

William Bayard (1729–1804). New York General Assembly, 1761–1768. Second cousin.

John Jay** Brother-in-law. See **JAY****.

William Alexander Duer (1780–1858). New York Supreme Court, 1822–1829. First cousin once removed.

John Duer (1782–1858). New York constitutional convention, 1821. U.S. attorney, 1827–1829. Judge, superior court, New York City, 1849–1858. First cousin once removed.

John Scott Harrison (1804–1878). U.S. House of Representatives, Ohio, 1853–1857. Grandnephew.

John Cleves Symmes (1742–1814). New Jersey Council, 1778. Chief judge, New Jersey Supreme Court, 1777–1787. Continental Congress, 1785–1786. Judge, Northwest Territory, 1788–1802. Brother-in-law (member of **Harrison** family).

Collateral Relatives

Henry Alexander Livingston (1776–1849). New York Assembly, 1827. New York Senate, 1838–1841. Grandson of Henry Livingston (1714–1799).

Goodhue Livingston, Jr. (b. 1897). Executive secretary to mayor of New York, 1943–1945. Planning commission, New York City, 1945–1961. Great-great-grandson of Robert R. Livingston (1746–1813).

Peter R. Livingston (1766–1847). Speaker, New York Assembly, 1823. New York Senate, 1820–1822, 1826–1829. Brother-in-law of Edward Livingston.

Other Connections

Peter Van Brugh Livingston (1710–1792) was
   father-in-law of **John Kean I;**
   a first cousin twice removed of **Hamilton Fish** (1808–1893).

Robert R. Livingston (1718–1775) was
   father-in-law of **John Armstrong;**
   father-in-law of **Richard Montgomery;**
   father-in-law of **Morgan Lewis.**

John Livingston (1680–1720) was son-in-law of **Fitz-John Winthrop.**

Philip Livingston (1686–1749) was a first cousin of **John Schuyler.**

Robert Livingston (1708–1790) was the father-in-law of **James Duane.**

William Livingston was a brother-in-law of **William Alexander.**

Gilbert Livingston was the father-in-law of **Smith Thompson****. See **THOMP-SON****.

McCALEB*

E. HOWARD McCALEB* (1897–1978). Court of appeals, 1936–1941, 1943–1946. Supreme Court, 1941–1943, 1946–1972 (chief justice, 1970–1972).

Edwin Howard McCaleb (b. 1843). City attorney, New Orleans, 1878–1880. State Democratic executive committee, 1888–1904. Grandfather.

Thomas W. Collens (1812–1879). District attorney, New Orleans, 1840–1842. Judge, New Orleans City Court, 1842–1846. Constitutional convention, 1852. District judge, 1856, 1867–1873. Great-grandfather.

Collateral Relatives

Theodore Howard McCaleb (1810–1864). U.S. district judge, 1841–1861. Uncle of Edwin Howard McCaleb.

David McCaleb (d. 1851). Sheriff, Pendleton District, South Carolina, *ca.* 1800. Father of Theodore Howard McCaleb.

Samuel McCaleb (1782–1843). Justice of the peace, 1824. Louisiana House of Representatives, 1826–1828. Treasurer, West Feliciana Parish, 1828. Brother of David McCaleb.

William McCaleb. Constitutional ratification convention, South Carolina. Father of David McCaleb.

William H. Hammett. Virginia House of Delegates. U.S. House of Representatives, Mississippi, 1843–1845. Son-in-law of David McCaleb.

Soloman (or Samuel) Downs (1801–1854). Senate, Ouachita Parish, 1836. U.S. attorney, 1845–1847. U.S. Senate, 1847–1853. Collector, Port of New Orleans, 1853–1854. Son-in-law of Samuel McCaleb.

Other Connections

A son of **David McCaleb** married a daughter of **Joseph E. Davis.**

David McCaleb is the father-in-law of **John J. Guion.**

McENERY*

SAMUEL DOUGLAS McENERY* (1837–1910). Lt. governor, 1880–1881. Governor, 1881–1888. Supreme Court, 1888–1897. U.S. Senator, 1897–1910.

Henry O'Neal McEnery. Registrar, federal land office, Monroe. Father.

John McEnery (1833–1891). Police jury, Ouachita Parish. Registrar, federal land office, Monroe, 1857–? House of Representatives, 1866. Unrecognized governor, 1873. Brother.

McKINLEY**

JOHN McKINLEY** (1780–1852). Alabama legislature, 1820, 1831, 1836. U.S. Senate, 1826–1831. U.S. House of Representatives, 1833–1835. Supreme Court, 1837–1852.

Andrew McKinley. Land office registrar, Kentucky. Son.

Alexander Pope Churchill. Kentucky legislature, 1839–? Son-in-law.

Relatives from Other Families

Benjamin Logan. Virginia General Assembly, 1780, 1781. Magistrate, 1781. Second sheriff, Harrodsburg, Kentucky. Brigadier general, 1786. Kentucky constitutional conventions, 1792, 1799. Kentucky legislature intermittently from 1792. Uncle.

Ben Logan (1789–1873). Kentucky House of Representatives, 1818. First cousin.

John Logan (d. 1826). Kentucky House of Representatives, 1815–1825. First cousin.

William Logan (1776–1822). Kentucky constitutinal convention, 1799. Speaker, House of Representatives, 1803. Judge, court of appeals, 1808, 1810. U.S. Senate, 1819–1820. First cousin.

Robert Logan Wickliffe. Kentucky House of Representatives. First cousin once removed.

John J. Hardin (1810–1847). Kentucky legislature, 1836–1842. U.S. House of Representatives, 1843–1845. First cousin once removed.

Caleb Wallace Logan (1819–1864). Kentucky legislature, 1850. Judge, chancery court, Louisville, 1856–*ca.* 1862. First cousin once removed.

John A. Logan (b. 1812). Kentucky House of Representatives, 1839. First cousin once removed.

Other Connections

John McKinley's daughter married a son of **Jeremiah T. Boyle.**

McLEAN**

JOHN McLEAN** (1785–1861). U.S. House of Representatives, Ohio, 1813–1816. Ohio Supreme Court, 1816–1822. General land office commissioner, 1822–1823. Postmaster general, 1825–1829. Supreme Court, 1830–1861.

Nathaniel McLean (1815/18–1905). Brigadier general, Ohio Volunteers, 1862–1865. Son.

William McLean (1794–1839). Receiver of public monies, Piqua, Ohio. U.S. House of Representatives, 1823–1829. Brother.

John McLean (b. 1815). Clerk, U.S. district court, Ohio. Son.

Relatives from Other Families

Joseph Pannhill Taylor (1796–1864). Brigadier general, USA. Son-in-law.

Other Connections

A son of **John McLean**** married a daughter of **Jacob Burnet.**

MARSHALL**

JOHN MARSHALL** (1755–1835). Virginia House of Burgesses, 1780, 1782–1788. Executive Council, 1782–1795. Constitutional ratification convention, 1788. U.S. House of Representatives, 1799–1800. Secretary of state, 1800–1801. Supreme Court, 1801–1835.

Thomas Marshall (1730–1802). Virginia House of Burgesses. Sheriff. Father.

Lewis Markham. Sheriff, Westmoreland County, Virginia. Great-grandfather.

Jacquelin Ambler (1742–1840). Treasurer, Virginia. Father-in-law.

Alexander Keith Marshall (1770–1825). Kentucky House of Representatives, 1797–1800. Brother.

Thomas Marshall (1761–1817). County clerk, Mason County, Kentucky. State constitutional convention. Brother.

James Markham Marshall (1764–1848). Ninth Kentucky convention for statehood. Brother.

Humphrey Marshall (1756/60–1841). Danville convention, Kentucky, 1787. Constitutional ratification convention, Virginia, 1788. Kentucky House of Representatives, 1793, 1807–1808, 1823. U.S. Senate, Kentucky, 1795–1801. First cousin and brother-in-law.

Thomas Alexander Marshall (1794–1871). Kentucky House of Representatives, 1827–1828, 1863. U.S. House of Representatives, 1831–1835. Court of appeals, 1835–1856. Chief justice, court of appeals, 1866–1867. First cousin once removed.

John J. Marshall (1785–1846). Kentucky House of Representatives, 1815, 1816, 1833. Senate, 1820–1824. Judge, circuit court, Louisville, 1836–1846. First cousin once removed.

Martin Pickett Marshall (1777–1853). Kentucky House of Representatives, 1805–1806. First cousin.

William Champe Marshall (1807–1873). Kentucky House of Representatives, 1834, 1840–1842. Mayor Augusta, Kentucky, Commonwealth attorney. First cousin once removed.

Thornton F. Marshall (b. 1819). Kentucky Senate, 1859–1863. First cousin once removed.

James Keith (1839–1918). Virginia legislature, 1869. Judge, *ca.* 1879–1895. Supreme Court of Appeals, 1895–1916. First cousin once removed.

George K. Taylor (1769–1815). Virginia legislature, 1795–1796, 1798–1799. U.S. court of appeals, 1801–1802. Brother-in-law.

Joseph Hamilton Daviess (1774–1811). U.S. attorney, Kentucky, 1800. Brother-in-law.

John Marshall (1798–1833). Virginia legislature? Son.

James Keith Marshall (1800–1862). Virginia Senate. Son.

Edward Carrington Marshall (1805–1882). Virginia legislature. Son.

Fielding Lewis Marshall (b. 1819). Virginia House of Delegates, 1869–1871. Grandson.

John Marshall (1811–1854). Virginia legislature. Grandson.

Charles A. Marshall. Kentucky legislature. Nephew.

Martin Pickett Marshall (1798–1883). Prosecuting attorney. Legislature, 1825–1827. Kentucky constitutional convention, 1849. Senate, 1861. Nephew.

Thomas Francis Marshall (1801–1864). Kentucky House of Representatives, 1832–1836, 1838–1839, 1854. U.S. House of Representatives, 1841–1843. Nephew.

Alexander J. Marshall (1803–1882). Clerk, Fauquier County, Virginia. Senate, CSA. Nephew.

William Ball Marshall (b. 1836). County attorney. Grandnephew.

William Lewis Marshall (1846–1920). Brigadier general and chief of engineers, 1907–1909. Grandnephew.

Relatives from Other Families

Alexander K. McClung (1812?–1855). Chargé to Bolivia. Nephew.

Thomas M. Duke (1795–1866). Judge, Texas. Nephew.

James K. Duke (b. 1839). Clerk, Montana Territorial House of Representatives. Grandnephew.

Basil Duke (b. 1837). Brigadier general, CSA. Grandnephew.

Duff Green (1791–1875). Missouri constitutional convention. House of Representatives. Senate. Brigadier general. U.S. consul, Galveston, Texas, 1844. First cousin once removed.

Jacquelin Burwell Harvie (b. 1788). Virginia Senate. Major general, Virginia Militia. Son-in-law.

William McClung (1758–1811/15). Virginia legislature. Kentucky Senate, 1796–1800. Danville convention, 1787. Judge, U.S. circuit court. Judge, U.S. district court, 1802–death. Brother-in-law.

Thomas Randolph (b. 1683?). Justice, Henrico County, Virginia, 1713–? Great-grandfather.

Thomas Mann Randolph (b. 1741). Virginia House of Burgesses, 1772. Senate, 1776. First cousin once removed.

Thomas Mann Randolph (1767?–1828). U.S. House of Representatives, Virginia, 1803–1807. Governor, 1819–1822. Second cousin.

William Randolph (1712–1745). Virginia House of Burgesses. Granduncle.

Collateral Relatives

Edward Colston (1786–1854). Virginia House of Delegates. U.S. House of Representatives, 1817–1819. Brother-in-law of Martin Pickett Marshall (1798–1883).

Robert Morris (1734–1806). Continental Congress, ?–1778. Pennsylvania Assembly, 1778–? U.S. superintendent of finance, 1781–1783. U.S. Senate, 1789–1795. Father-in-law of James Markham Marshall.

Joseph P. Foree (b. 1820). Mississippi House of Representatives, 1848. Probate judge. Kentucky House of Representatives, 1871–1872. County judge, Kentucky. Presiding judge, court of magistrates. Brother-in-law of William Ball Marshall.

John J. McAfee. Kentucky legislature. Son-in-law of Humphrey Marshall (1756/60–1841).

H. Marshall Buford. Judge, court of common pleas, Lexington, Kentucky. Grandson of Alexander Keith Marshall.

H. Snowdon Marshall (1870–1931). U.S. attorney, New York, 1913–1917. Grandson of Alexander J. Marshall.

Charles Edward Marshall (1821–1868). Kentucky House of Representatives, 1846. Son of John J. Marshall.

Humphrey Marshall (1812–1872). City council, Louisville, 1836. U.S. House of Representatives, Kentucky, 1849–1852, 1855–1859. Minister to China, 1852–1854. Brigadier general, CSA. Congress, CSA. Son of John J. Marshall.

George Catlett Marshall (1880–1959). Chief of staff, U.S. Army, 1939–1945. Secretary of state, 1947–1949. Secretary of defense, 1950–1951. Grandson of William Champe Marshall.

Other Connections

Martin Pickett Marshall (1798–1883) was a grandson of **Martin Pickett.**

James K. Marshall was a great-grandson of **Lewis Burwell.**

William Louis Marshall was a son-in-law of **Alfred H. Colquitt.**

William Ball Marshall was a great-grandson of **James Ball.**

H. Marshall Buford was a second cousin of **Frank Adair Monroe***. See **MONROE*.**

John Marshall** was a second cousin once removed of **Thomas Jefferson.**

Alexander K. Marshall was
a son-in-law of **Samuel McDowell;**
a great-grandfather of **James P. Harbeson.**

Fielding Lewis Marshall was
a son-in-law of **Richard Coke, Jr.;**
a first cousin twice removed of **Fielding Lewis.**

Humphrey Marshall (1812–1872) was
a first cousin of **James G. Birney** (and others);
a second cousin of **James Barbour.**

Note: Alexander Keith Marshall (1808–1884), U.S. House of Representatives, Kentucky (1855–1857), was probably the son of Alexander Keith Marshall, above.

MATTHEWS*

GEORGE MATTHEWS, JR.* (1774–1836). Judge, Orleans Territorial Court, 1806–1813. Supreme Court, 1813–1836.

George Matthews, Sr. (1739–1812). Governor, Georgia, 1787–1788, 1793–1796. U.S. House of Representatives, 1789–1791. Brigadier general, 1811. Father.

Note: Henry Mason Mathews [*sic*] (1834–1884), governor of West Virginia in 1876, was probably related to Justice Matthews.

MATTHEWS**

STANLEY MATTHEWS** (1824–1889). Clerk, Ohio House of Representatives, 1848–1849. Judge, court of common pleas, Cincinnati, 1851–1853. Senate, 1855–1858. U.S. attorney, 1858–1861. Judge, Supreme Court of Cincinnati, 1863–1865. U.S. Senate, 1877–1879. Supreme Court, 1881–1889.

Relatives from Other Families

Horace Gray** Son-in-law. See **GRAY****.

Harvey MaGee Watterson (1811–1891). Tennessee House of Representatives, 1835. Senate, 1845–1847. Brother-in-law.

Henry Watterson (1840–1921). U.S. House of Representatives, Kentucky, 1876–1877. Nephew. •

MERRICK*

EDWIN THOMAS MERRICK* (1808–1897). District judge, 1845–? Chief justice, Supreme Court, 1855–1865.

David Thomas Merrick (b. 1842). Inspector general, Second Louisiana Brigade, CSA. Son.

Edwin Thomas Merrick, Jr. (1880–1936). Atchafalaya Basin Levee Board, 1912–1928. Grandson.

Frank Merrick. Atchafalaya Basin Levee Board. School board, Pointe Coupee Parish. Great-grandson.

Edward Jemayson Merrick. Police jury, Pointe Coupee Parish. State Democratic central committee. Great-grandson.

Other Connections

Edward Jemayson Merrick is a son-in-law of **Aimée Bondy Garrett.**

MILLER*

HENRY CARLTON MILLER* (1828–1899). U.S. attorney, *ca.* 1858–1861. Confederate attorney, 1861–? Supreme Court, 1894–1899.

Branch W. Miller (d. 1834). District attorney, St. Tammany Parish. Reporter, Louisiana Supreme Court, 1831–1834. Louisiana Senate. Father.

Branch Knox Miller (1857–1906). Assistant district attorney, Orleans Parish, 1883–1884. Assistant city attorney, New Orleans, 1884–? Attorney, board of liquidation of city debt. State Democratic convention, 1883. Son.

MOISE*

HAROLD A. MOISE* (b. 1879). House of Representatives, Orleans Parish, 1908–1912. Judge, civil district court, 1937–1948. Supreme Court, 1949–1958.

James C. Moise (1849–1901). Assistant attorney general, 1884–1889. Judge, criminal district court, Orleans Parish, 1898–1901. Father.

Leonard Compton Moise (b. 1862). City attorney, Houma. District attorney, Terrebonne Parish. Uncle.

E. Warren Moise (b. 1811). Speaker, Louisiana House of Representatives. U.S. attorney. Attorney general, 1855–1859. Granduncle.

Harold A. Moise, Jr. Clerk, Louisiana Supreme Court, 1970s. Son.

MONROE*

FRANK ADAIR MONROE* (1844–1927). Judge, civil district court, New Orleans, 1876–1899. Supreme Court, 1899–1922 (chief justice, 1914–1922).

Victor Monroe (1813–1856). Federal judge, Washington Territory. Father.

Thomas Bell Monroe (1791–1865). U.S. district judge, Kentucky. Grandfather.

John Adair (1757–1840). Constitutional ratification convention, South Carolina. Kentucky constitutional convention, 1792. Kentucky House of Representatives, 1793–1795, 1798, 1800–1803, 1817. U.S. Senate, 1805–1806. Governor, Kentucky, 1820–1824. U.S. House of Representatives, 1831–1833. Great-grandfather.

Relatives from Other Families

Joshua G. Baker* (b. 1852). Brother-in-law. See **BAKER***.

William Polk (1752–1814). Judge. Great-grandfather.

H. Marshall Buford. Second cousin. See **MARSHALL****.

Collateral Relatives

Andrew Monroe (d. 1735). Sheriff, Westmoreland County, Virginia, 1731. Granduncle of Thomas Bell Monroe.

Spence Monroe (d. 1774). Circuit judge, Virginia. Son of Andrew Monroe.

James Monroe (1758–1831). Virginia House of Delegates, 1782. Continental Congress, 1783–1786. Virginia Assembly, 1786–1787, 1810–1811. U.S. Senate, 1790–1794. Minister to France, 1794–1796, 1803. Governor, Virginia, 1799–1802, 1811. Minister to Britain and Spain, 1803–1807. Secretary of state, 1811–1814. President, 1817–1825. President, Virginia constitutional convention, 1829. Son of Spence Monroe.

Joseph Jones Monroe (1764–1824). Clerk of district and circuit courts, Virginia. Son of Spence Monroe.

James Monroe (1799–1870). Alderman, New York City, 1833–1835. U.S. House of Representatives, 1839–1841. New York Senate, 1852–1855. Nephew of President James Monroe.

Joseph Jones (1727–1805). Virginia House of Burgesses, *ca.* 1775. Constitutional convention, 1776. House of Delegates, 1776–1777, 1780–1781, 1783–1785. Continental

Congress, 1777–1778, 1780–1783. Judge, general court, Virginia, 1778–1779. Major general, Virginia Militia. Uncle of President James Monroe.

Henry J. Leovy (b. 1826). City attorney, New Orleans, 1870–1872. Son-in-law of Thomas B. Monroe.

Other Connections

Frank Adair Monroe* was a great-great-grandson of **William Winder.**

MOORE**

ALFRED MOORE** (1755–1810). North Carolina Senate, 1782. Attorney general, 1782–1789. House of Commons, 1792. Judge, superior court, 1798. Supreme Court, 1800–1804.

Maurice Moore (1735–1777). Judge, North Carolina, 1758. House of Commons, 1757–1760, 1762, 1764–1771, 1773–1774. Governor's Council, 1760–1761. Father.

Maurice Moore (d. 1744). Speaker, North Carolina Assembly. Grandfather.

James Moore (1650?–1706). Member, South Carolina Council and Assembly. Chief justice. Governor, 1700–1703. Great-grandfather.

James Moore (1737–1777). House of Commons, North Carolina, 1764–1771, 1773. Provincial Congress, 1775. Brigadier general, Continental Army, 1776–1777. Uncle.

James Moore (1667–1740). Governor, North Carolina, 1719. Attorney general. Judge. Speaker, Assembly, 1721–1725. Granduncle.

Relatives from Other Families

Joseph Alston (1778/9–1816). South Carolina legislature, 1802–1812. Governor, 1812–1814. First cousin once removed (member of the Ashe family).

Collateral Relatives

Alexander Lillington. Colonial governor, North Carolina. Grandfather of Maurice Moore, ?–1744.

MORGAN*

PHILIP H. MORGAN* (1825–1900). District judge, Orleans Parish, 1853–1857. U.S. attorney, 1866–1867, 1869–1873. Supreme Court, 1873–1876. Minister to Mexico, 1880–1885.

Thomas Gibbs Morgan. Judge, Baton Rouge, *ca.* 1830s–1840s. Father.

George Morgan (1743–1810). Judge, civil district court, Illinois, 1768. Great-grand-father.

Thomas M. T. McKennan (1794–1852). Deputy attorney general, Washington County, Pennsylvania, 1814–1817. Town councilman, Washington County, Pennsylvania, 1818–1831. U.S. House of Representatives, 1842–1843. Uncle.

James Rennie Ford. Judge, Baton Rouge, Father-in-law.

James Morris Morgan (1845–1928). Consul general to Australasia, 1885–1888. Half brother.
George Washington Morgan (1820–1893). Prosecuting attorney, Knox County, Ohio, ?–1846. U.S. consul to Marseilles, 1856–1858. Minister to Lisbon, 1858–1861. Brigadier general, Ohio Volunteers, 1861–1863. U.S. House of Representatives, Ohio, 1867–1868, 1869–1873. First cousin once removed.

Collateral Relatives

Charles A. Finke. Judge, New York. Father-in-law of James Morris Morgan.
William John Duane (1780–1865). Pennsylvania House of Representatives, 1809–1810, 1812, 1819–1820. Prosecuting attorney. Mayor's court, Philadelphia, 1820–1823. Selectman, 1829–? Secretary of the treasury, four months in 1833. Uncle of George Washington Morgan.

Other Connections

James M. Morgan is a son-in-law of **G. A. Trenholm.**
Philip H. Morgan* was a first cousin twice removed of **Joseph Borden McKean.**

MORPHY*

ALONZO MORPHY* (d. 1856). Louisiana legislature. Attorney general, 1829. Supreme Court, 1839–1946.
Don Diego Morphy, Sr. (d. 1814). Spanish consul, New Orleans, ?–1814. Father.
Don Diego Morphy, Jr. (d. 1865). Spanish consul, Natchitoches, 1818. Half brother.
J. C. Sybrant. Swedish consul. Son-in-law.

MURPHY**

FRANK MURPHY** (1890–1949). U.S. attorney, 1919–1920. Judge, recorder's court, Detroit, 1923–1930. Mayor, Detroit, 1930–1933. Governor general, Phillippines, 1933–1936. Governor, Michigan, 1937–1938. U.S. attorney general, 1939–1940. Supreme Court, 1940–1949.
John F. Murphy (b. 1849). Prosecuting attorney, Huron County, Michigan. Postmaster, Harbor Beach, Michigan. U.S. circuit court commissioner. Father.
George Murphy (b. 1894). Judge, recorder's court, Detroit. Brother.

NELSON**

SAMUEL NELSON** (1792–1873). Postmaster, Cortland, New York, 1821. Constitutional convention, 1821. Circuit judge, 1823. Associate justice, New York Supreme Court, 1831–1837. Supreme Court, 1845–1872.
Rensselaer Russell Nelson (1826–1904). County attorney, Superior, Wisconsin, 1853–1855. Supreme Court, Minnesota Territory, 1857–1858. U.S. district judge, 1858–1896. Son.
? Russell. Judge. Father-in-law (second marriage).
? Woods. Judge. Father-in-law (first marriage).

NICHOLLS*

FRANCIS T. NICHOLLS* (1834–1912). Brigadier general, CSA, 1862. Governor, 1877–1880, 1888–1892. Chief justice, Supreme Court, 1892–1904. Associate justice, 1904–1911.

Thomas Clark Nicholls (1790–1847). Louisiana House of Representatives. District judge, 1836–? Judge, court of appeals, 1843–46. Father.

Edward C. Nicholls (1746?–1812). First judge of Attakapas County, Louisiana, 1805–? Grandfather.

Lawrence D. Nicholls. Clerk of court, Ascension Parish. Brother.

Robert Welman Nicholls I. Judge. Brother.

Thomas C. Nicholls III. Senate, 1846. Judge. Brother.

Isaac Edward Morse (1809–1866). Louisiana Senate, 1842–1844. U.S. House of Representatives, 1844–1851. Attorney general, Louisiana, 1853–1855. First cousin.

Robert Welman Nicholls II Judge, Helena, Arkansas. Nephew.

Collateral Relatives

David Craufurd (d. 1801?). Maryland Provincial Convention. Upper House of Burgesses, 1776. Judge, Prince George County, Maryland, after Revolution. Granduncle of Thomas C. Nicholls.

Relatives from Other Families

William W. (W. W.) Pugh (1811–1906). Louisiana House of Representatives, 1845, 1852–1858 (Speaker, 1854–1858). Superintendant of Education, Assumption Parish. Police jury and school board after Civil War. Brother-in-law.

Walter Guion (1849–1927). District judge, Assumption Parish, 1888–1900. Louisiana attorney general, 1904–1912. U.S. attorney, 1913–1917. U.S. Senate, 1918. Brother-in-law.

George Seth Guion (d. 1861). Judge, Concordia Parish. Father-in-law.

ODOM*

FRED M. ODOM* (b. 1871). Clerk, town council, 1901–1902. Clerk, police jury, Morehouse Parish, six years. District attorney, Morehouse Parish, 1908–*ca.* 1914. Supreme Court, 1931–1944.

W. M. Odom. House of Representatives, Morehouse Parish. Brother.

J. T. Scogin. Sheriff, Morehouse Parish, 1904–1912. Father-in-law.

OGDEN*

ABNER NASH OGDEN*. Supreme Court, 1853–1855.

Robert Nash Ogden. Judge, court of appeals, 1892–1900. Brother.

Horatio Nash Ogden. Attorney general, Louisiana, 1877–1879. Son.

R. N. Ogden. Speaker, Louisiana House of Representatives. Nephew.

John Nicholson Ogden (b. 1847). City attorney, Opelousas. District attorney, St. Landry Parish. Nephew.

Percy T. Ogden (b. 1878). City attorney, Crowley. District attorney, 1912 (five months). Senate, 1936–1940. Grandnephew.

Relatives from Other Families

Abner Nash (1740?–1786). Virginia House of Burgesses, 1761–1762. House of Commons, North Carolina, 1764–1765, 1770–1771, 1777–1778. Provincial Congress, 1774–1776. Provincial Council, 1775–1776. North Carolina Senate, 1779. Governor, 1780–1781. North Carolina House of Representatives, 1782, 1784. Continental Congress, 1782, 1783, 1785, 1786. Grandfather.

Frederick Nash (1781–1858). House of Commons, North Carolina, 1804–1805, 1814–1817, 1828–1829 (Speaker, 1814). Judge, superior court, 1818–1826, 1836–1844. Supreme Court, 1844–1858 (chief justice, 1852–?). Uncle.

Francis Nash (1) (1742?–1777). Justice of the peace and clerk of court, North Carolina, 1763. House of Commons, 1764–1765, 1771, 1773, 1775. Judge, 1774–1775. Provincial Congress, 1775. Brigadier general, 1777. Granduncle.

John Randolph (b. 1867). Police jury, Grant Parish, 1905–1908, 1919–1925. Parish and state Democratic committees. Son-in-law.

Other Connections

Percy T. Ogden was an uncle of **Henry P. Carmouche.**

A son of **Abner Nash Ogden** married a sister of **Jefferson Wells Gordon.**

O'NIELL*

CHARLES AUSTIN O'NIELL* (1869–1951). District judge, St. Mary Parish, 1908–1914. Supreme Court, 1914–1949 (chief justice, 1922–1949).

John A. O'Niell (1). (1818–1910). Sheriff, St. Mary Parish, 1871–1873. Treasurer, assessor, and school board, St. Mary Parish. Father.

John A. O'Niell (2). Secretary, police jury, St. Mary Parish. Brother.

Wilson McKerall O'Niell (b. 1898). Mayor, Franklin, 1945–1958, 1962–1966. Nephew.

Relatives from Other Families

Minos T. Gordy (1) (1829?–1911). Sheriff, St. Mary Parish, 1873–1884. Father-in-law.

Minos T. Gordy (2) (b. 1865). District attorney, Vermilion Parish, 1890–1900. Constitutional convention, 1898. District judge, 1900–1904. Brother-in-law.

Other Connections

Wilson McKerall O'Niell is
    a grandson of **Wilson McKerall;**
    a first cousin of **Edward H. Peterman.**

OVERTON*

WINSTON OVERTON* (1870–1934). District judge, 1908–1920. Constitutional convention, 1921. Supreme Court, 1921–1934.

Thomas Overton (1) (1835–1913). District attorney, 1884–1888. District judge. Father.

John Holmes Overton (1) (1797–1883). House of Representatives, Ouachita Parish, 1824. Judge, court of appeals. Grandfather.

Thomas Overton (2) (1753–1825). North Carolina legislature, Moore County. State inspector of revenue. Brigadier general (by North Carolina legislature). Great-grandfather.

John Holmes Overton (2) (1875–1948). U.S. House of Representatives, Louisiana, 1931–1932. U.S. Senate, 1932–1948. Brother.

Thomas Overton Brooks (1897–1961). U.S. House of Representatives, Louisiana, 1936–1961. Nephew.

Relatives from Other Families

George R. King*. Granduncle. See **KING***.

George King. Great-grandfather. See **KING***.

John E. King (1). First cousin once removed. See **KING***.

Valentine King Irion (b. 1862). Superintendent of Schools, St. Landry Parish. Board of the Louisiana State Normal School. Louisiana State Board Dentistry, *ca.* 1913. Second cousin.

Collateral Relatives (Louisiana Branch)

Walter Hampden Overton (1788–1845). Major general (by Louisiana legislature), 1815. U.S. House of Representatives, 1829–1831. Son of Thomas Overton (1753–1825), and half brother of John H. Overton (1797–1883).

Thomas Overton Moore (1804–1876). Louisiana House of Representatives, 1848. Senate, 1852. Governor, 1860–1864. Nephew of Walter H. Overton.

Collateral Relatives (Virginia Branch)

James Overton (1) (1688–1738). Justice, Hanover County, Virginia. Grandfather of Thomas Overton (2).

Robert Overton (1609–after 1668). Major general. Governor of Hull, England, *ca.* 1647. Governor of Edinburg, *ca.* 1650. Commissioner appointed by Parliament to administer the armed forces, 1659. Grandfather of James Overton (1).

James Overton (2) (1726/30–1816). Justice, Louisa County, Virginia, 1763, 1771, 1790. Son of James Overton (1), and father of Thomas Overton (2).

Waller Overton (1750–1827). Sheriff, Louisa County, Virginia. Son of James Overton (2).

John Overton (1). Private secretary to President Jackson. Son of Waller Overton.

Samuel Overton (1). Provisional governor of Florida (appointed by President Jackson). Son of Waller Overton.

Samuel Overton (2) (1768–1832). Exiseman, Eastern District of Virginia (under Washington and Adams). Son of James Overton (2).

William Taylor Barry (1784–1835). Ambassador to Spain. U.S. House of Representatives, Kentucky, 1810–1811. U.S. Senate, 1814–1816. U.S. postmaster general, 1829–1835. Son-in-law of Waller Overton.

Collateral Relatives (Tennessee Branch)

John Overton (2) (1776–1833). Supervisor of Revenue, 1795. Judge, superior court, 1804–1810. Tennessee Supreme Court, 1810–1816. Son of James Overton (2).

John Overton (3) (1821–1898). Justice of the peace. Tennessee legislature. Son of John Overton (2).

John Overton, Jr. (1842–1906). Tennessee legislature, 1873. Mayor of Nashville, 1881–1883. Son of John Overton (3).

Samuel Watkins Overton II (1894–1958). Tennessee House of Representatives, 1925. Senate, 1927. Mayor, Memphis, 1928–1940, 1949–1953. President, Memphis Board of Education, 1947–1949. Grandson of John Overton, Jr.

John Overton (4) (1880–1944). City Health Officer, Nashville. Grandson of John Overton (3).

Other Connections

John Holmes Overton (1) (Louisiana Branch) was
    a nephew of **Gabriel Holmes, Jr.;**
    father-in-law of **Joseph M. Moore.**

Walter Hampden Overton was
    first cousin once removed of **Jacob M. Dickinson, Jr.;**
    first cousin twice removed of **Luke Lea** (1879–1945);
    first cousin once removed of **Dabney Carr;**
    son-in-law of **James Fenwick Brent.**

James Overton (1) was
    an uncle of **Robert Harris;**
    great-grandfather of **James Overton Cosby.**

John Overton (2) (Tennessee Branch) was a grandson of **James White.**

Thomas Overton Moore was a great-grandfather of **David G. Stafford.**

Walter Hampden Overton and **Blount Breazeale** married sisters.

Thomas Overton Moore and **Gervais Baillio** married sisters.

PARLANGE*

CHARLES PARLANGE* (1852–1907). Clerk, constitutional convention, 1879. Louisiana Senate, 1880–1885; U.S. attorney, 1885–? Lt. governor, 1892. Supreme Court, 1893–1894.

Walter C. Parlange, Jr. Police jury, Pointe Coupee Parish, 1970s–1980s (president, 1985). Grandson of Charles Parlange.

PATERSON**

WILLIAM PATERSON** (1745–1806). Provincial Congress, New Jersey, 1775–1776. Attorney general, New Jersey, 1776–1783. Senate, 1776–1777. New Jersey constitutional convention, 1776. Constitutional convention, 1787. U.S. Senate, 1789–1790. Governor, 1790–1793. Supreme Court, 1793–1806.

Name unknown. Judge, court of appeals, New Jersey. Grandson.

Relatives from Other Families

Anthony Walton White (1750–1803). Adjutant general, New Jersey, 1793–1803. General, U.S. Army, 1794. Brother-in-law.

Anthony White. Judge. Father-in-law.

Stephen Van Rensslaer (1794–1839). New York Assembly, 1789–1790. Senate, 1791–1795. Lt. governor, 1795. Constitutional convention, 1801, 1821. Major general, New York Militia. U.S. House of Representatives, 1822–1829. President, New York Board of Agriculture, 1820. Son-in-law.

Other Connections

William Paterson★★ and **John Bubenhiem Bayard** married sisters.

PECKHAM★★

RUFUS W. PECKHAM★★ (1838–1909). District attorney, Albany County, New York, 1869–1872. New York Supreme Court, 1883–1886. Court of appeals, New York, 1886–1895. Supreme Court, 1895–1909.

Rufus Wheeler Peckham (1809–1873). District attorney, Albany County, New York, 1838–1841. U.S. House of Representatives, 1853–1855. New York Supreme Court, 1861–1869. Court of appeals, New York, 1870–1873. Father.

Wheeler Hazard Peckham (1833–1905). District attorney, New York, 1884. Brother.

Other Connections

Rufus Wheeler Peckham was a great-grandson of **George Hazard** (1700–1738).

PITNEY★★

MAHLON PITNEY★★ (1858–1924). U.S. House of Representatives, 1895–1899. New Jersey Senate, 1899–1901. New Jersey Supreme Court, 1901–1908. Chancellor, 1908–1912. Supreme Court, 1912–1922.

Henry Cooper Pitney (1817–1911). Vice chancellor, New Jersey, 1889–1907. Father.

POCHE★

FELIX PIERRE POCHE★ (1836–1895). Senate, St. James Parish, 1866–1868. Supreme Court, 1880–1890.

Jerome Evariste Poche (b. 1851). Attorney, St. James Parish, 1877–1879. School board, 1879–? Police jury. Brother.

PONDER★

AMOS LEE PONDER★ (1887–1959). District attorney, Tangipahoa Parish, 1924–1930. District judge, 1930–1937. Supreme Court, 1937–1959.

Amos L. Ponder. School superintendent, Sabine Parish, 1886–1895. Father.

William A. Ponder. Louisiana constitutional convention, 1879. House of Representatives, 1890–death. Grandfather.

Silas D. Ponder (1860–1933). Prosecuting attorney, Denton, Texas. Mayor, Many, Louisiana. State constitutional convention, 1913, 1921. Uncle.

William H. Ponder (b. 1896). District judge, Sabine Parish, 1936–1966. First cousin.

PORTER*

ALEXANDER PORTER, JR.* (1785–1844). Louisiana constitutional convention, 1811. House of Representatives, St. Mary Parish, 1816. Supreme Court, 1821–1833. U.S. Senate, 1833–1837.

Alexander James Porter (1822–1888). Alderman, Nashville, 1877–1881. Board of public works, Nashville, 1885–1887. Nephew of Alexander Porter, Jr.

Relatives from Other Families

Joshua G. Baker (1763–1816). Father-in-law. See **BAKER***.

Joshua Baker (1799–1885). Brother-in-law. See **BAKER***.

Other Connections

Alexander James Porter is
    a first cousin of **Donald Caffery;**
    a first cousin once removed of **Murphy James Foster;**
    a nephew of **John B. Murphy.**

POWELL**

LEWIS F. POWELL, JR.** (b. 1907). Chairman, school board, Richmond, Virginia. Supreme Court, 1971–1987.

Relatives from Other Families

Marvin Pierce Rucker (1881–1953). President, board of health, Manchester, Virginia. President, board of health, Richmond, 1946–1953. Father-in-law.

PROVOSTY*

OLIVIER OTIS PROVOSTY* (1852–1924). District attorney, Pointe Coupee Parish, 1873–1878. Senate, 1888–1890. Constitutional convention, 1898. Supreme Court, 1901–1925 (chief justice, 1922–1925).

August Provosty (1818–1868). Senate, Pointe Coupee Parish, ?–1842. House of Representatives, 1850–1861. Father.

Michel August Provosty (1778–1826). President, school board, Pointe Coupee Parish, *ca.* 1820. Grandfather.

Auguste A. Provosty (1848–1873). District attorney, Pointe Coupee Parish, 1872–1873. Brother.

Albin Provosty (1865–1932). District attorney, Pointe Coupee Parish, 1900–1908. Town council, New Roads. State Democratic central committee. Senate, 1912–1920. Constitutional convention, 1921. Brother.

Michel Provosty (1889–1958). City attorney, New Orleans. Judge, civil district court, Orleans Parish, 1932–1936. Son.

Olivier Provosty Carrier (1903–1981). Judge, civil district court, Orleans Parish, 1956–? Grandson.

LeDoux R. Provosty, Jr. (b. 1930). Rapides Parish Democratic committee, 1968–1972. Grandnephew.

Albin A. Provosty (b. 1943). Red River Waterway Commission, 1989– . Grandnephew.

Relatives from Other Families

Michel Alcide Becnel (1838–1891). Police jury, St. John the Baptist Parish, 1876–*ca.* 1891. Nephew.

Edgar LaCour Becnel (b. 1905). Chief deputy sheriff, Pointe Coupee Parish, 1960–? Grandnephew.

Nauman Scott, Jr. (b. 1916). U.S. district judge, 1970– . Grandnephew.

Zenon LeDoux, Jr. (1820–1850). Louisiana Senate, 1843–1845. Acting secretary of state, 1845. Constitutional convention, 1845. Attorney general, 1845. First cousin once removed.

Other Connections

August Provosty was a second cousin once removed of **Adolphe V. Coco.**

LeDoux Provosty and **Albin A. Provosty** are brothers-in-law of **Gustave A. Fritchie, Jr.**

REID*

ROBERT RAYMOND REID* (1855–1923). District judge, Tangipahoa Parish, 1894–1904. Constitutional convention, 1921. Supreme Court, 1923 (12 days in office).

Columbus Reid (1884–1953). District judge, Tangipahoa Parish, 1920–1930. Son.

Horace Reid (b. 1902). District judge, 1953–1962. Judge, court of appeals, 1963–1970. Son.

Robert R. Reid (b. 1910). Assistant attorney general, Louisiana, 1944–1948. Grandson.

ROGERS*

WYNNE GREY ROGERS* (b. 1874). Judge, civil district court, New Orleans, 1920–1921. Supreme Court, 1922–1946.

Wynne Rogers (b. 1845). Louisiana House of Representatives, 1874–1876. Louisiana Senate, 1880–1884. Judge, first city court, New Orleans, Judge, court of appeals, 1894–1897. Father.

Walter H. Rogers (b. 1843). Louisiana House of Representatives. District judge, 1876. Judge, court of appeals, 1880–1884. City attorney, New Orleans, 1884–1888. Attorney general, 1888–1892. Uncle.

ROST*

PIERRE ADOLPHE ROST* (1797–1868). Louisiana Senate, 1826. Supreme Court, 1839, 1846–1853. Confederate commissioner to Spain, 1861–1862.

Emile Rost (1839–1913). District judge, Jefferson, St. Charles and St. John, 1888–1903. Son.

Relatives from Other Families

Jean Noel Destrehan (1754–1823). President, Legislative Council, Territory of Orleans, 1806, 1810–1812. Constitutional convention, 1812. Senate, Orleans Parish, 1812–1817. Father-in-law.

Other Connections

Emile A. Rost was

a second cousin of **Charles Gayarré;**

a first cousin once removed of **Bernard Marigny.**

RUTLEDGE**

JOHN RUTLEDGE** (1739–1800). South Carolina House of Representatives, 1761–1776, 1781–1782, 1784, 1790. Attorney general, pro tem, 1764–1765. Stamp Act Congress, 1765. Continental Congress, 1774–1776, 1782–1783. President, General Assembly, 1776–1778. Governor, 1779–1782. Judge, Supreme Court of Chancery, 1784. U.S. constitutional convention, 1787. Constitutional ratification convention, South Carolina, 1788. U.S. Supreme Court, 1790–1791. South Carolina Supreme Court, 1791–1795. Chief justice, U.S. Supreme Court, 1795.

John Rutledge (d. 1750). South Carolina General Assembly, 1748. Father.

Andrew Rutledge (ante 1709–1755). Justice of the peace, 1734. Assembly, 1730. Speaker, South Carolina Assembly, 1751. Uncle.

Edward Rutledge (1749–1800). Continental Congress, 1774–1777. South Carolina legislature, 1782–1796. Constitutional convention, South Carolina, 1790. Governor, 1798–1800. Brother.

Hugh Rutledge (1745?–1811). Judge, court of admiralty, 1776, 1783. Speaker, South Carolina House of Representatives, 1777–1778, 1782–1785. Brother.

John Mathews (1744–1802). Speaker, South Carolina House of Representatives, 1776. South Carolina Supreme Court, 1776–1778. Continental Congress, 1778–1782. Governor, 1782–1783. Chancellor, 1785–1797. Brother-in-law.

John Rutledge, Jr. (1776–1819). U.S. House of Representatives, South Carolina, 1797–1803. Son.

Benjamin Huger Rutledge (1828–1893). Succession convention, 1861. South Carolina legislature. Grandnephew.

Relatives from Other Families

Roger Smith (1745–1805). Provincial Congress, South Carolina, 1775–1776. Brother-in-law.

Thomas Rhett Smith (1768–1830). South Carolina House of Representatives and Senate. Nephew.

John Fauchereau Grimke (1752–1819). Chief justice, South Carolina Supreme Court. Brother-in-law.

Other Connections

Edward Rutledge was a son-in-law of **Henry Middleton** (1717–1784).

Edward Rutledge and **Charles Cotesworth Pinckney** married sisters.

John Rutledge's brother married a sister of **Christopher Gadsden.**

ST. PAUL*

JOHN ST. PAUL* (b. 1867). Senate, Orleans Parish, 1896–1899. District judge, Orleans, 1899–1922. Supreme Court, 1922–1934.

Henri Honoré St. Paul (1814?–1888). Constitutional convention, 1852. Father.

SHIRAS**

GEORGE SHIRAS, JR.** (1832–1924). Supreme Court, 1892–1903.

Oliver Perry Shiras (1833–1916). U.S. district judge, Iowa, 1882–1903. Brother.

George Shiras III. Pennsylvania legislature. Son.

SIMON*

FLORENT EDOUARD SIMON* (1799–1866). Supreme Court, 1840–1849.

JAMES DUDLEY SIMON* (1897–1982). Senate, 1921–1925. District judge, St. Martin Parish, 1925–1954. Supreme Court, 1955–1960. Great-grandson.

Edouard H. P. Simon. Judge, Belgium. Father of Florent Edouard Simon.

Emile Edouard Joseph (Edward) Simon (1824–1913). District attorney, 1853. District judge, 1860s. Constitutional convention, 1879. Son of Florent E. Simon and grandfather of James D. Simon.

Arthur F. Simon (b. 1841). Justice of the peace, St. Landry Parish, before 1888. Son of Florent E. Simon and granduncle of James Dudley Simon.

James Etienne Simon (1866–1925). District attorney. District judge, 1904–? Father of James Dudley Simon* and grandson of Florent E. Simon*.

Relatives from Other Families

James E. Mouton (1846–1908). District judge, St. Martin and Iberia Parishes. Grandfather of James Dudley Simon.

Other Connections

A daughter of **Arthur Simon** married a son of **Felix Voorhies.** See **VOORHIES*.**

SLIDELL*

THOMAS SLIDELL* (1805–1860). Senate, 1844–1845. Supreme Court, 1846–1855 (chief justice, 1853–1855).

John Slidell (1793–1871). District attorney, New Orleans, 1829. U.S. House of Representatives, 1843–1845. U.S. Senate, 1853–1861. Brother.

Ranald Slidell MacKenzie (1840–1889). Brigadier general, USA. Nephew.

Relatives from Other Families

Matthew C. Perry (1794–1858). Commodore, USN, 1841–? Brother-in-law.

Other Connections

John Slidell and P. G. T. Beauregard married sisters.

SPENCER*

WILLIAM BRAINERD SPENCER* (1835–1882). U.S. House of Representatives, Louisiana, 1876–1877. Supreme Court, 1877–1880.

Joseph Spencer (1714–1789). Major general, Continental Army. Connecticut Assembly, 1750–1766. Continental Congress, 1779–1781. Great-grandfather.

Collateral Relatives

Jared Spencer. General court, Connecticut, elected six times after 1660. Great-grandfather of Joseph Spencer.

Relatives from Other Families

Thomas Sambola Jones (b. 1859). Superintendent of education, East Baton Rouge Parish. City judge. House of Representatives, 1912–1913, 1916–1920, 1924–1928. Minister to Honduras, 1919–1920. Son-in-law.

Lewis Cass (1782–1866). Ohio House of Representatives, 1806. U.S. marshall, Ohio, 1807–1812. Brigadier general, USA, 1813. Governor, Michigan Territory, 1813–1831. Secretary of war, 1831–1836. Minister to France, 1836–1842. U.S. Senate, Michigan, 1845–1848, 1849–1857. Secretary of state, 1856–1860. First cousin once removed.

Lewis Cass, Jr. (b. 1810?). Chargé to Papal States, 1849. Minister to Italy, 1854–1858. Second cousin.

Other Connections

Joseph Spencer was a granduncle of **John Sergeant.**

STEWART**

POTTER STEWART** (1915–1985). City council, Cincinnati, 1950–1953. U.S. court of appeals, 1954–1958. Supreme Court, 1958–1981.

James Garfield Stewart (1880–1959). City council, Cincinnati, 1933–1947 (and mayor, 1938–1947). Ohio Supreme Court, 1947–1959. Father.

STONE**

HARLAN FISKE STONE** (1872–1946). U.S. attorney general, 1924–1925. Supreme Court, 1925–1946 (chief justice, 1941–1946).

Frederick Stone (b. 1836). Selectman, assessor, tax collector, Chesterfield, New Hampshire. Selectman, Mille Valley, Massachusetts, 1884–*ca.* 1893. Father.

Collateral Relatives

Peter Stone (1741–1820). Selectman, Chesterfield, New Hampshire, 1784, 1785. Great-grandfather of Frederick Stone.

Simon Stone, Jr. Selectman, tax collector, Watertown, Massachusetts. Deputy, general court. Great-grandfather of Peter Stone.

Simon Stone (1585–1665). Selectman, Watertown, Massachusetts. Deputy, general court, 1636–1656. Father of Simon Stone, Jr.

STORY**

JOSEPH STORY** (1779–1845). Massachusetts legislature, 1805–1808, 1811. U.S. House of Representatives, 1808–1809. Supreme Court, 1812–1845.

William Story. Register, British vice admiralty court, Boston. Clerk, American Navy Board. Grandfather.

William Wetmore Story (1819–1895). Commissioner, U.S. courts, Massachusetts, Maine, and Pennsylvania. Reporter, U.S. circuit court, Massachusetts. Son.

William Wetmore. Judge. Father-in-law.

Relatives from Other Families

George Ticknor Curtis. Son-in-law. See **CURTIS****.

STRONG**

WILLIAM STRONG** (1808–1895). U.S. House of Representatives, Pennsylvania, 1847–1851. Pennsylvania Supreme Court, 1857–1868. Supreme Court, 1870–1880.

Martin Strong (1778–1838). Connecticut House and Senate. Judge. Uncle.

Theron Rudd Strong (1802–1873). District attorney, Wayne County, New York, 1835–1839. U.S. House of Representatives, 1839–1841. New York Assembly, 1842. First cousin.

SUMMERS*

FRANK W. SUMMERS* (b. 1914). District judge, Vermilion Parish, 1952–1954. Supreme Court, 1960–1980 (chief justice, 1979–1980).

George West Summers (1849–1930). President, school board, Vermilion Parish. Secretary, town council, Abbeville. Secretary, police jury, Vermilion Parish. Grandfather.

Henry Moore Summers (1813?–1865). City council, New Orleans. Recorder (judge), first district, New Orleans. Great-grandfather.

Elijah Ewing (b. 1820). Louisiana legislature, 1857–1860. Great-grandfather.

Relatives from Other Families

Severin LeBlanc, Sr. (b. 1833). School board, Vermilion Parish. Great-grandfather.

Rom P. LeBlanc (b. 1873). Secretary, police jury, Vermilion Parish, 1908–*ca*. 1925. House of Representatives, Vermilion Parish, 1896–1908. Mayor, Abbeville, 1921–? Granduncle.

SUTHERLAND**

GEORGE SUTHERLAND** (1862–1942). Utah Senate, 1896. U.S. House of Representatives, 1901–1903. U.S. Senate, 1905–1911, 1911–1917. Supreme Court, 1922–1938.

Alexander G. Sutherland (d. 1911). Justice of the peace. Postmaster, Utah. Father.

SWAYNE**

NOAH H. SWAYNE** (1804–1884). Prosecuting attorney, 1826–1829. Ohio legislature, 1829, 1836. U.S. attorney, 1830–1839. Supreme Court, 1862–1881.

Wager Swayne (1834–1902). Major general, Ohio Volunteers, 1866–1868. Board of education, Toledo, Ohio. Son.

TAFT**

WILLIAM HOWARD TAFT** (1857–1930). Superior court, Ohio, 1887–1890. U.S. solicitor general, 1890–1892. U.S. court of appeals, 1892–1900. Governor general, Philippines, 1900–1904. Secretary of war, 1904–1908. President, 1909–1913. Chief justice, Supreme Court, 1921–1930.

Alfonso Taft (1810–1891). City council, Cincinnati. Superior court, Ohio, 1865–1872. Secretary of war, 1876. U.S. attorney general, 1876–1877. Minister to Austria-Hungary, 1882–1884. Minister to Russia, 1884–1885. Father.

Peter Rawson Taft (1785–1867). Judge, superior court, Cincinnati. Grandfather.

Williamson Herron. Judge. Father-in-law.

Charles Phelps Taft (1843–1929). Ohio House of Representatives, 1871–1873. U.S. House of Representatives, 1895–1897. Half brother.

Robert A. Taft (1889–1953). Ohio House of Representatives, 1921–1926. Senate, 1931–1932. U.S. Senate, 1939–1953. Son.

Charles Phelps Taft (b. 1897). Prosecuting attorney, Hamilton County, Ohio, 1927–1928. City council, Cincinnati, 1938–1942, 1948–1951, 1955–? Son.

William Howard Taft III (b. 1915). Ambassador to Ireland, 1953–1957. Grandson.

Robert Taft, Jr. (b. 1917). Ohio House of Representatives, 1955–1962. U.S. House of Representatives, 1963–1965, 1967–1971. U.S. Senate, 1971–1976. Grandson.

Collateral Relatives

Charles Phelps. Judge. Grandfather of Charles Phelps Taft (1843–1929)

David Sinton Ingalls (b. 1899). Assistant secretary of the navy, 1929–1932. Grandson of Charles Phelps Taft (1843–1929).

Lloyd W. Bowers (1859–1910). U.S. solicitor general, 1909–1910. Grandfather of Robert Taft, Jr., and William Howard Taft III.

Thomas Wilson (1827–1910). Circuit judge, 1857–? Chief justice, Minnesota Supreme Court, 1864–1869. Minnesota House of Representatives, 1880. Senate, 1882–1885. U.S. House of Representatives, 1887–1889. Great-grandfather of Robert A. Taft, Jr., and William H. Taft, III.

Other Connections

Robert A. Taft and **Charles Phelps Taft** (b. 1897) were great-grandsons of **Eli Collins.**

William Howard Taft** and **H. F. Lippitt** married sisters.

TALIAFERRO*

JAMES GOVAN TALIAFERRO* (1797–1876). Judge, Catahoula Parish, 1840. Constitutional conventions, 1852, 1868. Secession convention, 1861. Supreme Court, 1866–1876.

Henry Bullard Taliaferro (1845?–1919). Parish judge. District judge. Son.

Robert W. Taliaferro (d. 1884). Postmaster, New Orleans. Son.

James G. Taliaferro (d. 1922). Clerk of court, Catahoula Parish. Grandson.

Taliaferro Alexander (d. 1924). Constitutional convention, 1898. Grandson.

Robert Monroe Taliaferro (1882–1951). Constitutional convention, 1921. Catahoula and state Democratic committees. District judge, 1924–? Court of appeals, ?–1951. Great-grandson.

Collateral Relatives

Henry Arthur Taliaferro (b. 1909). Treasurer, police jury, Catahoula Parish, mid-1950s to mid-1960s. Son of Robert Monroe Taliaferro.

Other Connections

James G. Taliaferro (d. 1922) is the father-in-law of **John A. Guss.**

Henry Arthur Taliaferro is a nephew of **Henry S. Holloman** and a first cousin of **Wood H.** and **Matthew C. Thompson** (all from the Thompson* family).

TANEY**

ROGER B. TANEY** (1777–1861). Maryland legislature, 1799–1800. Senate, 1816–1821. Attorney general, 1827–1831. U.S. attorney general, 1831–1833. Acting secretary of war, 1831. Chief justice, Supreme Court, 1836–1864.

Michael Taney. Maryland legislature. Father.

Octavius C. Taney. Maryland House of Delegates and Senate. Brother.

Relatives from Other Families

Francis Scott Key (1779–1843). U.S. attorney, District of Columbia. Brother-in-law.

TATE*

ALBERT TATE, JR.* (1920–1986). Judge, court of appeals, 1954–1970. Supreme Court, 1970–1980. Judge, U.S. court of appeals, 1980–1986.

Albert Tate, Sr. (b. 1893). Louisiana Commission on Aging, *ca.* 1960. Delegate, Democratic national convention, 1924. Father.

Rene L. DeRouen (1874–1942). Louisiana constitutional convention, 1921. U.S. House of Representatives, 1927–1941. Father-in-law.

Relatives from Other Families

Jack C. Fruge (b. 1923?). Senate, Avoyelles and Evangeline Parishes, 1964–1968. First cousin.

THOMPSON*

DAVID NEWTON THOMPSON* (1859–1945). District attorney, Catahoula Parish, 1892–1900. District judge, 1900–1908. Judge, court of appeals, 1908–1922. Supreme Court, 1922–1932.

Wood H. Thompson (b. 1888). District attorney, Franklin Parish, 1911–1920. Constitutional convention, 1921. Assistant attorney general, 1924–1932. Son.

Matthew Carey Thompson (b. 1885). House of Representatives, Catahoula Parish, 1908–1916. Son.

Relatives from Other Families

Jesse P. Holloman (1818–1873). Justice of the peace, Catahoula Parish. Father-in-law.
Millard F. Holloman. Treasurer, Catahoula Parish. Brother-in-law.
William Harrison Holloman (1843?–1923). President, Tensas Basin Commission. Brother-in-law.

THOMPSON**

SMITH THOMPSON** (1768–1843). New York legislature, 1800. Constitutional convention, 1801. New York Supreme Court, 1802–1818. Secretary of the navy, 1819–1823. Supreme Court, 1823–1843.

Ezra Thompson. Constitutional ratification convention, New York, 1788. Father.

Relatives from Other Families

Gilbert Livingston (1742–1800/06). Father-in-law. See **LIVINGSTON****.

Other Connections

Smith Thompson's daughter married a son of **Daniel Tompkins.**

TODD*

ROBERT B. TODD* (d. 1901). Supreme Court, 1880–1888.

David Todd. Judge, first district, Missouri. Father.

Levi Todd (1756–1807). Clerk, First Court of Quarter Sessions, 1777. Danville conventions of 1785–1787. Clerk, Fayette County, Kentucky, ?–1807. Major general, Kentucky. Grandfather.

Robert Smith Todd (1791–1849). Clerk, Kentucky House of Representatives, *ca.* 1821–*ca.* 1841. House of Representatives, Fayette County, three times. Senate, 1845–1849. Uncle.

Roger North Todd. Clerk, circuit court, Missouri. Uncle.

Robert Todd. Virginia General Assembly. Danville convention, 1785. Kentucky Senate. Judge, circuit court, Fayette District, Kentucky. Granduncle.

John Todd. Virginia General Assembly, 1777. Civil governor, Illinois County. Granduncle.

Levi Todd (2). Judge, Indiana. First cousin once removed.

J. Harvey Brigham. District judge, Morehouse Parish, 1880–? Brother-in-law.

David Todd (d. 1878?). School commissioner, Daviess County, Kentucky, 1868–*ca.* 1878. Second cousin.

Will H. Todd, Jr. (b. 1895). Alderman, Bastrop. House of Representatives, Morehouse Parish, 1936–1940. City attorney, Bastrop, 1934–? Grandson.

Relatives from Other Families

John Todd Stuart (1807–1885). Illinois House of Representatives, 1832–1836. U.S. House of Representatives, 1839–1843, 1863–1865. Illinois Senate, 1848–1852. First cousin.

Charles Carr. Judge, Fayette County, Kentucky. First cousin.

Robert Elisha Carr. Judge, St. Louis. First cousin.

Levi Todd Carr. Judge, California. First cousin.

Walter Chiles Carr. Judge, St. Louis. First cousin.

Emilie Todd Helm (d. 1930). Postmistress, Elizabethtown, Kentucky, *ca.* 1883–1895. First cousin.

Charles H. Breck. Judge, Madison County, Kentucky. First cousin.

Robert Todd Lincoln (1843–1926). Secretary of war, 1881–1885. Minister to Great Britain, 1889–1893. Second cousin.

John Todd Shelby (b. 1851). City attorney and alderman, Lexington, Kentucky. First cousin once removed.

Collateral Relatives

Nathaniel Henry Rhodes Dawson (1829–1895). Alabama House of Representatives, 1863–1864. Speaker of the House, 1880–1881. Son-in-law of Robert Smith Todd.

James C. Todd. Sheriff, Fayette County, Kentucky. Half brother of David Todd.

Lymann Beecher Todd (b. 1832). Postmaster, Lexington, Kentucky, *ca.* 1861–1869. Son of James C. Todd.

Robert Stuart Todd (b. 1856). County attorney, 1890–1897. School board, Owensboro, Kentucky. Son of David Todd (d. 1878?).

Other Connections

Robert Todd was the grandfather of **William Orlando Butler.**
John Todd's daughter married a brother of **Charles A. Wickliffe.**
Robert Smith Todd was the father-in-law of **Ninian W. Edwards.**
Levi Todd (1756–1807) and **Robert Parker** were half first cousins, and their children (Robert Smith Todd and Eliza Parker) married.

TODD**

THOMAS TODD** (1765–1826). Clerk, U.S. district court, Kentucky, 1786–1792. Clerk, court of appeals, 1792–1801. Judge, court of appeals, 1801–1806. Chief justice, Kentucky Supreme Court, 1806. Supreme Court, 1807–1826.
William Todd. High sheriff, Pittsylvania County, Virginia. Brother.
Charles Stewart Todd (1791–1871). Secretary of state, Kentucky, 1816. Legislature, 1817–1818. Minister to Russia, 1841–1846. Son.
John Harris Todd (b. 1796). Kentucky legislature, 1821–1823. Son.
Harry Innes Todd (b. 1818). Sheriff, Franklin County, Kentucky. Warden, Kentucky State Prison. Grandson.
Edmund L. Starling (1840–1910). Mayor, Henderson, Kentucky, 1868–1874. Board of trustees of schools, 1870–? Great-grandson.
Josiah T. Griffith (b. 1861). Clerk of court, Daviess County, Kentucky. Great-grandson.
George D. Todd (b. 1856). Mayor, Louisville, Kentucky, 1896. Great-grandson.
Chapman Coleman Todd (1848–1929). Rear admiral, USN. Great-grandson.
John H. Hanna. Minister to Russia. Son-in-law.

Other Connections

John H. Todd was
    a son-in-law of **Harry Innes;**
    the father-in-law of **Thomas L. Crittenden.**
Charles S. Todd was a son-in-law of **Isaac Shelby.**
Thomas Todd** and **James Madison** married sisters.
George D. Todd was a grandson of **James Davidson.**

Note: Charles S. Todd's daughter married a Judge Posey of Baton Rouge who was probably Reuben T. Posey of West Baton Rouge Parish and who may be related to the other Poseys of Louisiana.

TRIMBLE**

ROBERT TRIMBLE** (1776–1828). Kentucky legislature, Bourbon County, 1803. Supreme Court of Appeals, 1807–1809. District attorney, 1813. U.S. district judge, 1816–1826. Supreme Court, 1826–1828.

John Trimble (1783–1852). Judge, court of appeals. Kentucky legislature, 1826, 1833, 1835. Brother.

William W. Trimble (b. 1821). Judge. Nephew.

Benjamin Trimble. Judge, circuit court, Mississippi, 1867–1886. Nephew.

Robert Morgan Evans. Acting territorial governor of Indiana, 1805. Son-in-law.

Relatives from Other Families

Alexander White (1738–1804). Virginia House of Delegates, 1782–1786, 1788, 1799–1801. U.S. House of Representatives, 1789–1793. Granduncle.

Garrett Davis (1801–1872). Kentucky House of Representatives, 1833–1835. U.S. House of Representatives, 1839–1847. Constitutional convention, 1849. U.S. Senate, 1861–1872. Son-in-law.

Other Connections

Robert Trimble** was a third cousin of **John Blair Hoge.**

Note: Senator William Allen Trimble, brother of Governor Allen Trimble (both of Ohio), studied law under Robert Trimble**. The two Trimble families considered themselves related, but they were not sure how.

VINSON**

FREDERICK M. VINSON** (1890–1953). Commonwealth attorney, Kentucky, 1921–1924. U.S. House of Representatives, 1923–1929, 1931–1939. U.S. court of appeals, 1938–1943. Director, Office of Economic Stabilization, 1943–1945. Director, Office of War Mobilization, 1945. Secretary of the treasury, 1945–1946. Chief justice, Supreme Court, 1946–1953.

James Vinson (1856?–1927). County jailer (elected) 1885–*ca.* 1895. Marshall, Louisa, Kentucky, 1895–? Father.

VOORHIES*

CORNELIUS VOORHIES, JR.* (1804–1859). Louisiana House of Representatives, 1832–1844. District attorney, Avoyelles Parish, 1842–1844. Constitutional convention, 1845. District judge, 1846–1854. Supreme Court, 1854–1859.

ALBERT VOORHIES* (1829–1914). Judge, St. Martin Parish, 1855–1859. Supreme Court, 1859–1865. Lt. governor, 1866–1868. District attorney, St. Martin Parish. Senate, 1872–1876. House of Representatives, 1876–1878. Son.

Cornelius Voorhies, Sr. (1775–1835). Parish judge, 1816–1826. Sheriff, Avoyelles Parish, 1829–1837. Father.

Martin Voorhies (b. 1836). House of Representatives, St. Martin Parish, 1872–1876. Son.

Alfred Voorhies (b. 1830). House of Representatives, St. Martin Parish, 1882, 1886–1889. Son.

Felix Voorhies (1839–1919). House of Representatives, St. Martin Parish, 1874–1878. District judge, 1892–1900. Son.

Jean Sosthene Voorhies (b. 1883). Town council, Breaux Bridge. Grandson.

Edward G. Voorhies (1861–1911/12). Clerk of court, Lafayette Parish, 1898–*ca.* 1910. Grandson.

Charles Voorhies (b. 1859). Chief constable, St. Martin Parish, 1886–? Grandson.

Cornelius P. Voorhies (b. 1908). Senate, Iberia Parish, 1944–1948. Great-grandson.

Collateral Relatives

Bennett Voorhies, Jr. (b. 1925). State Democratic central committee, 1960–1968. Grandson of Edward G. Voorhies.

Henry C. Voorhies, Jr. Coroner, Lafayette Parish, ?–1980. Grandson of Edward G. Voorhies.

Other Connections

A daughter of **Alfred Voorhies** married a son of **Alfred Mouton.**

A son of **Felix Voorhies** married a daughter of **Arthur Simon.** See **SIMON*.**

Note: Cornelius Voorhies, Sr., the first Louisiana official in the family, was a descendant of Steven Coerte Van Voorhies (1600–1684), who came to Long Island from France and was said to have held office. His son Coerte Stevense Van Voorhies (1637–post 1702) was a magistrate and member of the General Assembly. His son Cornelius Coerte Van Voorhies (b. 1678) was also thought to have held office; he was the great-grandfather of Cornelius Voorhies, Sr. Senator David Walsey Voorhies (Indiana, 1877–1895) and his son Congressman Charles Stewart Voorhies (Tennessee, 1885–1889) were probably members of this family. The spelling of the name has varied over the generations.

WAITE**

MORRISON WAITE** (1816–1888). Ohio legislature, 1849–1850. Constitutional convention, 1873. Chief justice, Supreme Court, 1874–1888.

Henry Matson Waite (1787–1869). Connecticut House of Representatives, 1815, 1825–1826. Senate, 1832–1833. Connecticut Supreme Court, 1834–1857 (chief justice, 1854–1857). Father.

Remick Waite (b. 1758). Justice of the peace. Grandfather.

Richard Waite (1831–1907). Judge, Ohio. Brother.

William Alfred Buckingham (1804–1875). Mayor, Norwich, Connecticut, 1849–1850, 1856–1857. Governor, 1858–1866. U.S. Senate, 1869–1875. First cousin once removed.

Collateral Relatives

Marvin Waite (1746–1815). Connecticut legislature. Judge, county court. Half brother of Remick Waite.

John Turner Waite (1811–1899). State's attorney, New London, Connecticut, 1841–1844, 1846–1854. Senate, 1865, 1866. House of Representatives, 1867, 1871, 1873. U.S. House of Representatives, 1876–1887. Son of Marvin Waite.

Relatives from Other Families

Richard Ely Selden. Magistrate. Grandfather.

Samuel Selden (1723–1776). Deputy, Connecticut General Assembly, 1762–1769. Great-grandfather.

WASHINGTON**

BUSHROD WASHINGTON** (1762–1829). Virginia House of Delegates, 1787. Constitutional ratification convention, 1788. Supreme Court, 1799–1829.

John Augustine Washington (1735/6–1787). Virginia convention, 1776. Father.

Augustine Washington (1694?–1743). Justice of the peace. High sheriff, Virginia, 1727. Grandfather.

John Bushrod. Justice of the peace. Virginia House of Burgesses. Grandfather.

Gavin Corbin. President, Governor's Council, Virginia. Great-grandfather.

Lawrence Washington (1659–1697). Virginia House of Burgesses, 1685. High sheriff, 1692. Great-grandfather.

Caleb Butler. Justice of the peace, Westmoreland County, Virginia. Great-grandfather.

George Washington (1732–1799). Continental Congress, 1774, 1775. Commander in chief, Continental Army, 1775–1783. U.S. constitutional convention, 1787. President, 1789–1797. Uncle.

Samuel Washington (b. 1734). Justice of the peace. High sheriff. Uncle.

William Augustine Washington (b. 1757). Brigadier general, U.S. Army. Half first cousin and brother-in-law.

Bushrod Corbin Washington (b. 1790). House of Delegates, Virginia. Nephew.

Collateral Relatives

John Washington. Virginia House of Burgesses. Father of Lawrence Washington, (1659–1697).

Lawrence Washington (1718–1752). Virginia House of Burgesses, Fairfax County. Son of Augustine Washington (1694?–1743).

Augustine Washington (1720–1773). Virginia Assembly. Son of Augustine Washington (1694?–1743) by his first wife.

George Corbin Washington (1789–1854). Maryland legislature. U.S. House of Representatives, 1827–1833, 1835–1837. Son of William Augustine Washington.

Burdett Ashton (1747–1814). Virginia convention, 1788. Assembly. Son-in-law of Augustine Washington (1720–1773).

Benjamin Franklin Washington (1820–1872). Collector, Port of San Francisco. Great-grandson of Samuel Washington.

George **Washington** (1830–1890). Judge, Johnson County, Missouri. Great-grandson of Samuel Washington.

George **Washington** (1843–1905). Chairman, constitutional convention, Kentucky, 1890. First cousin once removed of Benjamin Franklin Washington.

Ramsey **Washington** (1869–1923). County attorney, Kentucky. Son of George Washington (1843–1905).

George Thomas **Washington** (1908–1971). Assistant U.S. solicitor general, 1946–1949. U.S. court of appeals, 1949–1965. Nephew of Ramsey Washington.

Other Connections

Augustine **Washington** (1720–1773) was the father-in-law of **Alexander Spotswood** (1746–1818).

Augustine **Washington** (1694?–1743) was a grandson of **Augustine Warner**.

Lawrence **Washington** (1718–1752) was a son-in-law of **William Fairfax**.

William Augustine **Washington** was

a first cousin once removed of **Aylett Buckner**;

a grandson of **William Aylett** (1673–1735).

George **Washington** (1732–1799) was

a brother-in-law of **Fielding Lewis**;

a second cousin once removed of **Howell Jackson****;

a great-grandson of **William Ball** (1615–1680). See **JACKSON****.

Bushrod Corbin **Washington** was a grandson of **Richard Henry Lee**.

Lawrence **Washington** (1659–1697) was a grandson of **Nathaniel Pope**.

Bushrod **Washington**** was a second cousin once removed of **James Barbour****. See **BARBOUR****.

WATKINS*

LYNN BOYD WATKINS* (1836–1901). District judge, 1871. Supreme Court, 1886–1901.

John Thomas Watkins (1854–1925). District judge, 1892–1904. U.S. House of Representatives, Louisiana, 1905–1921. Nephew.

John D. Watkins (1828–1873). District attorney, 1854–1859. Judge, 1859–1869. Senate, 1880–1884. Constitutional convention, 1879. Brother.

WAYNE**

JAMES MOORE WAYNE** (1790–1867). Georgia House of Representatives, 1815–1816. Mayor, Savannah, 1815–1816. Superior court, Georgia, 1824–1829. U.S. House of Representatives, 1829–1835. Supreme Court, 1835–1867.

Henry Constantine Wayne (1814–1883). Major general, Georgia Militia, 1864. U.S. circuit court commissioner, 1872–? Son.

Alexander Campbell. District attorney, Virginia. Father-in-law.

WHITE**

BYRON R. WHITE** (b. 1917). Deputy U.S. attorney general, 1961–1962. Supreme Court, 1962–1993.

Alfred White. Mayor, Wellington, Colorado. Father.

Robert L. Stearns (b. 1892). President, University of Colorado, 1939–? Chairman, Colorado Resources Development Commission, 1947. Father-in-law.

WHITE*,**

EDWARD DOUGLAS WHITE, JR.** (1845–1921). Louisiana Senate, 1874–1878. Louisiana Supreme Court, 1879–1880. U.S. Senate, 1891–1894. U.S. Supreme Court, 1894–1921 (chief justice, 1910–1921).

Edward Douglas White (1795–1847). Judge, city court, New Orleans, 1825–1828. U.S. House of Representatives, 1829–1834, 1839–1843. Governor, 1834–1838. Father.

James White (1749–1809). North Carolina General Assembly, 1785. Continental Congress, 1786–1788. Territorial (later Tennessee) legislature, 1794. Territorial delegate to Congress, 1794–1796. Judge, Attakapas District of Louisiana, 1804. Grandfather.

Trent Ringgold. U.S. marshall, District of Columbia (Monroe and Madison administrations). Grandfather.

Other Connections

Edward Douglas White, Jr.** was a great-great-grandson of **Thomas Ludwell Lee.**

WILSON**

JAMES WILSON** (1742–1798). Provincial convention, Pennsylvania. Continental Congress, 1774–1776, 1782–1783, 1785–1787. U.S. constitutional convention, 1787. Constitutional ratification convention, 1788. Supreme Court, 1789–1798.

Bird Wilson (1777–1859). President, Pennsylvania Court of Common Pleas, 1802–1817. Son.

WOODBURY**

LEVI WOODBURY** (1789–1851). Clerk, New Hampshire Senate, 1816. New Hampshire Supreme Court, 1817. Governor, 1823–1824. U.S. Senate, 1825–1831, 1841–1845. Secretary of the navy, 1831–1834. Secretary of the treasury, 1834–1841. Supreme Court, 1845–1851.

Peter Woodbury. New Hampshire legislature. Father.

Relatives from Other Families

Montgomery Blair (1813–1883). U.S. attorney, Missouri, 1839. Mayor, St. Louis, 1842–1843. Judge, court of common pleas, 1843–1849. Postmaster general, 1861–1864. Maryland House of Representatives, 1878. Son-in-law.

WOODS**

WILLIAM BURNHAM WOODS** (1824–1887). Mayor, Newark, Ohio, 1855. Legislature, 1857–1862. Chancellor, Alabama, 1868–*ca.* 1870. U.S. circuit court, 1869. Supreme Court, 1880–1887.

Charles Robert Woods (1827–1885). Brigadier general, Ohio Volunteers, 1863–? Major general. Brother.

INFORMATION ON NETWORKS 1–43

Data on the forty-three smaller kinship networks, discussed in the first part of Chapter 4, are presented here. As in Appendix A, * follows the surnames of Louisiana justices and ** follows the surname of United States justices. Some of the major positions are abbreviated as follows:

United States Senate: USS
U.S. House of Representatives: USHR
State Supreme Court: State SC

NETWORK 1

Justice:	Bradley**	Major positions:	1
Allied families:	1	USS:	0
Total families:	1	USHR:	0
Total officials:	5	Cabinet:	0
Earliest office:	1779	State SC:	1
Latest office:	1914	Governor:	0
Range:	136 years	Ambassador:	0
Total states:	1	Other:	0
Location:	New Jersey		

NETWORK 2

Justices:	Brewer**, Field**	Major positions:	4
Allied families:	0	USS:	0
Total families:	1	USHR:	1
Total officials:	4	Cabinet:	0
Earliest office:	1847	State SC:	2
Latest office:	1910	Governor:	0
Range:	64 years	Ambassador:	0
Total states:	2	Other:	1
Locations:	Kansas, California, Canada		

NETWORK 3

Justice:	Carleton*	Major positions:	5
Allied families:	1	USS:	0
Total families:	1	USHR:	2
Total officials:	10	Cabinet:	1
Earliest office:	1837	State SC:	0
Latest office:	1928	Governor:	1
Range:	92 years	Ambassador:	0
Total states:	4	Other:	1
Locations:	Louisiana, South Carolina,		
	Montana, Idaho, the Bahamas		

NETWORK 4

Justice:	Catron**	Major positions:	2
Allied families:	1	USS:	0
Total families:	2	USHR:	0
Total officials:	4	Cabinet:	0
Earliest office:	1815	State SC:	2
Latest office:	1865	Governor:	0
Range:	51 years	Ambassador:	0
Total states:	1	Other:	0
Location:	Tennessee		

NETWORK 5

Justice:	Chase**	Major positions:	11
Allied families:	1	USS:	4
Total families:	2	USHR:	2
Total officials:	6	Cabinet:	1
Earliest office:	1803	State SC:	1
Latest office:	1879	Governor:	3
Range:	77 years	Ambassador:	0
Total states:	3	Other:	0
Locations:	Ohio, Vermont, Rhode Island		

NETWORK 6

Justice:	Clifford**	Major positions:	6
Allied families:	1	USS:	2
Total families:	2	USHR:	3
Total officials:	7	Cabinet:	1
Earliest office:	Before 1824	State SC:	0
Latest office:	1959	Governor:	0
Range:	136 years	Ambassador:	0
Total states:	1	Other:	0
Location:	Maine		

NETWORK 7

Justices:	Curtis**, Story**	Major positions:	1
Allied families:	0	USS:	0
Total families:	2	USHR:	1
Total officials:	6	Cabinet:	0
Earliest office:	?	State SC:	0
Latest office:	1857	Governor:	0
Range:	?	Ambassador:	0
Total states:	1	Other:	0
Location:	Massachusetts		

NETWORK 8

Justice:	Derbigny*	Major positions:	2
Allied families:	1	USS:	0
Total families:	2	USHR:	0
Total officials:	4	Cabinet:	0
Earliest office:	1795	State SC:	0
Latest office:	?	Governor:	2
Range:	?	Ambassador:	0
Total states:	1	Other:	0
Locations:	Louisiana, France		

NETWORK 9

Justice:	Fenner*	Major positions:	2
Allied families:	1	USS:	1
Total families:	2	USHR:	1
Total officials:	11	Cabinet:	0
Earliest office:	1865	State SC:	0
Latest office:	1979	Governor:	0
Range:	115 years	Ambassador:	0
Total states:	2	Other:	0
Locations:	Louisiana, Tennessee		

NETWORK 10

Justices:	Harlan** (both)	Major positions:	2
Allied families:	1	USS:	0
Total families:	2	USHR:	1
Total officials:	8	Cabinet:	0
Earliest office:	Before 1807	State SC:	0
Latest office:	1971	Governor:	0
Range:	165 years	Ambassador:	0
Total states:	3	Other:	1
Locations:	Kentucky, Illinois, Ohio, Puerto Rico		

NETWORK 11

Justice:	Hyman*	Major positions:	1
Allied families:	1	USS:	0
Total families:	2	USHR:	0
Total officials:	6	Cabinet:	0
Earliest office:	1753	State SC:	0
Latest office:	1909	Governor:	1
Range:	157 years	Ambassador:	0
Total states:	1	Other:	0
Location:	Louisiana		

NETWORK 12

Justice:	Iredell**	Major positions:	6
Allied families:	1	USS:	2
Total families:	2	USHR:	0
Total officials:	4	Cabinet:	0
Earliest office:	1734	State SC:	0
Latest office:	1831	Governor:	3
Range:	98 years	Ambassador:	0
Total states:	1	Other:	1
Location:	North Carolina		

NETWORK 13

Justice:	Johnson**	Major positions:	14
Allied families:	1	USS:	1
Total families:	2	USHR:	3
Total officials:	12	Cabinet:	2
Earliest office:	1762	State SC:	0
Latest office:	1933	Governor:	2
Range:	172 years	Ambassador:	3
Total states:	2	Other:	3
Locations:	Maryland, Massachusetts		

NETWORK 14

Justice:	LaBauve*	Major positions:	0
Allied families:	1	USS:	0
Total families:	2	USHR:	0
Total officials:	7	Cabinet:	0
Earliest office:	1834	State SC:	0
Latest office:	1895	Governor:	0
Range:	62 years	Ambassador:	0
Total states:	1	Other:	0
Location:	Louisiana		

NETWORK 15

Justice:	LeBlanc*	Major positions:	0
Allied families:	1	USS:	0
Total families:	2	USHR:	0
Total officials:	11	Cabinet:	0
Earliest office:	1874	State SC:	0
Latest office:	1988	Governor:	0
Range:	115 years	Ambassador:	0
Total states:	1	Other:	0
Location:	Louisiana		

NETWORK 16

Justice:	Lemmon*	Major positions:	0
Allied families:	1	USS:	0
Total families:	2	USHR:	0
Total officials:	8	Cabinet:	0
Earliest office:	1904	State SC:	0
Latest office:	1988	Governor:	0
Range:	85 years	Ambassador:	0
Total states:	1	Other:	0
Location:	Louisiana		

NETWORK 17

Justice:	Merrick*	Major positions:	0
Allied families:	1	USS:	0
Total families:	2	USHR:	0
Total officials:	10	Cabinet:	0
Earliest office:	1855	State SC:	0
Latest office:	1937	Governor:	0
Range:	83 years	Ambassador:	0
Total states:	1	Other:	0
Location:	Louisiana		

NETWORK 18

Justice:	Moore**	Major positions:	13
Allied families:	1	USS:	0
Total families:	2	USHR:	4
Total officials:	16	Cabinet:	0
Earliest office:	1700	State SC:	2
Latest office:	1887	Governor:	6
Range:	188 years	Ambassador:	0
Total states:	3	Other:	1
Locations:	North Carolina, South Carolina, Tennessee		

NETWORK 19

Justice:	Peckham**	Major positions:	3
Allied families:	1	USS:	0
Total families:	2	USHR:	1
Total officials:	6	Cabinet:	0
Earliest office:	Before 1710	State SC:	2
Latest office:	1909	Governor:	0
Range:	200 years	Ambassador:	0
Total states:	2	Other:	0
Locations:	New York, Rhode Island		

NETWORK 20

Justice:	Summers*	Major positions:	0
Allied families:	1	USS:	0
Total families:	2	USHR:	0
Total officials:	6	Cabinet:	0
Earliest office:	1857	State SC:	0
Latest office:	1980	Governor:	0
Range:	124 years	Ambassador:	0
Total states:	1	Other:	0
Location:	Louisiana		

NETWORK 21

Justice:	Taney**	Major positions:	7
Allied families:	1	USS:	1
Total families:	2	USHR:	2
Total officials:	13	Cabinet:	1
Earliest office:	1728	State SC:	0
Latest office:	1861	Governor:	2
Range:	134 years	Ambassador:	0
Total states:	2	Other:	1
Locations:	Maryland, Louisiana, District of Columbia		

NETWORK 22

Justice:	Tate*	Major positions:	1
Allied families:	1	USS:	0
Total families:	2	USHR:	1
Total officials:	5	Cabinet:	0
Earliest office:	1921	State SC:	0
Latest office:	1986	Governor:	0
Range:	66 years	Ambassador:	0
Total states:	1	Other:	0
Location:	Louisiana		

NETWORK 23

Justice:	Waite**	Major positions:	4
Allied families:	1	USS:	1
Total families:	2	USHR:	1
Total officials:	10	Cabinet:	0
Earliest office:	1744	State SC:	1
Latest office:	1887	Governor:	1
Range:	144 years	Ambassador:	0
Total states:	2	Other:	0
Locations:	Connecticut, Ohio		

NETWORK 24

Justice:	Woodbury**	Major positions:	7
Allied families:	1	USS:	2
Total families:	2	USHR:	1
Total officials:	6	Cabinet:	2
Earliest office:	1796	State SC:	1
Latest office:	1873	Governor:	1
Range:	78 years	Ambassador:	0
Total states:	3	Other:	0
Locations:	New Hampshire, Missouri, Kentucky		

NETWORK 25

Justice:	Ellsworth**	Major positions:	11
Allied families:	2	USS:	2
Total families:	3	USHR:	4
Total officials:	10	Cabinet:	0
Earliest office:	1760	State SC:	2
Latest office:	1861	Governor:	0
Range:	102 years	Ambassador:	0
Total states:	2	Other:	3
Locations:	Connecticut, Massachusetts		

NETWORK 26

Justice:	Holmes**	Major positions:	5
Allied families:	2	USS:	0
Total families:	3	USHR:	0
Total officials:	9	Cabinet:	0
Earliest office:	1775	State SC:	2
Latest office:	1932	Governor:	0
Range:	158 years	Ambassador:	1
Total states:	1	Other:	2
Location:	Massachusetts		

NETWORK 27

Justice:	Morgan*	Major positions:	9
Allied families:	2	USS:	0
Total families:	3	USHR:	2
Total officials:	15	Cabinet:	2
Earliest office:	1756	State SC:	1
Latest office:	1919	Governor:	1
Range:	164 years	Ambassador:	1
Total states:	7	Other:	2
Locations:	Pennsylvania, Delaware, South Carolina, Louisiana, Illinois, Ohio, New York		

NETWORK 28

Justice:	Slidell*	Major positions:	2
Allied families:	2	USS:	1
Total families:	3	USHR:	1
Total officials:	9	Cabinet:	0
Earliest office:	Before 1780	State SC:	0
Latest office:	1904	Governor:	0
Range:	125 years	Ambassador:	0
Total states:	2	Other:	0
Locations:	Louisiana, Rhode Island		

NETWORK 29

Justice:	Taft**	Major positions:	22
Allied families:	2	USS:	4
Total families:	3	USHR:	5
Total officials:	19	Cabinet:	4
Earliest office:	1815	State SC:	1
Latest office:	1988	Governor:	5
Range:	174 years	Ambassador:	2
Total states:	4	Other:	1
Locations:	New York, Rhode Island, Minnesota, Ohio		

NETWORK 30

Justices:	Simon* (both), Voorhies* (both)	Major positions:	2
Allied families:	1	USS:	1
Total families:	3	USHR:	0
Total officials:	27	Cabinet:	0
Earliest office:	1816	State SC:	0
Latest office:	1980	Governor:	1
Range:	167 years	Ambassador:	0
Total states:	1	Other:	0
Locations:	Louisiana, Belgium		

NETWORK 31

Justice:	O'Niell*	Major positions:	0
Allied families:	3	USS:	0
Total families:	4	USHR:	0
Total officials:	12	Cabinet:	0
Earliest office:	1869	State SC:	0
Latest office:	1966	Governor:	0
Range:	98 years	Ambassador:	0
Total states:	1	Other:	0
Location:	Louisiana		

NETWORK 32

Justice:	Rost*	Major positions:	1
Allied families:	3	USS:	0
Total families:	4	USHR:	0
Total officials:	15	Cabinet:	0
Earliest office:	1722	State SC:	0
Latest office:	1903	Governor:	0
Range:	182 years	Ambassador:	1
Total states:	2	Other:	0
Locations:	Louisiana, Texas, France		

NETWORK 33

Justice:	Spencer*	Major positions:	0
Allied families:	3	USS:	0
Total families:	4	USHR:	0
Total officials:	10	Cabinet:	0
Earliest office:	Before 1700	State SC:	0
Latest office:	1928	Governor:	0
Range:	229 years	Ambassador:	0
Total states:	6	Other:	0
Locations:	Louisiana, Ohio, Michigan, Pennsylvania, New Jersey, Connecticut, Honduras		

NETWORK 34

Justice:	Trimble**	Major positions:	7
Allied families:	3	USS:	1
Total families:	4	USHR:	6
Total officials:	14	Cabinet:	0
Earliest office:	1782	State SC:	0
Latest office:	1889	Governor:	0
Range:	108 years	Ambassador:	0
Total states:	6	Other:	0
Locations:	Kentucky, Mississippi, Indiana, Virginia, Pennsylvania, West Virginia, District of Columbia		

NETWORK 35

Justices:	Matthews**, Gray**	Major positions:	5
Allied families:	2	USS:	1
Total families:	3	USHR:	2
Total officials:	8	Cabinet:	0
Earliest office:	1785	State SC:	2
Latest office:	1902	Governor:	0
Range:	118 years	Ambassador:	0
Total states:	4	Other:	0
Locations:	Kentucky, Tennessee, Ohio, Massachusetts, Canada		

NETWORK 36

Justices:	Thompson*, Taliaferro*	Major positions:	0
Allied families:	2	USS:	0
Total families:	4	USHR:	0
Total officials:	16	Cabinet:	0
Earliest office:	1840	State SC:	0
Latest office:	*ca.* 1965	Governor:	0
Range:	126 years	Ambassador:	0
Total states:	1	Other:	0
Location:	Louisiana		

NETWORK 37

Justice:	Ogden*	Major positions:	3
Allied families:	4	USS:	0
Total families:	5	USHR:	0
Total officials:	23	Cabinet:	0
Earliest office:	1761	State SC:	1
Latest office:	1988	Governor:	1
Range:	228 years	Ambassador:	0
Total states:	3	Other:	1
Locations:	Louisiana, North Carolina, Virginia		

NETWORK 38

Justices:	McCaleb*, Nicholls*	Major positions:	11
Allied families:	3	USS:	3
Total families:	5	USHR:	3
Total officials:	38	Cabinet:	1
Earliest office:	1776	State SC:	0
Latest office:	1983	Governor:	3
Range:	208 years	Ambassador:	0
Total states:	7	Other:	1
Locations:	Louisiana, Arkansas, South Carolina, Virginia, North Carolina, Maryland, Mississippi		

NETWORK 39

Justices:	Fournet*, DeBlanc*	Major positions:	0
Allied families:	3	USS:	0
Total families:	5	USHR:	0
Total officials:	25	Cabinet:	0
Earliest office:	1613	State SC:	0
Latest office:	1988	Governor:	0
Range:	325 years	Ambassador:	0
Total states:	1	Other:	0
Locations:	Louisiana, Canada		

NETWORK 40

Justice:	Fuller**	Major positions:	7
Allied families:	5	USS:	1
Total families:	6	USHR:	0
Total officials:	20	Cabinet:	1
Earliest office:	Before 1718	State SC:	1
Latest office:	1921	Governor:	2
Range:	204 years	Ambassador:	2
Total states:	2	Other:	0
Locations:	Maine, Massachusetts		

NETWORK 41

Justice:	Provosty*	Major positions:	0
Allied families:	5	USS:	0
Total families:	6	USHR:	0
Total officials:	24	Cabinet:	0
Earliest office:	*ca.* 1820	State SC:	0
Latest office:	1988	Governor:	0
Range:	169 years	Ambassador:	0
Total states:	1	Other:	0
Location:	Louisiana		

NETWORK 42

Justice:	Rutledge**	Major positions:	27
Allied families:	5	USS:	0
Total families:	6	USHR:	4
Total officials:	27	Cabinet:	0
Earliest office:	1725	State SC:	5
Latest office:	1872	Governor:	6
Range:	148 years	Ambassador:	3
Total states:	2	Other:	9
Locations:	South Carolina, Ohio		

NETWORK 43

Justices:	Bermudez*, Eustis*	Major positions:	22
Allied families:	5	USS:	2
Total families:	7	USHR:	10
Total officials:	53	Cabinet:	2
Earliest office:	*ca.* 1621	State SC:	1
Latest office:	1988	Governor:	3
Range:	368 years	Ambassador:	3
Total states:	6	Other:	1
Locations:	Louisiana, Virginia, Tennessee, Mississippi, Massachusetts, New York		

APPENDIX C

SOURCES OF BIOGRAPHICAL AND GENEALOGICAL
INFORMATION ON FAMILIES

The families of Louisiana justices are indicated with *; those of federal justices, with
**. All others are allied families. Frequently cited works are referred to by the follow-
ing abbreviations:

APD   Hess, Stephen. *America's
      political dynasties: From
      Adams to Kennedy.* Garden
      City, N.Y.: Doubleday, 1966.

BDAC *Biographical directory of the
      American Congress,
      1774–1961*

BDFJ *Biographical directory of the
      federal judiciary, 1789–1974.*
      Detroit: Gale Research,
      1976.

CAG   Virkus, Frederick A. *The
      compendium of American
      genealogy.* Baltimore:
      Genealogical, 1987.

DAB   *Dictionary of American
      biography*

DLB   *Dictionary of Louisiana
      biography.* New Orleans:

      Louisiana Historical Asso-
      ciation in cooperation with
      the Center for Louisiana
      Studies of the University of
      Southwestern Louisiana,
      1988.

HFK   Green, Thomas Marshall.
      *Historic families of Ken-
      tucky.* Baltimore: Regional,
      1964.

Louisiana Fortier, Alcée. *History of
      Louisiana.* Madison, Wis.:
      Century Historical Associ-
      ation, 1914. All references
      are to Vol. 3 unless other-
      wise noted.

NCAB *National cyclopedia of
      American biography*

ADAMS
APD, 11–48, 623–24.

ALEXANDER
APD, 545.
DAB, 1–2:167–68, 175–76.

ARMSTRONG
APD, 87–88, 98, 549–50, 646.

ASHE
APD, 646.

DAB, 1–2:385–88

NCAB, 4:421; 6:254, 438; 7:349; 12:163–64.

AYLETT

CAG, 2:98; 4:173, 388.

BAILLIO

DLB, 1:30.

Futch, Catherine Baillio. *The Baillio family.* Baton Rouge: privately published, 1961.

BAKER*

DLB, 1:31.

Louisiana, 1:59.

Reeves, Miriam G. *The governors of Louisiana,* 74–75. Gretna, La.: Pelican, 1972.

Seebold, Herman de Bachelle. *Old Louisiana plantation homes and family trees,* 2:150–51. N.p.: privately published, 1941.

Sobel, Robert, and John Raimo. *Biographical directory of the governors of the United States, 1789–1978,* 2:70–71. Westport, Conn.: Meckler Books, 1978.

BALDWIN**

BDFJ, 12.

Coleman, Kenneth, and Charles Stephen Gurr. *Dictionary of Georgia biography,* 1:47–48. Athens: University of Georgia Press, 1983.

DAB, 1–2:530–34, 609–13.

Gatell, Frank Otto. In *The justices of the United States,* ed. Leon Friedman and Fred L. Israel, 1:571–80. New York: Chelsea House, 1969. [Note: The title of every entry in this series is the name of the justice. For the sake of clarity and space, the names are not included here.]

NCAB, 2:257; 5:274; 9:178.

BALL

CAG, 3:99, 122, 131, 647.

Hardy, Stella Pickett. *Colonial families of the southern states of America,* 30–42. Baltimore: Genealogical, 1974.

BANCROFT

CAG, 1:79.

DAB, 1–2:560–61, 564–70.

King, Willard L. *Melville Weston Fuller,* 3. New York: Macmillan, 1950.

NCAB, 4:306; 5:269.

Sobel, Robert. *Biographical directory of the United States executive branch, 1774–1977,* 16. Westport, Conn.: Greenwood Press, 1977.

BARBOUR**

BDAC, 513–14.

DAB, 1–2:590–96.

Green, Raleigh T. *Genealogical and historical notes on Culpepper County, Virginia,* 52–53, 135–45. Baltimore: Regional, 1964.

HFK, 218–19.

The lawyers and lawmakers of Kentucky, 701–10. Chicago: Lewis, n.d. Reprint, Easley, S.C.: Southern Historical Press, 1982.

NCAB, 2:259–60.

BAYARD

APD, 273–98, 546, 582–87, 624–26.

Who was who in America, vol. 9: 1985–1989, 24. Chicago: Marquis, 1989.

BEALE

Biographical and historical memoirs of Louisiana, 1:144. Baton Rouge: Claitor's, 1975.

Louisiana, 593–94.

BEAUREGARD

King, Grace. *Creole families of New Orleans,* 452–60. New York: Macmillan, 1921.

Wakelyn, Jon L. *Biographical dictionary of the Confederacy,* 94–95. Westport, Conn.: Greenwood Press, 1977.

BECNEL

Thomas, Laverne III. *Ledoux: A pioneer Franco-American family,* 239–48. New Orleans: Polyanthus, 1982.

BERMUDEZ*

Arthur, Stanley Clisby. *Old families of Louisiana,* 59–67. Baton Rouge: Claitor's, 1971.

DLB, 1:66.

NCAB, 5:507.

BIRNEY

DAB, 1–2:290–94.

HFK, 70–71.

The lawyers and lawmakers of Kentucky, 703. Chicago: Lewis, n.d. Reprint, Easley, S.C.: Southern Historical Press, 1982.

BLACK**

BDFJ, 22.

Frank, John P. In *The justices of the United States,* ed. Leon Friedman and Fred L. Israel, 3:2321–47. New York: Chelsea House, 1969.

Hamilton, Virginia Van Der Veer. *Hugo Black: The Alabama years,* 8. Baton Rouge: Louisiana State University Press, 1972.

BLAIR**

APD, 218, 575.

BDFJ, 23.

CAG, 5:647, 684.

DAB, 1–2:335–38.

Israel, Fred L. In *The justices of the United States,* ed. Leon Friedman and Fred L. Israel, 1:109–15. New York: Chelsea House, 1969

NCAB, 3:231–32.

BLAIR

APD, 71, 632.

Appleton's cyclopedia of American biography. Vol. 1. N.p.: n.p., n.d.

DAB, 1–2:330.

Sobel, Robert. *Biographical directory of the United States executive branch, 1774–1977,* 28–29. Westport, Conn.: Greenwood Press, 1977.

BLANCHARD*

Barber, Patsy K. *Historic Cotile,* 43–47. N.p.: Baptist Message Press, 1967.

Biographical and historical memoirs of northwest Louisiana, 552. Chicago and Nashville: Southern, 1890. Reprinted by the North Louisiana Historical Society, 1976.

DAB, 1–2:351.

DLB, 1:77–80.

Shreveport men and women builders . . . Shreveport biographies. 61. J. Edward Howe Publisher, 1931.

Stafford, George Mason Graham. *General George Mason Graham of Tyrone plantation and his people,* 397–433. New Orleans: Pelican, 1947.

Who's who in Louisiana and Mississippi, 26. New Orleans: Times-Picayune, 1919.

BLAND

DAB, 1–2:354–57.

NCAB, 7:133–34; 10:160.

BLATCHFORD**

DAB, 1–2:359–60.

NCAB, 25:227.

Paul, Arnold M. In *The justices of the United States,* ed. Leon Friedman and Fred L. Israel, 2:1401–14. New York: Chelsea House, 1969.

BOAGNI

Perrin, William Henry, ed. *Southwest Louisiana, historical and biographical,* 9. Baton Rouge: Claitor's, 1971.

Information provided by Patricia L. Jones and Adele Comeaux in several conversations between 1987 and 1989.

BOLLING

CAG, 5:684.

Hardy, Stella Pickett. *Colonial families of the southern states of America,* 71–80. Baltimore: Genealogical, 1974.

Mackenzie, George Norbury. *Colonial families of the United States of America,* 2:136–41. Baltimore: Genealogical, 1966.

BOND*

DLB, 1:58, 88.

Thomson, James E., ed. *Louisiana today,* 306, 314, 387, 390. New Orleans: Louisiana Society, 1939.

BONDY
Thomas, Laverne III. *Ledoux: A pioneer Franco-American family,* 804–807. New Orleans: Polyanthus, 1982.

BOYLE
BDAC, 584.
DAB, 1–2:532–33.
HFK, 227.

BRADLEY**
BDFJ, 28, 308.
DAB, 1–2:571–73; 9–10:230–33.
Friedman, Leon. In *The justices of the United States,* ed. Leon Friedman and Fred L. Israel, 2:1181–1200. New York: Chelsea House, 1969.

BRANDEIS**
BDFJ, 29.
Mason, Alpheus Thomas. In *The justices of the United States,* ed. Leon Friedman and Fred L. Israel, 3:2043–59. New York: Chelsea House, 1969.
NCAB, D:266.
Paper, Lewis J. *Brandeis,* 17. Englewood Cliffs, N.J.: Prentice Hall, 1983.
Sobel, Robert. *Biographical directory of the United States executive branch, 1774–1977,* 262. Westport, Conn.: Greenwood Press, 1977.

BRASHEAR
Anders, Quintilla Morgan. *Some early families of Lafayette, Louisiana.* N.p.: n.p., 1969.
Broussard, Bernard. *History of St. Mary Parish.* Chap. 14. N.p.: privately published, 1977.
Kilpatrick, Susan M. *Belt Brashear and Amelia Duvall.* N.p.: privately published, n.d.
Sanders, Mary Elizabeth. *Selected annotated abstracts of marriage book 1, St. Mary Parish, Louisiana, 1811–1829,* 84–85. N.p.: privately published, 1973.
Sanders, Mary Elizabeth. *Selected annotated abstracts of St. Mary Parish, Louisiana, court records, 1811–1837,* 3:77–78. N.p.: privately published, 1978.

BREAZEALE
Arthur, Stanley Clisby. *Old families of Louisiana,* 347–51. Baton Rouge: Claitor's, 1971.
Biographical and historical memoirs of northwest Louisiana, 325. Chicago and Nashville: Southern, 1890. Reprinted by the North Louisiana Historical Society, 1976.
Chambers, Henry E. *A history of Louisiana,* 2:334–35, 3:290. Chicago and New York: American Historical Society, 1925.
Historical encyclopedia of Louisiana, 441. N.p.: Louisiana Historical Bureau, n.d.
Louisiana portraits, 44. New Orleans: National Society of the Colonial Dames of America in the State of Louisiana, 1975.
Stafford, George Mason Graham. *General George Mason Graham of Tyrone plantation and his people,* 355. New Orleans: Pelican, 1947.

Thomson, James E., ed. *Louisiana today,* 323. New Orleans: Louisiana Society, 1939.

Williamson, Frederick William, and George T. Goodman. *Eastern Louisiana,* 3:1065. Louisville, Ky.: Historical Record Association, 1939.

BRECK

BDAC, 591.

HFK, 214–15.

NCAB, 11:411.

BRENNAN**

BDFJ, 30.

Friedman, Stephen J. In *The justices of the United States,* ed. Leon Friedman and Fred L. Israel, 4:2849–65. New York: Chelsea House, 1969.

NCAB, I:29.

BRENT

BDAC, 594.

Conrad, Glenn R. William L. Brent, Jeffersonian Republican and Louisiana politician. *Attakapas Gazette* 11 (summer 1976): 67–72.

DLB, 1:108–109.

Louisiana portraits, 45. New Orleans: National Society of the Colonial Dames of America in the State of Louisiana, 1975.

Mackenzie, George Norbury. *Colonial families of the United States of America,* 7:109–11. Baltimore: Genealogical, 1966.

Stafford, George Mason Graham. *General George Mason Graham of Tyrone plantation and his people,* 307–60. New Orleans: Pelican, 1947.

BREWER**

BDFJ, 30.

DAB, 3–4:22–23; 5–6:360–62.

NCAB, 4:236–37.

Paul, Arnold M. In *The justices of the United States,* ed. Leon Friedman and Fred L. Israel, 2:1515–34. New York: Chelsea House, 1969.

See also **FIELD**.

BRIANT

Pourciau, Betty, ed. *St. Martin Parish history,* 134. Baton Rouge: Le Comité des Archives de la Louisiane, 1985.

BROWN

BDFJ, 33.

Green, John W. Six judges of the U.S. district court for Tennessee. *Tennessee Law Review* 17 (June 1943): 888–98.

BRYAN

DAB, 3–4:190–91.

NCAB, 12:452.

BUCKNER
Biographical and historical memoirs of Louisiana, 1:325–26. Baton Rouge: Claitor's, 1975.
CAG, 3:448.
Encyclopedia of Virginia biography, 1:198–99. New York: Lewis Historical, 1915.
Graybar, Lloyd J. The Buckners of Kentucky. *Filson Club Historical Quarterly* 58 (January 1984): 202–18.
Louisiana, 494–95.
NCAB, 16:341–42; 37:34–35.
Sobel, Robert, and John Raimo. *Biographical directory of the governors of the United States, 1789–1978,* 1:198–99. Westport, Conn.: Meckler Books, 1978.
Stickles, Arndt M. *Simon Bolivar Buckner,* 1–3. Chapel Hill: University of North Carolina Press, 1940.

BULLARD*
BDAC, 623.
Bonquois, Dora J. The career of Henry Adams Bullard, Louisiana jurist, legislator, and educator. *Louisiana Historical Quarterly* 23 (October 1940): 995–1106.
DLB, 1:127.
See also **GARLAND***.

BURGER**
BDFJ, 36.
Mackenzie, John P. In *The justices of the United States,* ed. Leon Friedman and Fred L. Israel, 4:3111–42. New York: Chelsea House, 1969.

BURNET
DAB, 3–4:292–96.

BURTON**
BDFJ, 37.
Kirkland, Richard. In *The justices of the United States,* ed. Leon Friedman and Fred L. Israel, 4:2617–27. New York: Chelsea House, 1969.
NCAB, 12:62; G:22–24.

BURWELL
Hardy, Stella Pickett. *Colonial families of the southern states of America,* 94–103. Baltimore: Genealogical, 1974.

BUTLER
Arthur, Stanley Clisby. *Old families of Louisiana,* 352–61. Baton Rouge: Claitor's, 1971.
BDAC, 640, 1320.
DAB, 3–4:371–72.
HFK, 252–70.
Louisiana, 77–79.

Louisiana portraits, 83. New Orleans: National Society of the Colonial Dames of America in the State of Louisiana, 1975.

NCAB, 6:183; 8:85.

Seebold, Herman de Bachelle. *Old Louisiana plantation homes and family trees*, 2:352–58. N.p.: privately published, 1941.

CAFFERY

Anders, Quintilla Morgan. *Some early families of Lafayette, Louisiana*. N.p.: n.p., 1969.

BDAC, 646.

Broussard, Bernard. *History of St. Mary Parish*, 7. N.p.: privately published, 1977.

Caffery, Lucille Roy. The political career of Senator Donelson Caffery. *Louisiana Historical Quarterly* 27 (July 1944): 783–853.

The Caffery family, 1737–1958 (mimeo).

Chambers, Henry E. *A history of Louisiana*, 3:7. Chicago and New York: American Historical Society, 1925.

DLB, 1:140–42.

Hartje, Robert G. *Van Dorn: The life and times of a Confederate general*. Nashville: Vanderbilt University Press, 1967.

Kilpatrick, Susan M. *Belt Brashear and Amelia Duvall*. N.p.: privately published, n.d.

Mayors of Lafayette, 1884–1980. Lafayette: Lafayette Founders Committee, n.d.

NCAB, F:534–35.

The story of Louisiana, 3:203, 205–207. New Orleans: J. F. Hyer, 1960.

Violette, E. M. Donelson Caffery: A Louisiana Democrat out of line. *Louisiana Historical Quarterly* 14 (October 1931): 521–32.

Wood, Sudie Rucker. *The Rucker family genealogy*. Richmond: Old Dominion Press, 1932:535–37.

CAMPBELL**

BDFJ, 41.

DAB, 3–4:456–59.

Gillette, William. In *The justices of the United States*, ed. Leon Friedman and Fred L. Israel, 2:927–39. New York: Chelsea House, 1969.

NCAB, 2:472–73.

CARDOZO**

BDFJ, 42.

Kaufman, Andrew L. In *The justices of the United States*, ed. Leon Friedman and Fred L. Israel, 3:2287–2307. New York: Chelsea House, 1969.

NCAB, D:50–52.

CARLETON*

Dart, William Kernan. The justices of the Supreme Court. *Louisiana Historical Quarterly* 4 (January 1921): 116.

See also **HUNT.**

CARMOUCHE

Carmouche, Edward Moss. *Kindred.* Lake Charles, La.: privately published, 1986.

DLB, 1:152–53.

Historical encyclopedia of Louisiana, 900, 1284. N.p.: Louisiana Historical Bureau, n.d.

Louisiana, 719–20.

CARR

Boddie, John Bennett. *Historical southern families,* 5:130–31. Baltimore: Genealogical, 1967.

DAB, 3–4:515–16.

Genealogies of Virginia families, 1:588–93. Baltimore: Genealogical, 1982.

HFK, 213.

NCAB, 11:449.

Virginia Magazine of History and Biography 2 (1895): 221–25; and 3 (1896): 208–17.

CASS

BDAC, 672.

NCAB, 5:3; 7:528.

CATRON**

BDFJ, 45.

Caldwell, Joshua W. *Sketches of the bench and bar of Tennessee,* 85–92. Knoxville: Ogden Brothers, 1898.

Chandler, Walter. The centenary of Associate Justice John Catron of the United States Supreme Court. *Tennessee Law Review* 15 (December 1937): 32–51.

DAB, 3–4:576–77.

Gatell, Frank Otto. In *The justices of the United States,* ed. Leon Friedman and Fred L. Israel, 1:737–49. New York: Chelsea House, 1969.

NCAB, 2:261–62.

CHASE**

APD, 650.

BDFJ, 46.

DAB, 3–4:27–34.

Friedman, Leon. In *The justices of the United States,* ed. Leon Friedman and Fred L. Israel, 2:1113–28. New York: Chelsea House, 1969.

CHIPMAN

DAB, 3–4:74.

CLAIBORNE

Arthur, Stanley Clisby. *Old families of Louisiana,* 143–48. Baton Rouge: Claitor's, 1971.

BDAC, 694.

Biographical and historical memoirs of Louisiana, 1:348–49. Baton Rouge: Claitor's, 1975.

Biographies of Louisiana judges, 93–94. New Orleans: Louisiana District Judges Association, 1985.

Boddie, John Bennett. *Historical southern families,* 5:168–69. Baltimore: Genealogical, 1967.

CAG, 1:19, 550; 3:123; 4:660; 7:633–34.

Chambers, Henry E. *A history of Louisiana,* 3:370. Chicago and New York: American Historical Society, 1925.

Curet, Bernard. *Our pride: Pt. Coupee,* 15. Baton Rouge: Moran, 1981.

Louisiana, 102–103.

NCAB, 3:219; 10:74; 11:391; 12:558; 38:455–56.

Reeves, Miriam G. *The governors of Louisiana,* 40–42. Gretna, La.: Pelican, 1972.

Riffel, Judy, ed. *A history of Pt. Coupee Parish and its families,* 168–71. Baton Rouge: Le Comité des Archives de la Louisiane, 1983.

CLARK**

BDFJ, 50.

Current biography yearbook 1945: 107–11.

NCAB, H:20–22.

Who was who in America, 1897–1942, 1007. Chicago: Marquis, 1943.

CLARK

Coleman, Kenneth, and Charles Stephen Gurr. *Dictionary of Georgia biography,* 1:190–94. Athens: University of Georgia Press, 1983.

CLARKE**

BDFJ, 51.

Burner, David. In *The justices of the United States,* ed. Leon Friedman and Fred L. Israel, 3:2077–87. New York: Chelsea House, 1969.

DAB, suppl. 3, pp. 167–68.

NCAB, A:248–49.

Warner, Hoyt L. *Life of Mr. Justice Clarke.* Cleveland: Western Reserve University Press, 1959.

CLARKSON

CAG, 1:78, 131, 208, 379, 639.

DAB, 3–4:166.

CLIFFORD**

BDFJ, 52.

Gillette, William. In *The justices of the United States,* ed. Leon Friedman and Fred L. Israel, 2:963–75. New York: Chelsea House, 1969.

CAG, 1:503–504.

DAB, 3–4:216–18.

COBB

Coleman, Kenneth, and Charles Stephen Gurr. *Dictionary of Georgia biography,* 1:202–205. Athens: University of Georgia Press, 1983.

DAB, 3–4:239–47.

Members of Congress since 1789, 42. Washington: Congressional Quarterly, 1985.

Sobel, Robert. *Biographical directory of the United States executive branch, 1774–1977*, 65–66. Westport, Conn.: Greenwood Press, 1977.

COCO

Biographical and historical memoirs of northwest Louisiana, 626–28. Chicago and Nashville: Southern, 1890. Reprinted by the North Louisiana Historical Society, 1976.

Gremillion, William Nelson, Sr., and Loucille Edwards Gremillion. *Commentaries on some Avoyelles families*, 24–28. San Antonio: privately published, 1976.

Gremillion, William Nelson, Sr., and Loucille Edwards Gremillion. *Some early families of Avoyelles Parish, Louisiana*, 1:74–83. Eunice, La.: Hebert, 1980.

COKE

BDAC, 718.

COLLINS

APD, 309.

COLQUITT

BDAC, 723.

CONY

King, Willard L. *Melville Weston Fuller*, 5. New York: Macmillan, 1950.

NCAB, 6:314–15.

Sobel, Robert, and John Raimo. *Biographical directory of the governors of the United States, 1789–1978*, 2:613–14. Westport, Conn.: Meckler Books, 1978.

The twentieth-century biographical dictionary of notable Americans. Vol. 2. Boston: Biographical Society, 1904.

COSBY

Anderson, W. P. *The early descendants of William Overton and Elizabeth Waters of Virginia and allied families*, 5:102–103. N.p.: privately published, 1938.

Biographical encyclopedia of Kentucky, 251–52. Cincinnati: J. M. Armstrong, 1878.

CAG, abridged, 567.

NCAB, 5:498.

Warner, Ezra J. *Generals in gray*, 64. Baton Rouge: Louisiana State University Press, 1959.

CRITTENDEN

BDAC, 755.

DAB, 3–4:545–49.

HFK, 247–49.

CROW

Anders, Quintilla Morgan. *Some early families of Lafayette, Louisiana*. N.p.: n.p., 1969.

The Caffery family, 1737–1958 (mimeo).

Kilpatrick, Susan M. *Belt Brashear and Amelia Duvall*, 56–71. N.p.: privately published, n.d.

CURTIS**

BDFJ, 62.

DAB, 3–4:609–11, 613–14.

Gillette, William. In *The justices of the United States*, ed. Leon Friedman and Fred L. Israel, 2:895–908. New York: Chelsea House, 1969.

NCAB, 1:395; 2:472.

CUSHING**

BDFJ, 62.

CAG, 2:289.

DAB, 3–4:632–35.

Johnson, Herbert Allan. In *The justices of the United States*, ed. Leon Friedman and Fred L. Israel, 1:57–70. New York: Chelsea House, 1969.

NCAB, 12:548.

The twentieth-century biographical dictionary of notable Americans. Vol. 3. Boston: Biographical Society, 1904.

DANIEL**

BDAC, 775.

BDFJ, 64–65.

DAB, 5–6:67–69.

NCAB, 2:174; 10:33.

The twentieth-century biographical dictionary of notable Americans. Vol. 3. Boston: Biographical Society, 1904.

DAVIDSON (in network 45-E)

Biographical cyclopedia of the Commonwealth of Kentucky, 427–29. Chicago and Philadelphia: John M. Greshman, 1896.

HFK, 188–89, 206–207.

DAVIDSON (in network 45-M)

Barber, Patsy K. *Historic Cotile*, 47–48. Baptist Message Press, 1967.

DAVIS**

BDFJ, 66.

DAB, 5–6:110–12, 119–21.

Henig, Gerald S. *Henry Winter Davis*. New York: Twayne, 1973.

King, Willard L. *Lincoln's manager: David Davis*. Cambridge: Harvard University Press, 1960.

Kutler, Stanley I. In *The justices of the United States*, ed. Leon Friedman and Fred L. Israel, 2:1045–53. New York: Chelsea House, 1969.

NCAB, 2:474–75.

The twentieth-century biographical dictionary of notable Americans. Vol. 3. Boston: Biographical Society, 1904.

DAVIS (in network 38)

BDAC, 784.

DAB, 5–6:137.

Rowland, Dunbar. *Courts, judges, and lawyers of Mississippi*, 1:51. Jackson, Miss.: Hederman Bros., 1935.

DAVIS (in network 34)

BDAC, 781–82.

DAB, 5–6:113–14.

NCAB, 2:225.

DAWKINS*

BDFJ, 68.

Biographies of Louisiana judges, 19–20. 1956. Reprint, Baton Rouge: Claitor's, 1971.

Chambers, Henry E. *A history of Louisiana*, 2:237, 240, 246. Chicago and New York: American Historical Society, 1925.

Louisiana, 120, 509.

Mackenzie, George Norbury. *Colonial families of the United States of America*, 5:167. Baltimore: Genealogical, 1966.

DAY**

BDFJ, 69.

DAB, 17–18:250–51.

NCAB, 3:522; 5:224; 32:22.

Sobel, Robert. *Biographical directory of the United States executive branch, 1774–1977*, 88–89. Westport, Conn.: Greenwood Press, 1977.

Watts, James F., Jr. In *The justices of the United States*, ed. Leon Friedman and Fred L. Israel, 3:1773–89. New York: Chelsea House, 1969.

DE BLANC*

Anders, Quintilla Morgan. *Some early families of Lafayette, Louisiana.* N.p.: n.p., 1969.

Arthur, Stanley Clisby. *Old families of Louisiana*, 211–13. Baton Rouge: Claitor's, 1971.

Historical encyclopedia of Louisiana, 1073. N.p.: Louisiana Historical Bureau, n.d.

Information provided by Catherine de Blanc, October 26, 1987.

DE LASSUS

Arthur, Stanley Clisby. *Old families of Louisiana*, 342–46. Baton Rouge: Claitor's, 1971.

DLB, 1:227.

DE LA VERGNE

Arthur, Stanley Clisby. *Old families of Louisiana*, 59–67. Baton Rouge: Claitor's, 1971.

Kendall, John S. *History of New Orleans*, 3:1000. Chicago and New York: Lewis, 1922.

Louisiana, 124–25.

Mackenzie, George Norbury. *Colonial families of the United States of America*, 2:227–28. Baltimore: Genealogical, 1966.

DE LA VILLEBEUVRE

Arthur, Stanley Clisby. *Old families of Louisiana,* 274–78. Baton Rouge: Claitor's, 1971.

King, Grace. *Creole families of New Orleans,* 343–49. New York: Macmillan, 1921.

Reeves, Miriam G. *The governors of Louisiana,* 16–18. Gretna, La.: Pelican, 1972.

DERBIGNY*

Arthur, Stanley Clisby. *Old families of Louisiana,* 342–46. Baton Rouge: Claitor's, 1971.

DLB, 1:238–39.

DESTREHAN

Arthur, Stanley Clisby. *Old families of Louisiana,* 414–16. Baton Rouge: Claitor's, 1971.

DLB, 1:241–42.

Harvey, Horace H., Katherine Harvey Roger, and completed by Louise Destrehan Roger D'Oliveira. *To reach afar: Memoirs and biography of the Destrehan and Harvey families of Louisiana.* Clearwater, Fla.: Hercules, 1974.

Seebold, Herman de Bachelle. *Old Louisiana plantation homes and family trees,* 2:180–83. N.p.: privately published, 1941.

DICKINSON

Boddie, John Bennett. *Historical southern families,* 5:174–84. Baltimore: Genealogical, 1967.

NCAB, 14:410–11.

DOUGLAS**

BDFJ, 75.

Douglas, William O. *Go east, young man: The early years.* New York: Random House, 1974.

Frank, John P. In *The justices of the United States,* ed. Leon Friedman and Fred L. Israel, 4:2447–70. New York: Chelsea House, 1969.

The story of Louisiana, 4:501–504. New Orleans: J. F. Hyer, 1960.

DUANE

APD, 551, 635.

CAG, 1:265–67.

DAB, 5–6:464–67.

DU BIGNON

CAG, 6:288.

DUER

APD, 551, 635.

DAB, 5–6:485–88.

DUGAS

Biographical and historical memoirs of Louisiana, 1:389–90. Baton Rouge: Claitor's, 1975.

Louisiana, 154.

DUKE

Hardy, Stella Pickett. *Colonial families of the southern states of America,* 194–200. Baltimore: Genealogical, 1974.

DUPRE

Biographical and historical memoirs of Louisiana, 2:477–78, 481. Baton Rouge: Claitor's, 1975.

Chambers, Henry E. *A history of Louisiana,* 2:378–79. Chicago and New York: American Historical Society, 1925.

DLB, 1:270–72.

Perrin, William Henry, ed. *Southwest Louisiana, historical and biographical,* 35. Baton Rouge: Claitor's, 1971.

Wakelyn, Jon L. *Biographical dictionary of the Confederacy,* 175. Westport, Conn.: Greenwood Press, 1977.

DUVALL**

BDFJ, 79–80.

CAG, 5:187.

DAB, suppl. 1, pp. 272–74.

Dillard, Irving. In *The justices of the United States,* ed. Leon Friedman and Fred L. Israel, 1:419–29. New York: Chelsea House, 1969.

Hardy, Stella Pickett. *Colonial families of the southern states of America,* 201–208. Baltimore: Genealogical, 1974.

Kilpatrick, Susan M. *Belt Brashear and Amelia Duvall,* 7–11. N.p.: privately published, n.d.

Mackenzie, George Norbury. *Colonial families of the United States of America,* 1:142–51. Baltimore: Genealogical, 1966.

NCAB, 2:468.

EDWARDS

APD, 654.

BDAC, 848, 849, 850, 974.

DAB, 5–6:29–30, 41–43

ELLSWORTH**

BDAC, 858–59.

CAG, 4:320.

DAB, 5–6:110–16.

NCAB, 1:22; 7:516; 10:335.

EUSTIS*

Current biography yearbook 1960: 42–44.

DAB, 5–6:191–94; 13–14:258–59.

DLB, 1:273, 289–90.

King, Grace. *Creole families of New Orleans,* 446–51. New York: Macmillan, 1921.

NCAB, 1:135, 462; 3:153; 5:372–73; 7:191, 509; 49:483.

Thomas, Laverne III. *Ledoux: A pioneer Franco-American family,* 590–91. New Orleans: Polyanthus, 1982.

Who was who in America, vol. 6: 1974–1976, 41. Chicago: Marquis, 1976.

FAIRFAX

Burke's presidential families of the United States of America, 48. London: Burke's Peerage, 1975.

DAB, 5–6:255–57.

Griffith, Lucille. *The Virginia House of Burgesses, 1750–1774,* 118–19, 124. Northport, Ala.: Colonial Press, 1963.

NCAB, 4:459.

FAVROT

Arthur, Stanley Clisby. *Old families of Louisiana,* 375–80. Baton Rouge: Claitor's, 1971.

Biographical and historical memoirs of Louisiana, 1:409. Baton Rouge: Claitor's, 1975.

Chambers, Henry E. *A history of Louisiana,* 2:76, 82–83. Chicago and New York: American Historical Society, 1925.

Kellough, Elizabeth, and Leona Mayeux. *Chronicles of West Baton Rouge,* 241–46. Baton Rouge: Kennedy Print Shop, 1979.

Louisiana, 158–60, 375–76.

The story of Louisiana, 2:63, 261. New Orleans: J. F. Hyer, 1960.

Thomas, Laverne III. *Ledoux: A pioneer Franco-American family,* 582. New Orleans: Polyanthus, 1982.

FENNER*

DLB, 1:298–99.

Dufour, Charles L. *Darwin Fenner: A life of service.* New Orleans: privately published, 1984.

NCAB, 16:224–25; 39:486–87;

Seebold, Herman de Bachelle. *Old Louisiana plantation homes and family trees,* 1:334, 355–56. N.p.: privately published, 1941.

FIELD**

McClosky, Robert. In *The justices of the United States,* ed. Leon Friedman and Fred L. Israel, 2:1069–89. New York: Chelsea House, 1969.

See also **BREWER****.

FIELD

Green, Raleigh T. *Genealogical and historical notes on Culpepper County, Virginia,* 57–58. Baltimore: Regional, 1964.

NCAB, 12:485.

FISH

APD, 558, 655.

Members of Congress since 1789, 61. Washington: Congressional Quarterly, 1985.

FLEMING

Biographies of Louisiana judges, 88–89. New Orleans: Louisiana District Judges Association, 1985.

Chambers, Henry E. *A history of Louisiana,* 3:242–43. Chicago and New York: American Historical Society, 1925.

Fruge, J. Cleveland, ed. *Biographies of Louisiana judges,* 89. Baton Rouge: Claitor's, 1971.

Pourciau, Betty, ed. *St. Martin Parish history,* 39. Baton Rouge: Le Comité des Archives de la Louisiane, 1985.

FORTIER

Arthur, Stanley Clisby. *Old families of Louisiana,* 44–48. Baton Rouge: Claitor's, 1971.

Chambers, Henry E. *A history of Louisiana,* 3:349–50. Chicago and New York: American Historical Society, 1925.

Louisiana, 166–70.

NCAB, 9:135.

FOSTER

BDAC, 908–909.

Broussard, Bernard. *History of St. Mary Parish,* 121. N.p.: privately published, 1977.

Citizen's guide to the Louisiana legislature, 51. Baton Rouge: Public Affairs Research Council, 1988.

Historical encyclopedia of Louisiana, 959–60. N.p.: Louisiana Historical Bureau, n.d.

Perrin, William Henry, ed. *Southwest Louisiana, historical and biographical,* 108. Baton Rouge: Claitor's, 1971.

Romero, Sidney James. The political career of Murphy James Foster, governor of Louisiana. *Louisiana Historical Quarterly* 28 (October 1945): 1129–1243.

Sanders, Mary Elizabeth. *Annotated abstracts of the successions of St. Mary Parish, Louisiana,* 165–66. N.p.: privately published, 1972.

Sanders, Mary Elizabeth. *Selected annotated abstracts of St. Mary Parish, Louisiana, court records, 1811–1837,* 64–65. N.p.: privately published, 1978.

Sanders, Mary Elizabeth. *Selected annotated abstracts of marriage book 1, St. Mary Parish, Louisiana, 1811–1829,* 16, 127. N.p.: privately published, 1973.

The story of Louisiana, 3:255–57. New Orleans: J. F. Hyer, 1960.

Correspondence with Mrs. Murphy James Foster, June 12, 1986.

FOURNET*

Fruge, J. Cleveland, ed. *Biographies of Louisiana judges,* 9–12. New Orleans: Louisiana District Judges Association, 1965.

Perrin, William Henry, ed. *Southwest Louisiana, historical and biographical,* 326–27. Baton Rouge: Claitor's, 1971.

Pourciau, Betty, ed. *St. Martin Parish history,* 7, 12, 169–71. Baton Rouge: Le Comité des Archives de la Louisiane, 1985.

The story of Louisiana, 3:230–31. New Orleans: J. F. Hyer, 1960.

Correspondence with Kenneth L. Fournet, November 26, 1985.

FRITCHIE

Thomas, Laverne III. *Ledoux: A pioneer Franco-American family,* 328. New Orleans: Polyanthus, 1982.

FRUGE

Fruge, J. Cleveland, ed. *Biographies of Louisiana judges,* 35–36. Baton Rouge: Claitor's, 1971.

FULLER**

BDFJ, 96.

DAB, 19–20:371–72.

King, Willard L. *Melville Weston Fuller.* New York: Macmillan, 1950.

NCAB, 1:31–32; 7:503; 16:287–88; 33:121–22.

Schiffman, Irving. In *The justices of the United States,* ed. Leon Friedman and Fred L. Israel, 2:1471–95. New York: Chelsea House, 1969.

The twentieth-century biographical dictionary of notable Americans. Vol. 4. Boston: Biographical Society, 1904.

GADSDEN

DAB, 7–8:82–84.

NCAB, 1:76.

The twentieth-century biographical dictionary of notable Americans. Vol. 4. Boston: Biographical Society, 1904.

GARLAND*

BDAC, 930.

Chambers, Henry E. *A history of Louisiana,* 3:137. Chicago and New York: American Historical Society, 1925.

DLB, 1:335–36.

Louisiana, 614.

Perrin, William Henry, ed. *Southwest Louisiana, historical and biographical,* 46. Baton Rouge: Claitor's, 1971.

See also **BULLARD***.

GAY

Arthur, Stanley Clisby. *Old families of Louisiana,* 72–80. Baton Rouge: Claitor's, 1971.

BDAC, 934–35.

NCAB, 16:224–25; 42:336.

Seebold, Herman de Bachelle. *Old Louisiana plantation homes and family trees,* 1:336–41. N.p.: privately published, 1941.

The story of Louisiana, 2:370–71, 609, 611. New Orleans: J. F. Hyer, 1960.

Thomas, Laverne III. *Ledoux: A pioneer Franco-American family,* 280. New Orleans: Polyanthus, 1982.

GAYARRÉ

DLB, 1:340–41.

King, Grace. *Creole families of New Orleans,* 239–90. New York: Macmillan, 1921.

GIRARD

Anders, Quintilla Morgan. *Some early families of Lafayette, Louisiana.* N.p.: n.p., 1969.

Biographical and historical memoirs of Louisiana, 2:482–83. Baton Rouge: Claitor's, 1975.

Mayors of Lafayette, 1884–1980. Lafayette, La.: Lafayette Founders Committee, n.d.

GOODRICH

BDAC, 956–57.

DAB, 7–8:397–403.

NCAB, 2:138; 4:303–304.

GORDON

Stafford, George Mason Graham. *The Wells family of Louisiana and allied families,* 89. Baton Rouge: Claitor's, 1976.

GORDY

Broussard, Bernard. *History of St. Mary Parish,* 117. N.p.: privately published, 1977.

Chambers, Henry E. *A history of Louisiana,* 3:345–46. Chicago and New York: American Historical Society, 1925.

DLB, 1:352.

Louisiana, 181–82.

GRAY**

BDFJ, 107–108.

DAB, 7–8:514–15, 518–19, 523–24.

Filler, Louis. In *The justices of the United States,* ed. Leon Friedman and Fred L. Israel, 2:1379–89. New York: Chelsea House, 1969.

The twentieth-century biographical dictionary of notable Americans. Vol. 4. Boston: Biographical Society, 1904.

GREEN

DAB, 7–8:538–42.

Hardy, Stella Pickett. *Colonial families of the southern states of America,* 238–47. Baltimore: Genealogical, 1974.

The lawyers and lawmakers of Kentucky, 703. Chicago: Lewis, n.d. Reprint, Easley, S.C.: Southern Historical Press, 1982.

GRIFFITH

Biographical cyclopedia of the Commonwealth of Kentucky, 160–62. Chicago and Philadelphia: John M. Greshman, 1896.

GRIMKE

CAG, 1:308.

The twentieth-century biographical dictionary of notable Americans. Vol. 4. Boston: Biographical Society, 1904.

GUION

Louisiana, 724, 756–58.

NCAB, 13:489; 24:382–83.

Sobel, Robert, and John Raimo. *Biographical directory of the governors of the United States, 1789–1978,* 2:809–10. Westport, Conn.: Meckler Books, 1978.

GUSS

Chambers, Henry E. *A history of Louisiana,* 3:220. Chicago and New York: American Historical Society, 1925.

HALE

APD, 657.

BDFJ, 112–13.

CAG, 1:504.

HARBESON

HFK, 109–10.

HARDIN

HFK, 177–83.

NCAB, 12:146–47.

HARLAN** (both justices)

BDFJ, 115–16.

CAG, 1:149, 928; 2:220.

DAB, 7–8:267–69.

Filler, Louis. In *The justices of the United States,* ed. Leon Friedman and Fred L. Israel, 2:1281–95, 4:2803–20. New York: Chelsea House, 1969.

Hartz, Louis. John M. Harlan in Kentucky, 1855–1877: The study of his pre-court political career. *Filson Club Historical Quarterly* 14 (January 1940): 17–40.

NCAB, 11:142–43; 45:534–35; I:27–29.

The twentieth-century biographical dictionary of notable Americans. Vol. 5. Boston: Biographical Society, 1904.

HARRIS

Boddie, John Bennett. *Historical southern families,* 5:128. Baltimore: Genealogical, 1967.

Mackenzie, George Norbury. *Colonial families of the United States of America,* 7:265–66. Baltimore: Genealogical, 1966.

HARRISON

APD, 217–38, 628–29.

HARVIE

BDAC, 1020.

Hardy, Stella Pickett. *Colonial families of the southern states of America,* 347. Baltimore: Genealogical, 1974.

HAZARD

CAG, 1:491.

HELM

HFK, 216–20.

McMurtry, R. Gerald. General Ben Hardin Helm: Kentucky brother-in-law of Abraham Lincoln. *Filson Club Historical Quarterly* 32 (July 1958): 311–28.

NCAB, 13:7.

HOGE

CAG, 7:463.

Goff, John S. Mr. Justice Trimble of the United States Supreme Court. *Register of the Kentucky Historical Society* 58 (January 1960): 6–28.

The twentieth-century biographical dictionary of notable Americans. Vol. 5. Boston: Biographical Society, 1904.

HOLLOMAN

Chambers, Henry E. *A history of Louisiana,* 3:102, 182. Chicago and New York: American Historical Society, 1925.

Material supplied by Rowena Spencer, M.D., December 28, 1988.

HOLMES

Boddie, John Bennett. *Historical southern families,* 5:139–40. Baltimore: Genealogical, 1967.

Sobel, Robert, and John Raimo. *Biographical directory of the governors of the United States, 1789–1978,* 3:1122–23. Westport, Conn.: Meckler Books, 1978.

HOLMES**

Bowen, Catherine Drinke. *Yankee from Olympus: Justice Holmes and his family,* 15. Boston: Little, Brown, 1944.

DAB, 9–10:160–61, 169–76.

Freund, Paul A. In *The justices of the United States,* ed. Leon Friedman and Fred L. Israel, 3:1755–62. New York: Chelsea House, 1969.

NCAB, 27:1–4.

HORNBLOWER

See **BRADLEY****.

HUGHES**

Danelski, David J., and Joseph S. Tulchin. *The autobiographical notes of Charles Evans Hughs.* Cambridge: Harvard University Press, 1973.

Hendel, Samuel. In *The justices of the United States,* ed. Leon Friedman and Fred L. Israel, 3:1893–1915. New York: Chelsea House, 1969.

NCAB, 23:178; 39:1–7; C:61–62.

Sobel, Robert. *Biographical directory of the United States executive branch, 1774–1977,* 177–78. Westport, Conn.: Greenwood Press, 1977.

HUNT

BDAC, 1097.

BDFJ, 134.

DAB, 9–10:382–83, 396–97.

Dart, William Kernan. The justices of the Supreme Court. *Louisiana Historical Quarterly* 4 (January 1921): 116.

DLB, 1:417–19.

NCAB, 4:244–45.

HYMAN*

Arthur, Stanley Clisby. *Old families of Louisiana,* 277. Baton Rouge: Claitor's, 1971.

DLB, 1:421–22, 572–73.

NCAB, 12:253.

INNES

HFK, 192–95.

IREDELL**

DAB, 9–10:492–93.

Israel, Fred L. In *The justices of the United States,* ed. Leon Friedman and Fred L. Israel, 1:121–32. New York: Chelsea House, 1969.

NCAB, 1:23–24; 4:423.

Sobel, Robert, and John Raimo. *Biographical directory of the governors of the United States, 1789–1978,* 3:1124. Westport, Conn.: Meckler Books, 1978.

IRION

BDAC, 1106.

Landers, John Poindexter, and Robert Downs Poindexter. *Poingdestre-Poindexter: A Norman family through the ages, 1250–1977.* Austin: privately published, 1977.

Louisiana, 217–19.

JACKSON** (Howell E.)

DAB, 9–10:561–62.

CAG, 3:607.

NCAB, 8:243–45.

Schiffman, Irving. In *The justices of the United States,* ed. Leon Friedman and Fred L. Israel, 2:1603–15. New York: Chelsea House, 1969.

JACKSON** (Robert H.)

BDFJ, 138–39.

Gernhart, Eugene C. *America's advocate: Robert H. Jackson,* 1–34. New York: Bobbs-Merrill, 1958.

Kurland, Philip B. In *The justices of the United States,* ed. Leon Friedman and Fred L. Israel, 4:2543–71. New York: Chelsea House, 1969.

NCAB, G:20–22.

JACKSON

DAB, 9–10:534–35.

NCAB, 5:401; 28:400–401.

The twentieth-century biographical dictionary of notable Americans. Vol. 6. Boston: Biographical Society, 1904.

JASTREMSKI

Baton Rouge story, 19. Baton Rouge: Baton Rouge Foundation for Historical Louisiana, 1967.

Louisiana, 222–23.

JAY**

APD, 553, 583.

BDFJ, 139–40.

CAG, 1:78, 639.

DAB, 9–10:4–12.

JEFFERSON

Burke's presidential families of the United States of America, 97–127. London: Burke's Peerage, 1975.

JOHNSON** (Thomas)

BDFJ, 142.

CAG, 1:245.

DAB, 9–10:90–91, 121–22.

Delaplaine, Edward S. *The life of Thomas Johnson.* New York: Grafton Press, 1927.

Johnson, Herbert Alan. In *The justices of the United States,* ed. Leon Friedman and Fred L. Israel, 1:149–58. New York: Chelsea House, 1969.

NCAB, 4:182.

Warner, Ezra J. *Generals in gray,* 155–57. Baton Rouge: Louisiana State University Press, 1959.

JOHNSON** (William)

DAB, 9–10:108–109, 128–29.

Morgan, Donald G. *Justice William Johnson, the first dissenter.* Columbia: University of South Carolina Press, 1954.

Morgan, Donald. In *The justices of the United States,* ed. Leon Friedman and Fred L. Israel, 1:355–72. New York: Chelsea House, 1969.

NCAB, 2:467; 12:164.

Sobel, Robert, and John Raimo. *Biographical directory of the governors of the United States, 1789–1978,* 4:1396–97. Westport, Conn.: Meckler Books, 1978.

The twentieth-century biographical dictionary of notable Americans. Vol. 6. Boston: Biographical Society, 1904.

JOHNSTON

DAB, 9–10:140, 150–51.

JONES

Chambers, Henry E. *A history of Louisiana,* 2:123–24. Chicago and New York: American Historical Society, 1925.

KEAN

APD, 588, 661.

Current biography yearbook 1985: 215–19.

KEY

DAB, 9–10:362–63.

Mackenzie, George Norbury. *Colonial families of the United States of America*, 1:302–304. Baltimore: Genealogical, 1966.

Sobel, Robert, and John Raimo. *Biographical directory of the governors of the United States, 1789–1978*, 2:558, 646. Westport, Conn.: Meckler Books, 1978.

The twentieth-century biographical dictionary of notable Americans. Vol. 6. Boston: Biographical Society, 1904.

KING*

DLB, 1:465.

Feldhauser, Goode King. General John Edwards King of Kentucky. In *Genealogies of Kentucky families from the Register of the Kentucky Historical Society*, 1:643–48. Baltimore: Genealogical, 1981.

Fontenot, Keith P. The life and times of Judge George King. *Attakapas Gazette* 19 (fall 1984): 107–15.

See also **IRION.**

LABAUVE*

Dart, William Kernan. The justices of the Supreme Court. *Louisiana Historical Quarterly* 4 (January 1921): 120.

Grace, Albert L. *The heart of the sugar bowl: The story of Iberville*, 95–98. Plaquemine, La.: privately published, 1946.

Riffel, Judy. *Iberville Parish history*, 267–69. Baton Rouge: Le Comité des Archives de la Louisiane, 1985.

LAMAR** (both justices)

CAG, 1:471, 575, 674, 1000; 3:562–63; 6:288, 787.

Cate, Wirt Armistead. *Lucius Q. C. Lamar: Secession and reunion*, 8–22, 70, and 509. Chapel Hill: University of North Carolina Press, 1935.

Coleman, Kenneth, and Charles Stephen Gurr. *Dictionary of Georgia biography*, 2:591–98. Athens: University of Georgia Press, 1983.

DAB, 9–10:549–54.

Members of Congress since 1789, 39, 95. Washington: Congressional Quarterly, 1985.

NCAB, 1:37; 6:187.

The twentieth-century biographical dictionary of notable Americans. Vol. 6. Boston: Biographical Society, 1904.

See also **RUCKER.**

LAND*

Biographical and historical memoirs of Louisiana, 2:485–87. Baton Rouge: Claitor's, 1975.

Biographical and historical memoirs of northwest Louisiana, 78–79. Chicago and Nashville: Southern, 1890. Reprinted by the North Louisiana Historical Society, 1976.

Louisiana, 241–42, 535–36.

Thomson, James E., ed. *Louisiana today,* 143, 173, 243, 378. New Orleans: Louisiana Society, 1939.

Who's who in Louisiana and Mississippi, 229–30. New Orleans: Times-Picayune, 1919.

LASTRAPES
Louisiana, 726–27.

LAUVE
Riffel, Judy. *Iberville Parish history,* 94, 278–84. Baton Rouge: Le Comité des Archives de la Louisiane, 1985.

LEA
Boddie, John Bennett. *Historical southern families,* 5:220–26. Baltimore: Genealogical, 1967.

LEBLANC*
Biographical and historical memoirs of Louisiana, 1:538–39. Baton Rouge: Claitor's, 1975.

Chambers, Henry E. *A history of Louisiana,* 2:332–33, 346. Chicago and New York: American Historical Society, 1925.

Citizen's guide to the 1972 Louisiana legislature, 54. Baton Rouge: Public Affairs Research Council, 1972.

Louisiana, 775–79.

Membership in the legislature of Louisiana, 1880–1980, 8–9. Baton Rouge: Louisiana Legislative Council, 1979.

The story of Louisiana, 2:407–409, 471–73. New Orleans: J. F. Hyer, 1960.

Thomson, James E., ed. *Louisiana today,* 350, 403. New Orleans: Louisiana Society, 1939.

LEDOUX
Thomas, Laverne III. *Ledoux: A pioneer Franco-American family,* 120–43. New Orleans: Polyanthus, 1982.

LEE
APD, 49–82, 630–32.

Correspondence with David Philip Halle, Jr., genealogist with the Society of the Lees of Virginia, September 6, 1989.

LEMMON*
Biographies of Louisiana judges, 21, 127. New Orleans: Louisiana District Judges Association, 1985.

LEONARD*
BDAC, 849, 1212.
DLB, 1:503–504.
NCAB, 5:387–88.

LEVY*

BDAC, 1214.

Biographical and historical memoirs of northwest Louisiana, 358–59. Chicago and Nashville: Southern, 1890. Reprinted by the North Louisiana Historical Society, 1976.

DLB, 1:508–509.

LEWIS (network 44)

APD, 549.

DAB, 11–12:214–15, 222–23.

LEWIS (network 45-B)

CAG, 1:557–58, 625–26, 687, 773–74.

DAB, 11–12:214.

HFK, 84–91.

NCAB, 5:122.

Who was who in America: Historical volume, 1607–1896, 383–84. Chicago: Marquis, 1967.

LINCOLN

Burke's presidential families of the United States of America, 293–303. London: Burke's Peerage, 1975.

DAB, 7–8:268–69; 11–12:266–67.

Purvis, Thomas L. The making of a myth: Abraham Lincoln's family background in the perspective of Jacksonian politics. *Journal of the Illinois State Historical Society* 75 (spring 1982): 148–60.

LIPPITT

APD, 308.

DAB, 11–12:289.

Sobel, Robert, and John Raimo. *Biographical directory of the governors of the United States, 1789–1978*, 4:1353–54, 1361–62. Westport, Conn.: Meckler Books, 1978.

LIVINGSTON**

APD, 83–122, 541–59, 633–35.

BDAC, 1226–27.

Birmingham, Stephen. *America's secret aristocracy*, 18–45. New York: Berkley Books, 1987.

Kallenbach, Joseph E., and Jessamine S. Kallenbach. *American state governors, 1776–1976*, 73. Dobbs Ferry, N.Y.: Oceana, 1976.

NCAB, 2:396–97; 3:306–307; 5:293; 13:177; 24:57–58.

Padgett, James A. The ancestry of Edward Livingston of Louisiana: The Livingston family. *Louisiana Historical Quarterly* 19 (October 1936): 900–937.

The Livingston family. *Louisiana Historical Quarterly* 19 (October 1936): 900–937.

Correspondence with Congressman Robert L. Livingston, December 17, 1986, and February 5, 1987.

LOGAN

HFK, 117–229.

NCAB, 4:526.

Talbert, Charles Gano. John Logan: 1747–1807. *Filson Club Historical Quarterly* 36 (April 1962): 128–50.

LONGSTREET

Biographical and historical memoirs of Mississippi, 359. Chicago: Goodspeed, 1891.

Rowland, Dunbar. *Courts, judges, and lawyers of Mississippi,* 1:130. Jackson, Miss.: Hederman Bros., 1935.

Wakelyn, Jon L. *Biographical dictionary of the Confederacy,* 288–89. Westport, Conn.: Greenwood Press, 1977.

LOWELL

DAB, 11–12:453–70.

McCALEB*

Biographical and historical memoirs of Louisiana, 2:212–14. Baton Rouge: Claitor's, 1975.

DAB, 11–12:560–61.

DLB, 1:530–31.

Fruge, J. Cleveland, ed. *Biographies of Louisiana judges,* 10–11. Baton Rouge: Claitor's, 1971.

Louisiana, 268–69.

NCAB, 26:390–91.

Ruffin, Minnie Markette, and Lilla McLure. General Soloman Weathersbee Downs. *Louisiana Historical Quarterly* 17 (January 1934): 5–47.

McCLUNG

BDFJ, 183.

Hardy, Stella Pickett. *Colonial families of the southern states of America,* 346. Baltimore: Genealogical, 1974.

HFK, 39, 108.

NCAB, 3:212.

McDOWELL

BDAC, 1295.

Gray, Laman. Ephraim McDowell, father of abdominal surgery: Biographical data. *Filson Club Historical Quarterly* 43 (July 1969): 216–29.

HFK, 17–26, 214.

NCAB, 2:173.

McENERY*

DAB, 11–12:39.

DLB, 1:534–35.

Historical encyclopedia of Louisiana, 206–207. N.p.: Louisiana Historical Bureau, n.d.

Kendall, John S. *History of New Orleans,* 1:345, 356; 2:496, 498–99. Chicago and New York: Lewis, 1922.

NCAB, 10:81–83.

Reeves, Miriam G. *The governors of Louisiana,* 83–85. Gretna, La.: Pelican, 1972.

McKEAN

BDAC, 1303.

DAB, 11–12:77–82.

McKERRAL

Broussard, Bernard. *History of St. Mary Parish,* 107–108. N.p.: privately published, 1977.

The story of Louisiana, 3:178–80. New Orleans: J. F. Hyer, 1960.

McKINLEY**

BDFJ, 187–88.

Gatell, Frank Otto. In *The justices of the United States,* ed. Leon Friedman and Fred L. Israel, 1:769–77. New York: Chelsea House, 1969.

HFK, 226–27.

NCAB, 2:470.

McLEAN**

BDAC, 1310–11.

BDFJ, 188.

DAB, 11–12:127–28.

Gatell, Frank Otto. In *The justices of the United States,* ed. Leon Friedman and Fred L. Israel, 1:535–46. New York: Chelsea House, 1969.

NCAB, 2:469–70.

The twentieth-century biographical dictionary of notable Americans. Vol. 7. Boston: Biographical Society, 1904.

Warner, Ezra J. *Generals in blue,* 304–305. Baton Rouge: Louisiana State University Press, 1964.

Weisenburger, Francis P. *The life of John McLean: A politician on the United States Supreme Court.* Columbus: Ohio State University Press, 1937.

MADISON

Burke's presidential families of the United States of America, 138–43. London: Burke's Peerage, 1975.

HFK, 67–69.

Sobel, Robert. *Biographical directory of the United States executive branch, 1774–1977,* 239–40. Westport, Conn.: Greenwood Press, 1977.

MARIGNY

Arthur, Stanley Clisby. *Old families of Louisiana,* 316–20. Baton Rouge: Claitor's, 1971.

MARSHALL**

Aronson, Sidney H. *Status and kinship in the higher civil service: Standards of selection in the administrations of John Adams, Thomas Jefferson, and Andrew Jackson,* 150–52. Cambridge: Harvard University Press, 1964.

Beveridge, Albert J. *The life of John Marshall.* Vol. 1. Boston and New York: Houghton Mifflin, 1916.

DAB, 11–12:309–14, 328–33.

Hardy, Stella Pickett. *Colonial families of the southern states of America,* 341–65. Baltimore: Genealogical, 1974.

NCAB, G:24–25.

Payne, Robert. *The Marshall story: A biography of General George C. Marshall,* 3–11. New York: Prentice Hall, 1951.

Pogue, Forrest C. *George C. Marshall: Education of a general,* 1–16. New York: Viking Press, 1963.

Sobel, Robert. *Biographical directory of the United States executive branch, 1774–1977,* 342. Westport, Conn.: Greenwood Press, 1977.

The twentieth-century biographical dictionary of notable Americans. Vol. 7. Boston: Biographical Society, 1904.

MASON

Green, Raleigh T. *Genealogical and historical notes on Culpepper County, Virginia,* 137. Baltimore: Regional, 1964.

MATTHEWS*

DAB, 11–12:403–404.

Dart, William Kernan. The justices of the Supreme Court. *Louisiana Historical Quarterly* 4 (January 1921): 113–14.

Louisiana, 291–92.

NCAB, 12:431.

Sobel, Robert, and John Raimo. *Biographical directory of the governors of the United States, 1789–1978,* 1:281. Westport, Conn.: Meckler Books, 1978.

MATTHEWS**

BDFJ, 180.

DAB, 11–12:418–20.

Filler, Louis. In *The justices of the United States,* ed. Leon Friedman and Fred L. Israel, 2:1351–61. New York: Chelsea House, 1969.

NCAB, 2:476–77.

The twentieth-century biographical dictionary of notable Americans. Vol. 7. Boston: Biographical Society, 1904.

MAYES

Rowland, Dunbar. *Courts, judges, and lawyers of Mississippi,* 1:126–28, 178–82. Jackson, Miss.: Hederman Bros., 1935.

MERRICK*

DLB, 1:564–65.

Riffel, Judy, ed. *A history of Pt. Coupee Parish and its families,* 263–64. Baton Rouge: Le Comité des Archives de la Louisiane, 1983.

Thomas, Laverne III. *Ledoux: A pioneer Franco-American family,* 807. New Orleans: Polyanthus, 1982.

MIDDLETON

APD, 664.

BDAC, 1326–27.

Sobel, Robert, and John Raimo. *Biographical directory of the governors of the United States, 1789–1978,* 4:1392–93. Westport, Conn.: Meckler Books, 1978.

Sobel, Robert. *Biographical directory of the United States executive branch, 1774–1977,* 250–51. Westport, Conn.: Greenwood Press, 1977.

The twentieth-century biographical dictionary of notable Americans. Vol. 7. Boston: Biographical Society, 1904.

MILLER*

Biographical and historical memoirs of Louisiana, 2:255–56. Baton Rouge: Claitor's, 1975.

DLB, 1:569.

Louisiana, 797–800.

NCAB, 4:542.

MOISE*

Biographical and historical memoirs of Louisiana, 2:260. Baton Rouge: Claitor's, 1975.

Louisiana, 305–306, 729.

Correspondence with Mrs. Harold A. Moise, October 17, 1985.

MONROE*

BDAC, 457–58, 1354.

Biographical and historical memoirs of Louisiana, 1:544. Baton Rouge: Claitor's, 1975.

Burke's presidential families of the United States of America, 154–58. London: Burke's Peerage, 1975.

CAG, 1:31–33.

DLB, 1:575.

Louisiana, 17–19.

NCAB, 13:3–4.

Seebold, Herman de Bachelle. *Old Louisiana plantation homes and family trees,* 1:77–79. N.p.: privately published, 1941.

MONTGOMERY

APD, 98.

DAB, 13–14:98–99.

Dictionary of national biography, 38:320–21. London: Smith, Elder, 1894.

MOORE**
BDFJ, 198.

DAB, 13–14:112–13, 128–29, 133–34.

CAG, 7:653.

Friedman, Leon. In *The justices of the United States*, ed. Leon Friedman and Fred L. Israel, 1:269–79. New York: Chelsea House, 1969.

NCAB, 2:467; 6:438; 10:246, 251, 452; 12:154.

The twentieth-century biographical dictionary of notable Americans. Vol. 7. Boston: Biographical Society, 1904.

MOORE
BDAC, 1350.

Biographical and historical memoirs of Louisiana, 2:190. Baton Rouge: Claitor's, 1975.

Biographical and historical memoirs of northwest Louisiana, 647–48. Chicago and Nashville: Southern, 1890. Reprinted by the North Louisiana Historical Society, 1976.

Chambers, Henry E. *A history of Louisiana*, 2:24. Chicago and New York: American Historical Society, 1925.

Sanders, Mary Elizabeth. *Annotated abstracts of the successions of St. Mary Parish, Louisiana*, 107–108. N.p.: privately published, 1972.

Sanders, Mary Elizabeth. *Selected annotated abstracts of marriage book 1, St. Mary Parish, Louisiana, 1811–1829*, 26–27, 81–83. N.p.: privately published, 1973.

MORGAN*
Ashbury, Samuel E. Extracts from the reminiscences of General George W. Morgan. *Southern Historical Quarterly* 30 (January 1927): 178–81.

Biographical and historical memoirs of Louisiana, 1:284. Baton Rouge: Claitor's, 1975.

CAG, 1:265–67, 641.

DAB, 11–12:88–89; 13–14:169–72, 186.

DLB, 1:582.

NCAB, 13:596–97.

MORPHY*
Arthur, Stanley Clisby. *Old families of Louisiana*, 54–58. Baton Rouge: Claitor's, 1971.

Dart, William Kernan. The justices of the Supreme Court. *Louisiana Historical Quarterly* 4 (January 1921): 117.

MOUTON
Chambers, Henry E. *A history of Louisiana*, 3:91, 109. Chicago and New York: American Historical Society, 1925.

DLB, 1:587–90.

Mayors of Lafayette, 1884–1980. Lafayette, La.: Lafayette Founders Committee, n.d.

Mouton, J. Franklin, III, ed. *The Moutons*, 3, 9, 14, 24. N.p.: privately published, 1978.

Perrin, William Henry, ed. *Southwest Louisiana, historical and biographical*, 238–41. Baton Rouge: Claitor's, 1971.

MURPHY**

BDFJ, 203.

DAB, suppl. 4, pp. 610–14.

Fine, Sidney. *Frank Murphy: The Detroit years.* Ann Arbor: University of Michigan Press, 1975.

Frank, John P. In *The justices of the United States,* ed. Leon Friedman and Fred L. Israel, 4:2493–2506. New York: Chelsea House, 1969.

Howard, J. Woodford, Jr. *Mr. Justice Murphy: A political biography,* 3–16 and *passim.* Princeton: Princeton University Press, 1968.

NCAB, F:32–33.

Sobel, Robert, and John Raimo. *Biographical directory of the governors of the United States, 1789–1978,* 2:763. Westport, Conn.: Meckler Books, 1978.

NASH

CAG, 2:308.

DAB, 13–14:386–88.

DLB, 2:595.

HFK, 226.

NCAB, 4:419–20.

NELSON**

BDFJ, 205–206.

DAB, 13–14:420–23.

Gatell, Frank Otto. In *The justices of the United States,* ed. Leon Friedman and Fred L. Israel, 2:817–29. New York: Chelsea House, 1969.

NCAB, 2:470–71; 25:143–44.

NEWTON

BDAC, 1387.

NCAB, 4:312–13.

Stafford, George Mason Graham. *General George Mason Graham of Tyrone plantation and his people,* 397–413. New Orleans: Pelican, 1947.

NICHOLLS*

Aucoin, Sidney Joseph. The political career of Isaac Johnson, governor of Louisiana, 1846–1850. *Louisiana Historical Quarterly* 28 (July 1945): 957.

Conrad, Glenn R. The obituary of William Weeks. *Attakapas Gazette* 10 (fall 1975): 142.

DAB, 13–14:487–88.

DLB, 2:602–603.

Louisiana portraits, 193. New Orleans: National Society of the Colonial Dames of America in the State of Louisiana, 1975.

NCAB, 10:82.

The Nicholls family in Louisiana. *Louisiana Historical Quarterly* 6 (January 1923): 5–18.

Rees, Grover. *A narrative history of Breaux Bridge once called "La Point,"* 16. St. Martinville, La.: Attakapas Historical Association, 1976.

Reeves, Miriam G. *The governors of Louisiana,* 65–66, 80–81. Gretna, La.: Pelican, 1972.

Russell, R. Dana. *The Pughs of Bayou Lafourche,* 44. Austin: Plain View Press, 1985.

Sobel, Robert, and John Raimo. *Biographical directory of the governors of the United States, 1789–1978,* 2:573–74. Westport, Conn.: Meckler Books, 1978.

ODOM*
Louisiana, 647–48.

OGDEN*
Louisiana, 336–39.

O'NIELL*
Historical encyclopedia of Louisiana, 955. N.p.: Louisiana Historical Bureau, n.d.
NCAB, 42:442–43.
The story of Louisiana, 3:178–80. New Orleans: J. F. Hyer, 1960.

OVERTON*
Anderson, W. P. *The early descendants of William Overton and Elizabeth Waters of Virginia and allied families.* Vol. 5. N.p.: privately published, 1938.

Biographical and historical memoirs of northwest Louisiana, 644–45. Chicago and Nashville: Southern, 1890. Reprinted by the North Louisiana Historical Society, 1976.

Boddie, John Bennett. *Historical southern families,* 5:124–229. Baltimore: Genealogical, 1967.

Chambers, Henry E. *A history of Louisiana,* 3:176. Chicago and New York: American Historical Society, 1925.

DAB, 13-14:138–39.

Kallenbach, Joseph E., and Jessamine S. Kallenbach. *American state governors, 1776–1976,* 377–78. Dobbs Ferry, N.Y.: Oceana, 1976.

Louisiana, 340–41.

Mackenzie, George Norbury. *Colonial families of the United States of America,* 7:265–66. Baltimore: Genealogical, 1966.

Moore, Claude Hunter. *Thomas Overton Moore: A Confederate governor.* Clinton, N.C.: Commercial, 1960.

NCAB, 14:410–11.

Who was who in America, vol. 3, 1951–1960, 658. Chicago: Marquis, 1966.

PARKER
Baker, Jean H. *Mary Todd Lincoln.* New York: W. W. Norton, 1987.

Chambers, Henry E. *A history of Louisiana,* 2:4–5. Chicago and New York: American Historical Society, 1925.

DAB, suppl. 2, pp. 514–15.

Louisiana, 787.

NCAB, 29:80–81.

PARLANGE*

Curet, Bernard. *Our pride: Pt. Coupee, 72–75.* Baton Rouge: Moran, 1981.

Dart, William Kernan. The justices of the Supreme Court. *Louisiana Historical Quarterly* 4 (January 1921): 123.

DLB, 2:631.

Seebold, Herman de Bachelle. *Old Louisiana plantation homes and family trees,* 2:37–38. N.p.: privately published, 1941.

PATERSON**

APD, 279.

BDFJ, 215–16.

DAB, 13–14:293–95.

Lewis, William Draper. *Great American lawyers,* 1:225–45. Philadelphia: John C. Winton, 1907.

PAVY

Chambers, Henry E. *A history of Louisiana,* 2:377; 3:235, 285–86. Chicago and New York: American Historical Society, 1925.

Louisiana, 650.

Information provided by Patricia L. Jones and Adele Comeaux in several conversations between 1987 and 1989.

PECKHAM**

BDAC, 1439.

BDFJ, 218.

DAB, 13–14:385–87.

NCAB, 11:409–10.

Skolnik, Richard. In *The justices of the United States,* ed. Leon Friedman and Fred L. Israel, 3:1685–1703. New York: Chelsea House, 1969.

The twentieth-century biographical dictionary of notable Americans. Vol. 8. Boston: Biographical Society, 1904.

PENDLETON

APD, 666.

CAG, 1:674.

Green, Raleigh T. *Genealogical and historical notes on Culpepper County, Virginia,* 94–107. Baltimore: Regional, 1964.

PERRY

DAB, 13–14:484, 486–89, 490–92.

Morison, Samuel Eliot. *"Old Bruin": Commodore Matthew C. Perry.* Boston: Little, Brown, 1967.

The twentieth-century biographical dictionary of notable Americans. Vol. 8. Boston: Biographical Society, 1904.

PETERMAN

Broussard, Bernard. *History of St. Mary Parish,* 117. N.p.: privately published, 1977.

The story of Louisiana, 3:180–82. New Orleans: J. F. Hyer, 1960.

PICKETT

Hardy, Stella Pickett. *Colonial families of the southern states of America,* 414–38. Baltimore: Genealogical, 1974.

HFK, 60–61.

PINCKNEY

DAB, 13–14:611–20.

Williams, Frances Leigh. *A founding family: The Pinckneys of South Carolina.* New York: Harcourt Brace Jovanovich, 1978.

PITNEY**

BDFJ, 221.

CAG, 1:949.

DAB, 13–14:642–43.

Mangum, Frank W. In *The justices of the United States,* ed. Leon Friedman and Fred L. Israel, 3:2001–2009. New York: Chelsea House, 1969.

NCAB, 15:61–62.

POCHE*

Biographical and historical memoirs of Louisiana, 2:314–16. Baton Rouge: Claitor's, 1975.

POLK

Armstrong, Zella. *Notable southern families,* 1:173–79. Baltimore: Genealogical, 1974.

BDAC, 1467.

Biographical and historical memoirs of northwest Louisiana, 586. Chicago and Nashville: Southern, 1890. Reprinted by the North Louisiana Historical Society, 1976.

Burke's presidential families of the United States of America, 243–45. London: Burke's Peerage, 1975.

CAG, 1:31.

Chambers, Henry E. *A history of Louisiana,* 3:94. Chicago and New York: American Historical Society, 1925.

DAB, 15–16:39–45.

Louisiana, 767–70.

NCAB, 2:109; 6:265; 9:341–42; A:417.

The story of Louisiana, 2:215–17. New Orleans: J. F. Hyer, 1960.

PONDER*

Biographies of Louisiana judges, 3. 1956. Reprint, Baton Rouge: Claitor's, 1971.

Fruge, J. Cleveland, ed. *Biographies of Louisiana judges,* 186–87. Baton Rouge: Claitor's, 1971.

Louisiana, 563–64.

NCAB, 47:150.

POPE

Arthur, Stanley Clisby. *Old families of Louisiana*, 173–75. Baton Rouge: Claitor's, 1971.

BDAC, 1470.

Burke's presidential families of the United States of America, 39. London: Burke's Peerage, 1975.

CAG, 2:93, 317, 411; 4:162; 5:339.

DAB, 15–16:76–78.

DLB, 2:658.

NCAB, 26:270–71.

PORTER*

Blackburn, Florence, and Fay Brown, *Franklin through the years*, 101. Franklin, La.: privately published, 1972.

Broussard, Bernard. *History of St. Mary Parish*, 127–33. N.p.: privately published, 1977.

The Caffery family, 1737–1958 (mimeo).

DLB, 2:658.

NCAB, 8:133–34, 158–59.

Stephenson, Wendell Holmes. *Alexander Porter, Whig planter of old Louisiana*. Baton Rouge: Louisiana State University Press, 1934.

POSEY

BDAC, 1472.

Biographical and historical memoirs of Louisiana, 2:319. Baton Rouge: Claitor's, 1975.

Kilpatrick, Susan M. *Belt Brashear and Amelia Duvall*, 72–74. N.p.: privately published, n.d.

NCAB, 13:265–66.

Perrin, William Henry, ed. *Southwest Louisiana, historical and biographical*, 67–68. Baton Rouge: Claitor's, 1971.

POWELL**

Current biography yearbook 1965: 324–26.

See also **RUCKER****.

PRICE

BDAC, 1481.

The Caffery family, 1737–1958 (mimeo).

Historical encyclopedia of Louisiana, 231. N.p.: Louisiana Historical Bureau, n.d.

Sanders, Mary Elizabeth. *Selected annotated abstracts of marriage book 1, St. Mary Parish, Louisiana, 1811–1829*, 110–11, 127–28. N.p.: privately published, 1973.

Sanders, Mary Elizabeth. *Annotated abstracts of the successions of St. Mary Parish, Louisiana*, 74–75, 147. N.p.: privately published, 1972.

PROVOSTY*

Biographical and historical memoirs of Louisiana, 2:323. Baton Rouge: Claitor's, 1975.

Chambers, Henry E. *A history of Louisiana,* 3:346. Chicago and New York: American Historical Society, 1925.

DLB, 2:666.

Lafayette *Daily Advertiser,* 4 January 1989, 14.

The story of Louisiana, 2:136, 138. New Orleans: J. F. Hyer, 1960.

Thomas, Laverne III. *Ledoux: A pioneer Franco-American family,* 210–333. New Orleans: Polyanthus, 1982.

Material provided by Ledoux R. Provosty, Jr., in 1977 for another project.

PUGH

Biographical and historical memoirs of Louisiana, 2:323–24. Baton Rouge: Claitor's, 1975.

CAG, 3:435–36.

Chambers, Henry E. *A history of Louisiana,* 2:171–72; 3:129. Chicago and New York: American Historical Society, 1925.

Floyd, William Barrow. *The Barrow family of old Louisiana,* 27. Lexington, Ky.: privately published, 1963.

Louisiana, 367–68.

Martindale-Hubbell law directory, F:3118 B. Summit, N.J.: Martindale-Hubbell 1982.

NCAB, 44:420–21.

Correspondence with John F. Pugh, Jr., April 7, 1986.

RANDOLPH (network 37)

Biographical and historical memoirs of northwest Louisiana, 520–21. Chicago and Nashville: Southern, 1890. Reprinted by the North Louisiana Historical Society, 1976.

Chambers, Henry E. *A history of Louisiana,* 2:325–26; 3:281–82. Chicago and New York: American Historical Society, 1925.

RANDOLPH (network 45-A)

Adams, Henry. *John Randolph.* Boston: Houghton Mifflin, 1889.

Daniels, Jonathan. *The Randolphs of Virginia.* Garden City, N.Y.: Doubleday, 1972.

Genealogies of Virginia families, 4:226–55. Baltimore: Genealogical, 1982.

Kirk, Russel. *John Randolph of Roanoke.* Indianapolis: Liberty Press, 1978.

Sobel, Robert. *Biographical directory of the United States executive branch, 1774–1977,* 282–83. Westport, Conn.: Greenwood Press, 1977.

The twentieth-century biographical dictionary of notable Americans. Vol. 9. Boston: Biographical Society, 1904.

REID*

Biographical and historical memoirs of Louisiana, 2:331, 333. Baton Rouge: Claitor's, 1975.

Fruge, J. Cleveland, ed. *Biographies of Louisiana judges,* 21. New Orleans: Louisiana District Judges Association, 1965.

The story of Louisiana, 2:227. New Orleans: J. F. Hyer, 1960.

Williamson, Frederick William, and George T. Goodman. *Eastern Louisiana,* 2:650–52. Louisville: Historical Record Association, 1939.

ROBERTSON

DAB, 15–16:28.

Hardy, Stella Pickett. *Colonial families of the southern states of America,* 73–74. Baltimore: Genealogical, 1974.

Sobel, Robert, and John Raimo. *Biographical directory of the governors of the United States, 1789–1978,* 2:557; 4:1637–38. Westport, Conn.: Meckler Books, 1978.

ROGERS*

Biographical and historical memoirs of Louisiana, 2:344–45. Baton Rouge: Claitor's, 1975.

Chambers, Henry E. *A history of Louisiana,* 3:332–33. Chicago and New York: American Historical Society, 1925.

NCAB, 11:471.

Thomson, James E., ed. *Louisiana today,* 124. New Orleans: Louisiana Society, 1939.

ROST*

Arthur, Stanley Clisby. *Old families of Louisiana,* 415–16. Baton Rouge: Claitor's, 1971.

DLB, 2:697.

NCAB, 11:468.

RUCKER

CAG, 1:808; 4:299; 7:372, 714.

NCAB, 19:251; 42:51–52.

Wood, Sudie Rucker. *The Rucker family genealogy.* Richmond: Old Dominion Press, 1932.

See also **LAMAR****.

RUTLEDGE**

Barry, Richard. *Mr. Justice Rutledge of South Carolina,* 128–30. New York: Duell Sloan and Pearce, 1942.

BDFJ, 242.

DAB, 15–16:257–60.

Friedman, Leon. In *The justices of the United States,* ed. Leon Friedman and Fred L. Israel, 1:33–49. New York: Chelsea House, 1969.

Sobel, Robert, and John Raimo. *Biographical directory of the governors of the United States, 1789–1978,* 4:1389–90. Westport, Conn.: Meckler Books, 1978.

The twentieth-century biographical dictionary of notable Americans. Vol. 9. Boston: Biographical Society, 1904.

Webber, Mabel. John Rutledge and his descendants. *South Carolina Historical and Genealogical Magazine* 31 (January 1930): 7–25; and 31 (April 1930): 93–106.

ST. DENIS

Arthur, Stanley Clisby. *Old families of Louisiana,* 149–56. Baton Rouge: Claitor's, 1971.

ST. PAUL*

The story of Louisiana, 2:212–14. New Orleans: J. F. Hyer, 1960.

Thomas, Laverne III. *Ledoux: A pioneer Franco-American family,* 326–30. New Orleans: Polyanthus, 1982.

SCHUYLER

APD, 543–45.

DAB, 15–16:471–80.

NCAB, 1:97–99.

Sobel, Robert. *Biographical directory of the United States executive branch, 1774–1977,* 149–50. Westport, Conn.: Greenwood Press, 1977.

SCOTT

BDFJ, 440.

Chambers, Henry E. *A history of Louisiana,* 2:209. Chicago and New York: American Historical Society, 1925.

Citizen's guide to the 1984 Louisiana legislature, 72. Baton Rouge: Public Affairs Research Council, 1984.

Correspondence with John W. Scott, December 9, 1986.

SELDEN

CAG, 6:598.

SERGEANT

APD, 667.

BDAC, 1581.

SHELBY

Armstrong, Zella. *Notable southern families,* 2:305–29. Baltimore: Genealogical, 1974.

DAB, 16–17:59–63.

The lawyers and lawmakers of Kentucky, 623–24. Chicago: Lewis, n.d. Reprint, Easley, S.C.: Southern Historical Press, 1982.

McBride, Robert Martin, and Daniel Merritt Robison. *Biographical directory of the Tennessee General Assembly, Volume I, 1796–1861,* 666–69. Nashville: Tennessee State Library and Archives and Tennessee Historical Commission, 1975.

NCAB, 19:100–101.

SHIRAS**

BDFJ, 251.

DAB, 17–18:118–19.

NCAB, 2:477.

Paul, Arnold M. In *The justices of the United States,* ed. Leon Friedman and Fred L. Israel, 2:1577–92. New York: Chelsea House, 1969.

SIMON*

Bienvenu, Willie Z. *The family Bienvenu of St. Martinville and associated families.* St. Martinville: privately published, 1980.

DLB, 2:743–44.

Perrin, William Henry, ed. *Southwest Louisiana, historical and biographical,* 78. Baton Rouge: Claitor's, 1971.

Pourciau, Betty, ed. *St. Martin Parish history,* 243–44. Baton Rouge: Le Comité des Archives de la Louisiane, 1985.

Thomson, James E., ed. *Louisiana today,* 296, 383. New Orleans: Louisiana Society, 1939.

SLIDELL*

DAB, 11–12:90–91, 95–96; 17–18:209–11.

DLB, 2:746–47.

NCAB, 7:496.

Sears, Louis Martin. *John Slidell.* Durham: Duke University Press, 1925.

SMITH (network 40)

King, Willard L. *Melville Weston Fuller,* 59, 69. New York: Macmillan, 1950.

NCAB, 6:307–308.

SMITH (network 42)

Biographical directory of the Senate of South Carolina, 1776–1964, 310–12. Columbia: South Carolina Archives Department, 1964.

Webber, Mabel. John Rutledge and his descendants. *South Carolina Historical and Genealogical Magazine* 31 (January 1930): 13.

SONIAT DU FOSSAT

Arthur, Stanley Clisby. *Old families of Louisiana,* 260–61. Baton Rouge: Claitor's, 1971.

Biographical and historical memoirs of Louisiana, 2:398–99. Baton Rouge: Claitor's, 1975.

DLB, 2:754.

King, Grace. *Creole families of New Orleans,* 221–35. New York: Macmillan, 1921.

Louisiana, 404–406.

SPENCER*

BDAC, 1683.

CAG, abridged compendium, 567–68.

DAB, 17–18:450–51.

NCAB, 16:390; 20:193–94; 21:417; 33:312–13.

SPOTSWOOD

CAG, 3:302.

SPRAGUE

NCAB, 9:396, 402–403.

STAFFORD

DLB, 2:762–63.

Stafford, George Mason Graham. *General Leroy Augustus Stafford*. Baton Rouge: Claitor's, 1969.

STEWART**

BDFJ, 262.

Israel, Jerold H. In *The justices of the United States*, ed. Leon Friedman and Fred L. Israel, 4:2921–38. New York: Chelsea House, 1969.

NCAB, 45:92–93; I:29–30.

STONE**

BDFJ, 263.

CAG, 1:992.

DAB, suppl. 4, pp. 793–97.

Mason, Alpheus Thomas. *Harlan Fisk Stone: Pillar of the law*. New York: Viking Press, 1956.

Mason, Alpheus Thomas. In *The justices of the United States*, ed. Leon Friedman and Fred L. Israel, 3:2221–37. New York: Chelsea House, 1969.

NCAB, F:29–30.

STONE

APD, 669.

The twentieth-century biographical dictionary of notable Americans. Vol. 10. Boston: Biographical Society, 1904.

STORY**

BDFJ, 264.

DAB, 17–18:102–11.

Dunne, Gerald T. In *The justices of the United States*, ed. Leon Friedman and Fred L. Israel, 1:435–53. New York: Chelsea House, 1969.

NCAB, 2:468–69; 5:417–18.

STRONG**

BDFJ, 264.

CAG, 1:846, 992.

DAB, 17–18:153–55.

Kutler, Stanley I. In *The justices of the United States*, ed. Leon Friedman and Fred L. Israel, 2:1153–61. New York: Chelsea House, 1969.

NCAB, 21:4–5.

STUART

DAB, 17–18:160–62, 173–74.

HFK, 220–26.

Warner, Ezra J. *Generals in gray*, 296–97. Baton Rouge: Louisiana State University Press, 1959.

SUMMERS*

Fruge, J. Cleveland, ed. *Biographies of Louisiana judges,* 16–17. Baton Rouge: Claitor's, 1971.

History of Vermilion Parish, Louisiana, 145–46, 283, 293. Vermilion Historical Society, 1983.

Correspondence with Justice Frank W. Summers, December 28, 1988.

SUTHERLAND*

BDFJ, 266.

Burner, David. In *The justices of the United States,* ed. Leon Friedman and Fred L. Israel, 3:2133–43. New York: Chelsea House, 1969.

DAB, suppl. 3, pp. 753–56.

Paschal, Joel Francis. *Mr. Justice Sutherland.* Princeton: Princeton University Press, 1951.

SWAYNE*

BDFJ, 267.

DAB, 17–18:239–41.

Gillette, William. In *The justices of the United States,* ed. Leon Friedman and Fred L. Israel, 2:989–99. New York: Chelsea House, 1969.

The twentieth-century biographical dictionary of notable Americans. Vol. 10. Boston: Biographical Society, 1904.

TAFT*

APD, 299–337, 585–93, 640–41.

Burke's presidential families of the United States of America, 434–38. London: Burke's Peerage, 1975.

DAB, 1–2:508.

NCAB, 1:271; 22:148; C:309.

TALIAFERRO*

Chambers, Henry E. *A history of Louisiana,* 2:131; 3:197–98. Chicago and New York: American Historical Society, 1925.

DLB, 2:778–79

NCAB, 11:518.

The story of Louisiana, 4:326–28, 343–44. New Orleans: J. F. Hyer, 1960.

Genealogies of Virginia families, 4:719–71. Baltimore: Genealogical, 1982.

TANEY*

Arthur, Stanley Clisby. *Old families of Louisiana,* 116. Baton Rouge: Claitor's, 1971.

BDFJ, 270.

CAG, 1:960.

Gatell, Frank Otto. In *The justices of the United States,* ed. Leon Friedman and Fred L. Israel, 1:635–55. New York: Chelsea House, 1969.

TATE*

BDAC, 802.

The story of Louisiana, 2:531–32; 3:426–27. New Orleans: J. F. Hyer, 1960.

Thomson, James E., ed. *Louisiana today,* 302, 386. New Orleans: Louisiana Society, 1939.

TAYLOR (network 45-I)

CAG, 5:421–22.

Sanders, Mary Elizabeth. *Selected annotated abstracts of marriage book 1, St. Mary Parish, Louisiana, 1811–1829,* 127–28. N.p.: privately published, 1973.

Perrin, William Henry, ed. *Southwest Louisiana, historical and biographical,* 82. Baton Rouge: Claitor's, 1971.

Kilpatrick, Susan M. *Belt Brashear and Amelia Duvall,* 72–73, 99. N.p.: privately published, n.d.

TAYLOR (network 45-C)

Burke's American families of the United States of America, 2249–58. London: Burke's Peerage, 1975.

Burke's American families with British ancestry, 2936–37. Baltimore: Genealogical, 1977.

CAG, 5:421–22.

Green, Raleigh T. *Genealogical and historical notes on Culpepper County, Virginia,* 74–75. Baltimore: Regional, 1964.

THOMPSON**

BDFJ, 275.

CAG, 6:708.

DAB, 17–18:471–72.

Dunne, Gerald T. In *The justices of the United States,* ed. Leon Friedman and Fred L. Israel, 1:475–509. New York: Chelsea House, 1969.

THOMPSON*

Chambers, Henry E. *A history of Louisiana,* 2:341–42; 3:329. Chicago and New York: American Historical Society, 1925.

The story of Louisiana, 4:53–56. New Orleans: J. F. Hyer, 1960.

Williamson, Frederick William, and George T. Goodman. *Eastern Louisiana,* 2:837–38. Louisville: Historical Record Association, 1939.

TODD**

Biographical cyclopedia of the Commonwealth of Kentucky, 427–29. Chicago and Philadelphia: John M. Greshman, 1896.

Biographical encyclopedia of Kentucky, 195, 518–19. Cincinnati: J. M. Armstrong, 1878.

Burke's presidential families of the United States of America, 53, 138. London: Burke's Peerage, 1975.

CAG, 1:770

DAB, 17–18:569–70, 574–75.

Israel, Fred L. In *The justices of the United States,* ed. Leon Friedman and Fred L. Israel, 1:407–12. New York: Chelsea House, 1969.

O'Rear, Edward C. Justice Thomas Todd. *Register of the Kentucky Historical Society* 38 (April 1940): 112–19.

Price, Mary Starling. Edmund L. Starling, author of a history of Henderson Co. *Filson Club Historical Quarterly* 4 (January 1930): 17–23.

Who was who in America, 1897–1942, 1243. Chicago: Marquis, 1943.

TODD*

Baker, Jean H. *Mary Todd Lincoln.* New York: W. W. Norton, 1987.

Biographical encyclopedia of Kentucky, 748. Cincinnati: J. M. Armstrong, 1878.

Chambers, Henry E. *A history of Louisiana*, 2:248. Chicago and New York: American Historical Society, 1925.

Helm, Katherine. *Mary, wife of Lincoln.* New York: Harper, 1928.

HFK, 208–27.

The lawyers and lawmakers of Kentucky, 337–39, 734–37. Chicago: Lewis, n.d. Reprint, Easley, S.C.: Southern Historical Press, 1982.

McMurtry, R. Gerald. General Ben Hardin Helm: Kentucky brother-in-law of Abraham Lincoln. *Filson Club Historical Quarterly* 32 (July 1958): 334.

Membership in the legislature of Louisiana, 1880–1980, 90. Baton Rouge: Louisiana Legislative Council, 1979.

NCAB, 9:544; 4:339.

Thomson, James E., ed. *Louisiana today*, 369. New Orleans: Louisiana Society, 1939.

TOMPKINS

BDAC, 721.

Dunne, Gerald T. In *The justices of the United States*, ed. Leon Friedman and Fred L. Israel, 1:486. New York: Chelsea House, 1969.

Sobel, Robert. *Biographical directory of the United States executive branch, 1774–1977*, 332–33. Westport, Conn.: Greenwood Press, 1977.

TRENHOLM

DAB, 13–14:172.

NCAB, 4:382; 28:376–77.

TRIMBLE**

BDFJ, 279.

Biographical cyclopedia of the Commonwealth of Kentucky, 149–50. Chicago and Philadelphia: John M. Greshman, 1896.

Biographical encyclopedia of Kentucky, 167. Cincinnati: J. M. Armstrong, 1878.

DAB, 17–18:642–43.

Goff, John S. Mr. Justice Trimble of the United States Supreme Court. *Register of the Kentucky Historical Society* 58 (January 1960): 6–28.

HFK, 23.

Israel, Fred L. In *The justices of the United States*, ed. Leon Friedman and Fred L. Israel, 1:513–18. New York: Chelsea House, 1969.

The lawyers and lawmakers of Kentucky, 105–106. Chicago: Lewis, n.d. Reprint, Easley, S.C.: Southern Historical Press, 1982.

NCAB, 2:469.

VAN CORTLAND

APD, 634.

BDAC, 1745–46.

Burt, Nathaniel. *First families*, 88. Boston: Little, Brown, 1970.

DAB, 19–20:162–65.

See also **LIVINGSTON****.

VAN RENSSLAER

DAB, 19–20:207–12.

NCAB, 2:51, 397, 483–84; 7:524–25; 11:285.

VIAL

Fortier, Alcee. *Louisiana*. Vol. 3. Atlanta: Southern Historical Association, 1909 (not to be confused with the more frequently cited 1914 edition).

Historical encyclopedia of Louisiana, 1173–74, 1404–1405. N.p.: Louisiana Historical Bureau, n.d.

Thomson, James E., ed. *Louisiana today*, 338, 397. New Orleans: Louisiana Society, 1939.

Correspondence with David J. Vial, August 28 and September 11, 1985.

VINSON**

BDFJ, 285.

DAB, suppl. 5, pp. 711–15.

Hatcher, John Henry. Fred Vinson: Boyhood and education in the Big Sandy Valley. *Register of the Kentucky Historical Society* 72 (July 1974): 243–61.

Kirkendahl, Richard. In *The justices of the United States*, ed. Leon Friedman and Fred L. Israel, 4:2639–49. New York: Chelsea House, 1969.

Sobel, Robert. *Biographical directory of the United States executive branch, 1774–1977*, 341–42. Westport, Conn.: Greenwood Press, 1977.

VOORHIES*

CAG, 1:873; 3:461; 4:290, 517, 653; 5:191; 6:163, 595, 598; 7:447, 538.

DAB, 19–20:291–92.

Grant, Ruth T. The men, the years: Where have they gone? The life of Felix Voorhies. *Attakapas Gazette* 15 (fall 1980): 103–109.

Louisiana, 446–47.

Membership in the legislature of Louisiana, 1880–1980, 146. Baton Rouge: Louisiana Legislative Council, 1979.

NCAB, 2:359; 5:136.

Perrin, William Henry, ed. *Southwest Louisiana, historical and biographical*, 248, 349, 352. Baton Rouge: Claitor's, 1971.

Pourciau, Betty, ed. *St. Martin Parish history*, 265–68. Baton Rouge: Le Comité des Archives de la Louisiane, 1985.

Saucier, Corinne L. *History of Avoyelles Parish*, 128, 360. New Orleans: Pelican, 1943.

Interview with Cynthia Voorhies, November 22, 1988.

Interviews with Bennet Voorhies, Jr., November 29, 1988, and May 10, 1989.

WAITE**

BDAC, 1761.

BDFJ, 287.

CAG, 1:230; 6:598.

DAB, 3–4:228–29; 19–20:322–24.

Filler, Louis. In *The justices of the United States,* ed. Leon Friedman and Fred L. Israel, 2:1243–57. New York: Chelsea House, 1969.

NCAB, 26:11–12; 30:330.

Trimble, Bruce R. *Chief Justice Waite: Defender of the public interest,* 1–26, and *passim.* Princeton: Princeton University Press, 1938.

Waite, John Turner. Henry Matson Waite. *Northeast Historical and Genealogical Register* 24 (April 1870): 101–105.

WALKER

Aronson, Sidney H. *Status and kinship in the higher civil service: Standards of selection in the administrations of John Adams, Thomas Jefferson, and Andrew Jackson,* 95, 151, 228. Cambridge: Harvard University Press, 1964.

Doherty, Herbert J., Jr. Andrew Jackson's cronies in Florida politics. *Florida Historical Quarterly* 34 (July 1955): 3–29.

Green, Raleigh T. *Genealogical and historical notes on Culpepper County, Virginia,* 135–45. Baltimore: Regional, 1964.

Pyburn, Nita Katharine. David Shelby Walker (1815–1891): Educational statesman of Florida. *Florida Historical Quarterly.* 34 (October 1955): 159–71.

The twentieth-century biographical dictionary of notable Americans. Vol. 10. Boston: Biographical Society, 1904.

WARNER

Burke's presidential families of the United States of America, 39. London: Burke's Peerage, 1975.

HFK, 84–85.

WASHINGTON**

BDAC, 1780.

BDFJ, 291–92.

Burke's presidential families of the United States of America, 38–63. London: Burke's Peerage, 1975.

NCAB, 8:169–70.

Sobel, Robert. *Biographical directory of the United States executive branch, 1774–1977,* 347–48. Westport, Conn.: Greenwood Press, 1977.

WATKINS*

BDAC, 1782.

Biographical and historical memoirs of northwest Louisiana, 698–700. Chicago and Nashville: Southern, 1890. Reprinted by the North Louisiana Historical Society, 1976.

Dart, William Kernan. The justices of the Supreme Court. *Louisiana Historical Quarterly* 4 (January 1921): 122.

WATTERSON

APD, 670.

BDAC, 1783–84.

DAB, 19–20:551–55.

WAYNE**

BDFJ, 293.

Coleman, Kenneth, and Charles Stephen Gurr. *Dictionary of Georgia biography,* 2:1043–44. Athens: University of Georgia Press, 1983.

Gatell, Frank Otto. In *The justices of the United States,* ed. Leon Friedman and Fred L. Israel, 1:601–11. New York: Chelsea House, 1969.

Lawrence, Alexander A. *James Moore Wayne, southern Unionist,* 7–8, and *passim.* Chapel Hill: University of North Carolina Press, 1943.

NCAB, 2:176.

WESTON

NCAB, 7:503.

The twentieth-century biographical dictionary of notable Americans. Vol. 4. Boston: Biographical Society, 1904.

WHITE** (Byron)

BDFJ, 300.

Current biography yearbook 1962: 458–60.

Israel, Fred L. In *The justices of the United States,* ed. Leon Friedman and Fred L. Israel, 4:2951–61. New York: Chelsea House, 1969.

NCAB, J:42.

Who's who in American education 15 (1951–52): 1161.

WHITE* ** (Edward Douglas)

APD, 671.

BDAC, 1802–1804.

DAB, 19–20:95–98.

DLB, 2:838–40.

Highsaw, Robert B. *Edward Douglas White: Defender of the conservative faith.* Baton Rouge: Louisiana State University Press, 1981.

Klinkhamer, Marie Carolyn. *Edward Douglas White, chief justice of the United States.* Ph.D. dissertation, Catholic University of America, 1943.

NCAB, 10:76.

WHITE (network 34)

BDAC, 1801.

CAG, 2:252; 7:463.

DAB, 19–20:85.

NCAB, 2:220; 3:510.

WHITE (network 44-B)

APD, 279.

NCAB, 1:69–70.

WHITE (network 45-K)

BDAC, 1804.

Boddie, John Bennett. *Historical southern families,* 5:164. Baltimore: Genealogical, 1967.

WICKLIFFE

BDAC, 1812, 1862.

Biographical and historical memoirs of Louisiana, 2:454–55. Baton Rouge: Claitor's, 1975.

Biographical encyclopedia of Kentucky, 128–29, 131–32. Cincinnati: J. M. Armstrong, 1878.

DAB, 19–20:183–84.

HFK, 183–84.

Landry, Thomas R. The political career of Robert Charles Wickliffe, Governor of Louisiana, 1856–1860. *Louisiana Historical Quarterly* 25 (July 1942): 670–727.

NCAB, 1:354–56; 6:8; 10:77–78; 11:425.

Sobel, Robert. *Biographical directory of the United States executive branch, 1774–1977,* 172–73. Westport, Conn.: Greenwood Press, 1977.

Sobel, Robert, and John Raimo. *Biographical directory of the governors of the United States, 1789–1978,* 2:517–18. Westport, Conn.: Meckler Books, 1978.

WILSON**

BDFJ, 304.

DAB, 19–20:320–21, 326–30.

McClosky, Robert G. In *The justices of the United States,* ed. Leon Friedman and Fred L. Israel, 1:79–96. New York: Chelsea House, 1969.

Smith, C. P. *James Wilson: Founding father.* Chapel Hill: University of North Carolina Press, 1956.

WINDER

CAG, 1:31.

DAB, 19–20:380–82.

NCAB, 9:298–99; 10:487.

WINTHROP

APD, 546.

DAB, 19–20:407–17.

WILLIAMS (network 25)

DAB, 19–20:259–60, 266, 286–95.

WILLIAMS (network 40)

NCAB, 6:312–13.

Sobel, Robert, and John Raimo. *Biographical directory of the governors of the United States, 1789–1978,* 2:610. Westport, Conn.: Meckler Books, 1978.

WOODBURY**

BDAC, 1845.

DAB, 19–20:488–89.

Gatell, Frank Otto. In *The justices of the United States,* ed. Leon Friedman and Fred L. Israel, 2:843–54. New York: Chelsea House, 1969.

NCAB, 2:471.

The twentieth-century biographical dictionary of notable Americans. Vol. 10. Boston: Biographical Society, 1904.

WOODS**

BDFJ, 308.

DAB, 19–20:501–502, 505–506.

Filler, Louis. In *The justices of the United States,* ed. Leon Friedman and Fred L. Israel, 2:1327–36. New York: Chelsea House, 1969.

NCAB, 2:476.

Warner, Ezra J. *Generals in blue,* 571–73. Baton Rouge: Louisiana State University Press, 1964.